GUIDE FOR
THE CHRISTIAN ASSEMBLY

THIERRY MAERTENS – JEAN FRISQUE

GUIDE FOR THE
CHRISTIAN ASSEMBLY

REVISED EDITION

22nd to 34th SUNDAYS

Notre Dame, Indiana 46556

Translated from the French by MOLAISE MEEHAN, O.S.B.

Nihil Obstat: V. Descamps
can. libr. cens.

Imprimatur: J. Thomas, *vic. gen.*
Tournai, July 31, 1970

© Copyright, 1972, Fides Publishers, Inc.
Notre Dame, Indiana

LCCCN: 72-114245

ISBN: 0-8190-0007-8

1773

Translated from the original French edition,
Guide de l'assemblée chrétienne, Casterman, 1970.
An edition of St. Andrews Abbey, Bruges.

CONTENTS

TWENTY-SECOND SUNDAY

A. THE WORD

I. Jeremiah
20:7-9
1st reading
1st cycle

Jeremiah's temperament appears to have been quite depressive. Previously, at the beginning of Joachim's reign, a violent *demarche* against the temple cult had involved him in a trial for sacrilege, from which he emerged acquitted (Jr 26:24), but deeply wounded. Now, confronted by his destiny, he composes his "confessions," a literary genre that is new in the Jewish tradition, and that echoes all the tensions produced in his sensitive soul by God's call (Jr 16:1-13, etc.). Our reading today is an extract from an autobiographical ensemble (Jr 20:7-18) where he curses the day of his birth, tells of his confusion in face of the hate that surrounds him, and actually likens God's call to a sort of seduction.

It would be wrong of course to take these confessions as merely the outcome of depression. The fact that the first person singular is used (as it is in many psalms) is no justification for a merely individualist interpretation. The first person is in fact customary in collective prayers by the people, particularly when the assembly is conscious if its mediating role between God and the people. The prophet then is exercising a liturgical role in his confessions. Having proclaimed God's will to the people, he proceeds from his own personal experience to formulate a prayer of intercession before God. In the form of lamentation he describes the misery of Israel.

a) The great majority of vocation narratives emphasize the *deception* of the recipient. We have in Moses' case (Ex:32) desertion, discouragement for Elias (1 K 19), for Jonah deception (Jon 4) and for Jeremiah depression (Jr 20, etc.). It is especially painful to

1

feel oneself ostracized from a community, because one has reminded people of certain duties or given spiritual witness. The
hesitation of the prophet before his mission and its demands
(v. 9) is also that of the people, troubled about its destiny. This
becomes positive to the extent that a man realizes the gulf that
stretches between his will and that of God. There may be agony
of the spirit or a crisis of faith, but it remains one of God's abso-
ulate transcendence.

b) In verse 7a we have the key to the whole passage. Yahweh
has *seduced* him as he has seduced the people, his spouse. The
resulting tension for both prophet and people is but the inevitable
upheaval once human life is touched by the mystery of God. The
man for whom God is but an idea or a definition will probably
never experience the agony of encounter. He will never have to
strip and annihilate himself so that he may be aligned to God's
will.

But, even in his blinding mystery, God never obliterates freedom. A man can allow himself to be "seduced" because he is sur-
rendering to one with the right to take. Here we have the basis
of Jesus' obedience on the cross, which the eucharistic celebration
summons us to share.

II. Deuteronomy   These verses are taken from the conclusion to
  4:1-2, 6-8   the first great discourse in Deuteronomy
  1st reading   (1:1–4:40). They contain some of the major
  2nd cycle   themes of the whole book.

a) Moses' discourse is set down at a time when the exile is
looming on the horizon. Is not Israel about to be dispossessed
of her lands precisely as the Canaanites were, for infidelity and
impiety? It becomes imperative then to restore the unifying
bonds between God and the people.

A first means towards that is intensive teaching of the Law and traditions (v. 6). They will help the people towards a way of life that differs from other nations. They will be manifestly a people united to their God in a particular way (vv. 7-8). The legislator, bearing a mandate from God, appeals to the hearts of the people so that they will come to realize the profound link between *law* and *life*, between teaching and the happiness expected, which God alone can give (v. 1).

b) Once this link is truly lived, the believer begins to discern the merciful choice of God, and above all his *nearness* (v. 7). This is the first time a legislative text stresses nearness. Previously the emphasis was on distance and separation (Ex 33:20).

Here we have an important point. Israel has had an extraordinary history, marked indelibly by the Exodus events. Yet life should not be invariably backward-looking. She cannot go on living by ceaseless commentaries on, and repetitions of, the book which is her life, the code of the Sinai alliance. The lesson of Deuteronomy is that it is only through concrete involvement in God's here and now that full fidelity will be shown to the covenant and to Exodus. The covenant must be lived, not commented on.

Likewise, it is the Church's task to live the resurrection, not comment on it. The Pasch is now. If we take this attitude God will be "near" to his people, his Testament will be always new and Christ an actuality in ecclesial life.

III. **Sirach 3:17-18, 20, 28-29**
1st reading
3rd cycle

The verses in this reading are taken from two distinct portions of the book of Sirach. They follow one another and are linked by a common inspiration. The first deals with humility (2:17-24) the second with pride (2:26-29).

To understand the author's thought we must keep in mind his concept of *wisdom*. It is typically Jewish: enough knowledge to direct a practical attitude, and enough good sense to deal with events however taxing. He is altogether suspicious of speculation, especially of that current in Hellenist circles.

His attitude indeed is basically the sapiental one in general. He realizes that Wisdom is unique and that it resides in God (Si 1:8-10). It possesses the whole secret of creation and that of God, but does not reveal itself fully to man (Si 18:2-6, 47:17-20). It is man's lot to achieve merely a certain level of wisdom: further pretensions would be presumptuous (cf. v. 24).

He is not anti-intellectual; but he is convinced that authentic knowledge of God is impossible without daily fidelity to him. Furthermore, the pursuit of this wisdom requires more than human enterprise. God shares the search and makes it a way of sharing his life and his mystery (Si 21:13).

IV. Romans 12:1-2
2nd reading
1st cycle

Paul has just concluded his doctrinal section, and, following his custom, concludes the letter with paraentic exhortations. Three considerations receive main attention: Christian relations with one another (Rm 12:3-13), with others (Rm 12:14–13:14) and the relations between the strong and the weak (Rm 14:1–15:13). The first two verses of Chapter 12 give us the doctrinal basis for his whole treatment.

a) The wording of the first verse sends us back to Chapter 6, where he explained how the Christian gives his body to the service of justice (Rm 6:12-23). He now gives a *sacrificial* emphasis to this service.

By "body" he means the human person and the structure of his life. All of this is regarded as a sacrificial offering which may not be withdrawn, because it no longer belongs to the one who offered it. It is taken over by the Spirit, as at one time fire would consume a sacrifice. The Spirit makes it living, holy and pleasing to God: living, because the victim does not die with offering, like the victim of a holocaust, but lives more intensely; holy, through contact with the sanctifying Spirit; pleasing to God, like the aroma of ancient sacrifices (Ex 29:18, Lv 1:9, 13).

The whole point of this passage is the affirmation that henceforward moral performance has a cultic dimension. Once the whole structure of a man's life is taken up by the Spirit, it becomes the material of a new sacrifice, because this was the matter of Christ's sacrifice on the cross.

The idea of a spiritualized sacrifice, which had indeed been already contemplated in Daniel 3:38-40, issues in this concept, where moral and liturgical performance, life and rite, are mingled.

b) The participation by the Spirit in man's activity gives man himself a new vision (v. 2) of the world and humanity. He is now the new man, no longer the heir of Adam but the co-heir of Christ. His manner of living presupposes a conversion, which Paul describes as a transformation or *renewal of judgment*. He is, that is to say, accepting the role of a Christian in the world, and binding himself freely, independently of any outside pressure, even that of the law. His conduct represents his response to divine love in the context that he finds himself. Here he discerns, and does, the will of God.

c) The renewal of judgment draws the Christian into a radical *nonconformism* (v. 2). He belongs to another world, a nonterrestrial one, and thus need not adapt himself to the terrestrial. Confronted with the sort of publicity and propaganda that "molds" the masses, he can find solace in his faith. Confronted by majority views, he will find in his faith the courage to belong if necessary to a rejected minority. Confronted by the enticements of money and power, he will find the courage to stand for deeper and more spiritual values.

To be a Christian in the world, live in the world, live with others, is in itself worship, worship of God. Calvary was not a liturgy, but a slice of human life that Jesus molded to a cult. What saved us was not a cultic act, but a human act, set in the world and in history (cf. He 7:13).

Thus we who live in temporal society, in active revolt always against every form of injustice, have our authentic cult. Can this be reduced completely to the service of humanity and the world? Is there any place for the liturgy strictly speaking, as an act of thanksgiving to God?

There are those theologians of secularization who would be for suppression of official liturgy in favor of a worship "of the market-place," as if the sacred were altogether contained in the profane. However, it is only eschatologically that profane and sacred are destined to coincide. The Church is not yet the Kingdom, and, until she is, these two domains must remain in tension, looking towards a future reconciliation. In any "secular cult" of secular relationships, God can be no more than implicit. We need the explicit, and this is the function of what we call liturgy.

If we opt for the spiritual cult in the secular world, we cannot reject the explicit thanksgiving which makes secular life the gift of God, and social life the promise of the Kingdom. If we share the eucharistic life, it will be meaningless unless we find there the divine element in secular life. Without secular cult, in other words, liturgical worship, for all its sentiments about God, becomes empty formalism. Without secular cult, it will never equip participants for mission in the secular world.

Liturgy consequently must be involved with the world and with history. It must include a "secular cult" that confesses the mystery of Christ. It is so that the world is destined to become the Kingdom of God, and secular history the history of salvation.

V. James 1:17-18, The letter of James is made up of eight short
    21b-22, 27 instructions which were the inspiration for
    2nd reading homilies in the primitive communities. Having
    2nd cycle dealt with trial (Jm 1:2-12) and with the
source of temptation (Jm 1:13-18), the author considers the Christian's attitude to the Word of God (Jm 1:19-27).

He is particularly solicitous about moral behavior, and is concerned to define what the specific attitude of the Christian should be when faced with trial and weakness. A fundamental attitude is reception of the Word and its application in the performance of works (vv. 22-27; cf. 2:20-26). Our reading today is concentrated on this point.

The catechesis put forward in the letter of James is quite primitive. It is designed for Christian communities which are still altogether Jewish in origin and concerned with Jewish problems only.

a) Judaeo-Christian communities were constantly worried about the problems raised by passage from Judaism to the religion of Jesus (Jm 4:11). James reminds them that they should *receive the Word* and put it in practice (vv. 21b-22; cf. Pr 2:1; 7:1-3). This will deal adequately with their problems.

Rather more than a doctrine, the Word means a mysterious presence of God among those who hear it. It is "planted" in a person the moment that he receives it (v. 21). Here James has recourse to the ancient counsels offered by the sages to their disciples: not to give way to anger in order that the Word may be free to work (Pr 14:17, 29; 16:32); to receive teaching with "docility," with the modesty that is of the humble, rejecting all arrogance and pride (Jm 3:13-14; 4:6, Si 1:27, 45:4).

Like a seed, the Word carries within itself the principle of growth (cf. Mt 13), provided no obstacle is placed in the way and that it is sown in fertile ground. In this instance the fertile ground will be characterized by silence (v. 26), for the intemperance of human speech will not allow God to be heard, and by devotion (v. 27), which means worship and prayer, but above all charity and love.

b) The Word being then none other than the divine life in man, "keeping" it will not mean burying it like a treasure. It must expand into Trinitarian life, as other New Testament texts will go on to affirm (Jn 8:51-55; 14:21-24; 17:6-19, 1 Jn 2:5; 5:2-3). It should bear fruit in *"works"* (vv. 22-27; cf. Mt 7:21-26). It has nothing in common with Corinthian gnosis, which is just specula-

tion without moral involvement, or with Jewish reasoning, which
no longer entails doing the will of God.

God judges the efficacy of the Word in any person by the
"works" it produces (Tb 12:9; Jb 34:10-11; Jr 17:10, 31:29-30).
These constitute religion that is pure and without flaw.*

VI. Hebrews As in Galatians 4:24-26, Paul here asserts his
12:18-19, opposition to the mountains of Sinai and Sion
22-24 in order to withdraw his listeners from their
2nd reading nostalgic attachment. It is wrong for these
3rd cycle Jewish converts to keep longing for the tangible mountain, whether it be that of Sinai or
its successor Sion. From now on for them there should be only
one place of assembly: the spiritual Sion.

a) As with other ancient religions, in Judaism *mountains* were
of capital importance (cf. Is 2:2; 11:9; 25:6-7). The very fact that
they were elevated towards heaven, the presumed dwelling place
of God, was enough to sacralize them, especially when natural
phenomena invested them with a halo (vv. 18-19).

Such an attitude of course would be normal in a culture or
religion where man felt himself to be less than nature, and saw
God behind the phenomena of nature. He would revere the
mountain to show his fear of nature and to acknowledge the God
who was master of nature's mysterious, uncontrollable ways.

Christ however, by triumphing over death, nature's essential
law, has delivered man from this alienation. By the grace of God
he is freed. Consequently he need no longer seek encounter with
God through the medium of nature. Men will no longer congre-
gate around holy mountains; religion will not be characterized by
fear of natural phenomena (He 12:20-21).

The place of cult for the delivered man (the first-born that is,
v. 23) is the assembly of free men in the company of the angels.

*See the doctrinal theme: *works*, p. 70.

The angels were regarded as having power over the laws of nature, and are now on the same level as men (v. 22). In the company above all though of Jesus the mediator, whose triumph over death has enabled man to overcome evil and purify himself from sin (v. 24).

b) The argumentation reflects the opposition, which is latent throughout the letter, between *the celestial and the terrestrial*. The author's hope is based essentially on Christ's entry to the "celestial" world (that is to say, on his divinity). There he presents himself as the precursor of humanity (cf. v. 25; He 4:4; 6:20; 7:26; 8:1-2; 9:12-14; 11:12). In all this the author is concerned to spiritualize the hope of Christians, that has been too associated with the terrestrial Sion. In the future the assembly will gather round the divinized Lord, not a material mountain. Israel acquired the title, first-born, at Sinai (Ex 4:22-23; Jr 31:9; Si 36:11). Christians in turn can now claim the title (v. 23) as they gather round the new Sion, which is Jesus, the truly first-born (He 1:6). After the Sinai assembly, the name of the chosen people was written in the book of life (Ex 32:32-33) and subsequently in the registers of the terrestrial Jerusalem. But now it is written in the "heavenly" book (v. 23), that is the divine life itself. The Sinai assembly was due to the mediation of angels (v. 22; cf. Ac 7:38, 53; Ga 3:19; He 2:2). The Christian assembly takes place around the person of the unique and definitive mediator (v. 24), according to a covenant that is greater (cf. Ex 24:8; He 9:19-20; 10:29).

c) The purpose of the passage is to convince Christians that their *hope* should be spiritualized. Just as Sinai (or Sion which replaced Sinai: Ps 67/68:17; Is 2:2-3; Jr 31:11-12; Ga 4:21-26) was the place of "assembly" for the tribes (v. 23; cf. Ac 7:38; Dt 4:10; 9:10; 18:16), so now in the Church, the spiritual Sion, the assembly of the nations is convoked. It cannot be that the right of the first-born will be lost again, as Esau lost it (He 12:16-17; cf. v. 25).

Christians are dispersed throughout the world, but no longer hope, as the Jews did, for a universal reassembly in geographical terms. They constitute the first-born of a kingdom, the capital of which is no longer terrestrial.

VII. Matthew
16:21-27
Gospel
1st cycle

Here we have the first prophecy of the passion (vv. 21-22), with a statement of the conditions necessary in order to follow Jesus in the new way he is about to undertake. We have reached an important turning in the training of the disciples. This is clear from the phraseology adopted by Matthew: "he began to show . . ." (v. 21). The teaching is new, and doubtless it is in order to bring the apostles to a proper state of mind that Jesus has reprimanded them for their lack of faith (Mt. 16:5-12). To his remarks Matthew adds something he has already recounted (10:38-39), with emphasis this time on the ecclesial import. Matthew in fact shows considerable anxiety to stress the ecclesial lessons of the paschal mystery.

a) About the authenticity of the terms in which Jesus foretells his paschal mystery, exegetes are not quite agreed. It is clear that the primitive communities were anxious to give these predictions precise form. They had to conform *a posteriori* to the actual events, and they were very exactly stylized as formulas of faith. Among elements attributable to the primitive communities we might single out the reference to the *third day* (Mt 16:21; 17:23; 20:19). This is a refinement, under paschal influence, of an older phrase, probably Jesus' own: "after three days" (Mk 8:31; 9:31; 10:34). It was meant to indicate, not a precise day, but just a short interval (similar usage: Ho 6:2; Lk 13:32-33).

b) The predictions never give the actual *manner of death*. The mention of crucifixion is found in a single instance only (Mt 20:19). The reference to the "cross" in verse 24 cannot be taken as proof that he was foretelling the manner of death. Indeed he seems sometimes to have a presentiment of death by stoning (Mt 23:37). There can be no doubt that he foresaw his death, even if the details furnished, the reference to authorities (v. 21) and the sufferings (Mk 10:33-34), seem subsequent additions. It is equally certain that he foresaw his resurrection in one form or other. His reference to death and resurrection are far too numerous, and far too natural, to be the work of the primitive community (cf. Jn 2:19; Mt 12:40).

c) One of the doctrinal elements in the predictions is the affirmation that the sufferings and resurrection are a fulfillment of the Scriptures. That is the force of the formula "he was destined" (v. 21; cf. Mk 8:31; Mt 17:22, etc.). Generally in the New Testament it is used to describe the inevitable advent of the last times. It refers for the most part to events so decisive in salvation history that they affect its accomplishment (Mk 13:7, 10; Mt 24:6, etc.). Thus the tragic destiny of the Son of man is regarded as decisive for the *history of humanity*.

d) The biblical inspiration of all predictions is very evident, both in the original elements and the additions made by the primitive community. This sets the paschal event in the context of salvation history. In today's reading for instance we have the verb "suffer" (v. 21; cf. Mt 17:12; Mk 8:31; 9:12, Ac 1:3; 3:18; 17:3; 1 P 2:21-23; 4:1) which reflects Isaiah 53:4, 11, where it means "bearing a heavy burden," "being overwhelmed by trials." It stresses the link between the mystery of Christ and that of the *suffering Servant*.

e) To refer to the *resurrection* Matthew uses the verb "awaken" (*egeiresthai*), while Mark uses the word, probably primitive, "arise" (*anistasthai;* cf. Ho 6:2; Wi 4:20; 5:23; and above all Is 52:13, in reference to the Servant). By substituting "awaken" for "arise" Matthew may have wished to indicate that Christ's resurrection would bring an eschatological age of renewal. He would be emphasizing the ecclesiological import of the mystery. The word "arise" on the other hand has christological implications (the exaltation after crucifixion).

f) Jesus was not content with showing the eschatological necessity of his own suffering. He also wants to prepare his disciples for a life of similar trial. To emphasize this detail Matthew makes an anthology as it were, which is somewhat contrived, of previous sayings.

The phrases "renounce" "take up the cross" and "follow Christ" are really synonymous. They indicate in different ways what is the essential element of *Christian life*. If Jesus himself has to expect the punishment of the cross for his nonconformist ideas, he warns his followers that if they remain faithful to his teaching they can expect no better lot. All security must be renounced, and the counsels of the master must be accepted (this is the rabbinic meaning of the phrase "follow" someone), not alone in theory but in practice ("carry the cross," v. 24).

Saving one's life in this context means abandoning the group of followers, as too dangerously revolutionary, for reasons of security. Losing one's life means loyalty at this time, at the risk of one's life, to the group (v. 25). But one can only take that risk by maintaining absolute solidarity with Jesus' person ("for my sake").

If, throughout terrestrial life, this solidarity is maintained, it will ensure active participation in his resurrection and his eschatological kingdom (the theme of "life" contrasted with that of "the world" in v. 26). In this fashion the paschal mystery is fulfilled for every Christian. Christ's death and resurrection become the lot of the disciples, who carry the cross in order that they may share glory with him.

g) The glory that has been promised Jesus and his disciples (vv. 27-28) is described by introducing the theme of the *Son of Man*. In the prediction of the passion strictly speaking the theme had not been mentioned, by contrast with the other synoptics and with Matthew 17:22, 20:18, but now at the end of this passage it comes very appositely. The prediction of the passion is inspired not only by the suffering Servant theme; into the eschatological purview comes also the theme of the Son of man.

The Son of Man in Daniel 7 has often been interpreted as a symbol of the Remnant of the chosen of Israel, the nucleus of the new humanity. The image was subsequently individualized until it came finally to designate the Messiah (Mt 17:22; 20:18, etc.). Because of Matthew's placing, not in the prediction text, but at the end of his description of the common suffering of Jesus and his followers, one is inclined to wonder whether he is not still adhering to a collective interpretation; a symbol of the new humanity that escapes death and judgment to constitute the eschatological Kingdom. If such a view is possible, it is essential to remember that in Matthew also the Son of Man is an individual person, and that it is only through this person that humanity can eventually be included in the image, or, in any case, come to share the Kingdom.

VIII. Mark 7:1-8, 14-15, 21-23
Gospel
2nd cycle

Christ continues with the training of the apostles. He has instructed them in their missionary and eucharistic role (Mk 6:31-44), has revealed to them his power over evil (Mk 6:45-52), and made them open to universalism (Mk 6:53-56). They understand at once that the structures of the old religion cannot meet the missionary and universalist needs of the new. A discussion develops, which is at once concerned with pharisaic traditions. It is certainly not in its historical context at this point, because it is situated in Palestine, and just now Jesus is outside the frontiers (Mk 6:53). By placing it here Mark displays his concern with apostolic training and initiation to Christian life. Having dealt with the missionary and eucharistic dimensions, he now turns to the ethical.

a) The discussion between Jesus and the apostles about the *Pharisees* is centered on two concrete points. First, ritual ablutions before eating, of which Mark provides his non-Jewish readers with several examples (vv. 3-4). Second, the sacred offering of property which dispensed from the support of parents (vv. 10-11). There is little point in giving time to the analysis of these customs.

They are only mentioned to stress the point of verse 8, which is oddly repeated in verse 9, and illustrated by the citation of Isaiah 29:13 (v. 7). The tradition of men has tended to destroy the Word of God.

Like the first Adam the Pharisee considers that he has wrested from God the knowledge of good and evil. He employs this in his attempt to live a life of holiness. But it involves him in a perpetual state of conflict, each act being a decision between good and evil. He is always being torn in the toils of a knowledge that is not really his. And he is constantly causing agony to human beings by presuming to judge between those who do good and those who are slaves to evil. Only God can do that (Mt 7:1; cf. Rm 12:14-21).

Jesus wants the Pharisees to forsake this scrupulosity about good and evil, and rediscover unity with the Word of God itself. Instead of distinguishing between good and evil, and passing judgment on men's actions, they should be trying to know God himself so as to be known by him.

b) This is the meaning of verse 8, where Jesus contrasts *commandment* with tradition. The latter is purely juridical: it analyzes "cases," imposes "attitudes," and controls merely external behavior.*

The commandment however is personal; it uses the second person; it emanates from a person and can only be understood through communion with that person. It reaches down to the very depths of one's being. There is no question of introducing new precepts that cancel the traditions. What the commandment enjoins is a new way of fulfilling them in freedom. They must be lived in faith and in communion with God.

c) Thus Christ's criticism of the law is not really criticism of the law in itself. It had in it sufficient dynamism to reach the level of spiritualization that he sought. The Jews however, above all the Pharisees, by their overly material interpretation, had strangled the dynamism. Thus, as a result of his polemic, *pharisaism,*

*See the doctrinal theme: *faith and tradition,* p. 19.

which was originally synonymous with piety and perfection, came to be the symbol of hypocrisy.

Yet Christianity owes much to this tradition: many apostles to begin with, among them Saint Paul; the basic doctrine of the resurrection; the canon of Scripture from which primitive cathechesis was to draw so much. Pharisaism had led to elaborate complication of legal precepts, but pharisaic circles nevertheless were the first to emphasize the importance of charity in the law as a whole. During a time when pagan influence was overwhelming, they became uncompromising guardians of Jewish observance and really saved the soul of the people. Their efforts in this direction militated against messianism, which was thought too dangerous politically, and their insistence on cultic practices created an imbalance at the expense of human brotherhood and social justice.

It was inevitable that Jesus should clash with such an attitude. Religion for him was centered on the person rather than the law. He was wholly directed towards a purified messianism and regarded brotherliness as more important than cultic practice (Mt 15:18-20). He countered them by returning to the spirit of the primitive law and loosening the rigidities in order to spiritualize it. There is a considerable distance between this and rejection of all pharisaism as hypocrisy (something that was indeed severely condemned in pharisaic circles themselves). We should remember this, even if, in the heat of polemic, some primitive communities did not.

The tragedy of the Pharisees is that of humanity, really, whenever it pretends to a knowledge that is outside its compass. We have it wherever people are judged on the basis of a knowledge of good and evil that ignores God. It is only God who can make the proper allowances in passing judgment.

Christ was the first man who could make the knowledge of good and evil subserve a higher knowledge: that of God and his will. Living in conformity with God's will set him free from all casuistry about good and evil, and made him close to the sinner.

The Christian when he examines his conscience should not so much analyze the good and the evil. He should try to determine whether in his heart he finds the Word of God, and the person of Jesus who lives in him and for him (1 Co 4:3-4). Each day reception of the Eucharist recalls him to this task.

IX. Luke   Chapter 14 of Saint Luke is altogether given
   14:1, 7-14   over to the Lord's "table-talk," a normal liter-
   Gospel   ary genre in antiquity. The first verse is a gen-
   3rd cycle   eral introduction, and gives us the circum-
stances of time and place: a Sabbath, in the home of a Pharisee. He then describes the cure of the man with dropsy (vv. 2-6), and continues with two parables, the first about choice of place (vv. 7-11), the other about choice of guests (vv. 12-14). Finally comes the parable of the banquet (vv. 15-24). In order to give unity to the ensemble, Luke represents Christ as making these remarks in that order to the guests, to the host and one of the guests.

a) The "table-talk" that we have from contemporary pagan literature depicts the guests gathered at a meal round about the host. They are usually of the aristocracy, or from philosophic circles (see Plato's *Symposium*). Luke begins in the same way by showing us a number of prominent Pharisees, but at once he introduces the man with dropsy, to show that the meal of Christ is never one reserved to the elite.

During the course of the banquet it was customary for each guest to give a discourse concerning the subject under discussion, or to describe its applications. The discourse of Jesus is like this. The subject is humility. He describes its manifestations (vv. 7-10) and goes on to give its definition (v. 11).

In compiling the chapter Luke is thinking principally of the difficulties encountered by Christian gatherings of his time. Because these were detached from the temple and ran the risk of falling under pagan influence, it was imperative to provide a standard of procedure from the Gospel. That is the reason for this chapter, and also for James 2:1-4, and 1 Corinthians 11:20-21.

The lesson is conveyed against a background of Jewish custom, where there was a tendency to indicate the consequences of particular attitudes. Thus putting oneself in the last place might be a means of getting the first place. This could possibly be sapiental in origin (Pr 25:6-7).

When Luke gives us the two narratives that we have in today's Gospel (he is the only one to do this), he is anxious to provide a theology for the Sunday *assembly*. Jesus is removing all barriers of legal uncleanness with which the Jews surrounded their assemblies. His will be different, open to all. It can only be the assembly of salvation if all members feel at home.

b) One of the problems the early communities had to face most frequently was the sort of reception the poor should receive. To begin with Luke gives an answer set in the rabbinic and sapiental tradition (vv. 12-15). Remembering the consequences which particular attitudes could have, it was better to invite the poor, just as it was better to put oneself in the last place (vv. 10-12; cf. Pr 25:6-7). However, he quickly abandons this interested viewpoint for a more eschatological one.

Realizing that Christ has inaugurated the final times, he likens these, in Jewish fashion, to a great banquet for the poor (Is 55:1-5). It must be recognized that sometimes he succumbs to the optimistic view of some of his sources concerning material poverty. The view, that is, that this was the only title valid for entry to the Kingdom (Lk 12:13-21; 16:1-15; 19-31; 14:12-14; 20:45–21:4).

Matthew on the other hand, who is writing after some years of experience in the Church, affirms that sociological poverty is not necessarily a better title than any other to salvation (cf. the qualification added to the beatitude about the poor: Mt 5:3). For him the problem is why some of those admitted to the banquet (already called, that is, already Christian) cannot continue to be there after their mistake.

We can then distinguish three stages of development in the parable. When he delivered it, Jesus was proclaiming that the messianic banquet which had been awaited since Isaiah 55:1-3 was now an actuality; the invitations had been already made. As a result of problems in the primitive Christian assemblies, Luke interprets to the point of stressing sociological poverty as a condition for entry to the Kingdom. Matthew again qualifies this condition by adding a reference to the "justice" required.

Once we realize this we see the significance of Luke's answer to the question: who will be gathered at the banquet. It will be an assembly of the poor, the sick, the crippled, in a quite literal sense. These poor who are the successors of the "poor of Israel" are chosen not so much because of material poverty, but because of the attitude this makes possible. The wealth on the other hand of those originally invited precludes such an attitude.*

*See the doctrinal theme: *assembly of the poor*, p. 24.

B.   DOCTRINE

1. Theme of Faith and Tradition

More and more Christians are beginning to experience a real malaise where traditional formulations of the faith are concerned. What they want is a clear-cut, reasoned expose of what it means. They have a feeling that many elements of the traditional formulation stem from a religious perception that may be valid enough in itself but is thoroughly unsuited to modern requirements. Above all, anything traceable to a mythic sensibility should be reinterpreted and reduced to its clear content. Some would even go further. They want the kind of rationalization that will cover all the horizons of the faith, failing to see that this would mean reducing Christianity to a purely human philosophy or wisdom. This sort of process, we have often discovered, is liable to extract merely what is useful or acceptable, leaving aside doctrinal elements that are really essential.

Undue emphasis on the subjective viewpoint leads of course to actual subjectivism in religion. It is very evident that whenever the individual conscience is made the total norm, faith in Jesus Christ is undermined. We must be careful on the other hand of erecting barriers for the understanding by confusing real objectivism with formulations that actually are out-dated.

Faith is a personal commitment, but it depends on real data that Scripture describes as the "commandment of God" (1st reading and Gospel, 2nd cycle). The commandment is a living reality. Throughout their own history, the believers gradually gained more insight into it, until one day it assumed the visage of the man-God. The tradition which transmitted this commandment is radically different from the "tradition of men" (Mk 7:8). The latter will always tend to make of the commandment something delimited and circumscribed.

The objective basis of faith in Israel

In all traditional religions men have tended to show great respect for purely verbal and ritual formulations. Refusing as they do to accept the event and history, they celebrate everything that points to the recurring cycle. The kind of communication with the sacral that is yearned for can only be provided by the enduring, the stable, the solid. And so, from very primitive ages, rigorous ritual formulations are handed down. They are unchangeable, and provide the only avenue to religious experience. Men must accept the sacred formulas, be modeled by them, and so drawn into the great cosmic rhythm. Any attempt at change will automatically cut people off from the world of the gods.

The Jewish viewpoint was altogether different, because the regime of faith was erected around history and the event. The human predicament itself gradually made the Jew aware of the depth of his aspirations, which nothing but the intervention of a Totally-Other God could satisfy. His whole religious norm is fidelity to that living God, who has been active throughout Jewish history. Instead of cosmic stability, what nourishes him is the history of divine interventions and great liberating events. It was the sacred texts which described these turning points in his history that were constantly studied and interpreted.

However there was one dimension to this religious approach which seemed indeterminable. It was clear that salvation must depend on a divine initiative, but it was also clear that human response must be forthcoming. What could be the nature of that human fidelity? This was the agonizing question that troubled Israel collectively, and that finally led to messianism hope. At each turning point in her history, Israel would worry about her future and try to take the path indicated by the lessons of contemporary events. It was at the moment of the exile, for instance, or shortly afterwards, when all traditional securities had been lost, that the image of the suffering Servant took shape.

The event of Jesus as objective basis of faith

The Jesus-Event became the definitive basis of faith. He fulfilled the hope of Israel by confronting the event *par excellence:* death. He fully plumbed the mystery of the human predicament by accepting in the trend of events all that is most disconcerting to man. No one ever exeprienced more totally, or more lucidly, the incapacity of the creatural world to satisfy the yearning for the absolute of human freedom. But his very plumbing of the human predicament, which man was summoned to share through total renunciation, went side by side with a fulfillment of human aspiration that surpassed all hope. His response to the divine initiative was the perfect one because it was that of God's Son. In the decisive event of the Cross, that culminating point of his obedience as God and man, he wrought salvation. It was an obedience that revealed the unfathomable depths of love and the true grandeur of man's destiny: that he is called to be a child of God while fully embracing the creatural condition.

In such unexpected fashion was Israel's hope fulfilled. In giving faith its objective basis, Jesus did not go beyond the spiritual framework of Israel, but simply took his place within it. He brought the spiritual pilgrimage of his people to its goal. By his fidelity as man-God he accomplished the Law, and in this process it became evident what was transitory. That which was lasting though, reached an unprecedented degree of fulfillment. Throughout the vicissitudes of a life shared with his fellowmen he was fully himself, and never more so than when dying on the Cross. Because he was both God and man, this death as a criminal was seen to be the very *apogie* of love, the event which marked the perfect encounter between God and man. It was the perfect Pasch that opened the way to eternal life as Risen Lord.

The Church of the Risen Lord, living tradition of the Pasch

The basis of faith then is a Person: Jesus, who accomplished salvation in the paschal Event of the Cross. The Church's mission is to make this event actual for all peoples, everywhere. As he fulfilled Israel's hope, so must she the hope of other peoples. She must engraft this paschal event into their search so that they too will find the fulfillment that transcends their expectations. The only thing that enables her to do this is the presence with her of the Risen Lord. Were she not the Body of Christ, it would be impossible. On earth, the sign of her involvement is involvement of the hierarchic ministry.

Because the Risen Lord is with her, the mystery of his obedience and love is hers too. That is really the Good News of salvation that she offers to all mankind. All her members are under grave obligation to display this in their lives, because otherwise the mystery would remain hidden. If she is going to provide answers for all peoples, she must share their quest, and her members must demonstrate that it is only in the paschal Event they find fulfillment.

In that sense the Church is, and ought to be, the living tradition of Christ's Pasch. The transcedence of the mystery she carries with her is that of the Cross. From the second century onwards she was always aware that authentication of her message depended upon the link with apostolic witness. The thrust of that had been that Israel's pilgrimage reached fulfillment in the death and resurrection of Christ. The post-apostolic Church found in the Scriptures the same message, the one that she implanted in all the diverse cultures that she encountered.

Expressions of faith and diversity of cultures

Confessions of faith are as old as Christianity. The earliest formulations of the Christian creed that we find are in the New Testament. What they affirm is the basic historicity of Christianity: human salvation is Jesus of Nazareth, dead and risen again for all humanity. This is the immutable credo of the Church that must be transmitted. At every moment of history the Church will be the presence of the Risen Lord insofar as she is the living proclamation of his death. Set in the midst of the world she represents the paschal event, but this is the actualization of an event in history when the great encounter between God and man took place once for all. It is an event which dominates all history, but

an event in history. Any attempt to tamper with it would undermine the very foundations of Christianity.

From the time however of its very first formulations, the
Church's credo also affirmed, more or less explicitly, some insights
about the mystery of Christ. She was not content with proclamation of the fact; she wanted to penetrate the transcendent mystery.
Contrary to the view taken by some, we maintain that there was
a dogmatic content even in the most primitive credo, some attempt
to express the dimension of transcendence. Dogma was not a
product of Church history, as she encountered different cultures.
Once this is granted, it is obvious that the credo underwent
gradual development, as insight into the mystery deepened; that
it required many centuries to give us the formula we now know.
The Nicaeo-Constantinople credo adds nothing to the primitive
one; it does indicate deeper insight.

In a larger context, arising from the credo, the ferment of
theological speculation in the Church led to deeper understanding
of the implications of the paschal event. It clarified, in its fashion,
the mystery of the recapitulation of all things in Christ. Modern
man's requirements, with regard to formulation of the faith, are
certainly demanding, but if they are satisfied insofar as this is
legitimate, new avenues of understanding could be opened up.
It could well be that the Church would find here a means of
making her catholicity more evident.

The eucharistic celebration a sharing of Christ's Pasch

All the aspects of the objective basis of faith we have been discussing have relevance in the eucharistic celebration. For the
Church it is the moment *par excellence* of the Risen Lord's presence, the memorial of his Pasch. The proclamation of the Word
and the sharing of the Bread are designed to strengthen the faith
of believers, transcendentally as well as historically. The celebration is always being renewed, and enables Christians to make their
own what was accomplished once for all on the Cross. They can
bear witness by their lives to the mystery of obedience and love
out of which the Church was born.

In the celebration indeed, the problems about formulation of the faith are constantly present. The believers assembled there will be encountering some precise formulations. They may be venerable, but they are not always relevant. The Church has been constantly absorbing liturgical formulas that are the product of the different cultures she encountered. Since Vatican II a movement has been started that augurs well for the future. We may yet see the day when our eucharistic celebrations will take on the particular coloring of all the diversified cultures, while maintaining the essential structure intact. The Church will then be demonstrating the dynamism that is properly hers.

2. Theme of the Assembly of the Poor

The Second Vatican Council, in describing the role of the Church as "light" among the nations, stresses with remarkable emphasis two dimensions of the Christian vocation. In the first place membership of the Church means sharing the faith; the Christian is someone who is qualified by baptism to live the faith in Christ Jesus to the full. Secondly, this membership implies responsibility; the Christian must bring his particular, and irreplaceable, stone to the ecclesial edifice. He must take his part in the accomplishment of the Church's mission, disseminating the charity of Christ.

The third evangelist (Gospel, 3rd cycle, and Lk 14:15-24, which follows immediately) is concerned to demonstrate that poverty is a necessary characteristic of those who respond to God's invitation, a basic condition that is for Church membership. It, rather than anything else, reveals the Church as God's universal assembly.

It is very imperative nowadays, at a time when men tend to challenge the Church's claim that she assembles men of all races and nations, that Christians be aware of their responsibilities through baptism. She is always assured of the Lord's presence, but at every different period of history her members must determine the concrete tasks to be undertaken. It is thus that, until the end of time, Christ will continue the divine work of universal assembly.

The Kingdom of Yahweh, the reassembly of the poor

Man has a natural tendency to see salvation in terms of assembly. It seems to be a sign of favor from the gods, whereas dispersion is a sign of disfavor. The former gives security and solidarity; the latter creates insecurity and weakness. Liturgies which offer men communion with the sacral world enjoin assemblies. They facilitate passage from the profane to the sacral.

The Jewish people, when they saw Yahweh's salvation in terms of a reassembly, shared this sentiment. Their very history was punctuated by great assemblies: the desert, the Promised Land, the regathering after the exile. The great universalist visions of the prophets, set in the messianic future, were all in terms of a vast assembly of the nations at Jerusalem, with the chosen people at the center. This was anticipated as much as possible in Jewish liturgy. There were frequent assemblies of all the people. It was so in the desert. It was so during the Palestinian period, when all the tribes would be gathered together. These assemblies marked crucial moments in Israel's history, or times of pilgrimage at Jerusalem.

For pagan man the ideal assembly was itself the security he sought, and thus never extended further than a single people, or a group of peoples linked socially or politically. The Jewish ideal on the other hand went further. The assembly over which Yahweh, the God of faith, presides derives its security from God himself. And the great gathering anticipated for the Day of Yahweh comprises all nations, with Israel in the privileged place. Nor was simple membership of the people a passport to the assembly of salvation. The prophets emhasized the other conditions. Only those who remained faithful to the covenant and observed the law would enter the Kingdom: the poor of Yahweh, the small Remnant.

Jesus of Nazareth, architect of universal assembly

The Father's plan of universal assembly for his scattered children was realized in Jesus. In many essential points however this assembly differed from the Jewish concept.

To begin with, the Kingdom of the Father, which is the assembly of salvation, no longer offers the security of a secular assembly. It is not of this world, and it is absolutely universalist. Every human being is called to enter on a basis of equality, and there is no one with a special place.

Yet, though all are called to enter, the conditions for entry are demanding. A radical poverty is required. In this Jesus echoes the prophetic teaching and carries it further still. The poverty he speaks of however has this characteristic, that it confers no privilege. It can be the possession of any man, provided he acknowledge his sinfulness and throw himself on the divine mercy.

Another essential difference is what might be called the novelty of the divine salvific plan as revealed by Jesus. The universal assembly of the children of God called for human cooperation, and here Jesus himself played a decisive part. In the Old Covenant it had seemed possible that God could use particular men, at most, as instruments in the work of reassembly. They might not know they were being used: Cyrus for instance had no thought of fulfilling Yahweh's plan. With the New Covenant there is a striking difference. Jesus inaugurated it, and not only does he realize he is a divine instrument, he is the principal architect of the reassembly. The whole enterprise from now on is seen to be both divine and human. God has the great initiative, but the assembly takes place around the man-God, the "recapitulator" of all things.

The Cross is the secret of the reassembly willed by God. The man-God played the decisive role, because his encounter with death was the supreme act of love, of total self-renunciation.

Ecclesial reassembly and Christian communities

Christ inaugurated the work of universal assembly, and in the Church it is continued. It is important that we understand what precisely this assembly is, by what agency and means it is gathered, and the relationship it has with the Christian communities scattered throughout the universe.

The Church is primarily the family of God's children, humanity assembled in the Kingdom as the Body of Christ. The Kingdom however is not of this world, and the assembly that it constitutes is not sociological. Israel was a people in secular terms: the Church is not, she is the people of God. Throughout all time she will be working towards the realization of this. Following Christ, and by his grace, all men are called to be God's partners in the building of the Kingdom. Those who become members of the assembly must themselves become "assemblers."

There is no security in this ecclesial assembly: its basic meaning is to be found in love and self-renunciation. The believer is "assembled," and is himself an "assembler," insofar as he imitates Jesus in confronting death, wherever it appears, with the same obedience and with total renunciation. The responsibility he assumes is that of practising brotherly love without limits. He must turn above all to the poor and the deprived. This is going to make him vulnerable. There will be no security in the assembly gathered on such principles. Sometimes he will have to struggle with despair, and hope against hope.

It might seem that the individual Christian communities of the institutional Church, as they gather for eucharistic celebrations, ought to be described as sociological assemblies where members can find the securities they will not find in the Kingdom. This would not be accurate. The condition of the Christian in this world is that of a person dispersed among men. The initiation into the mystery of Christ that is provided for him by the ritual assembly is essentially a challenge to faith, an initiation into the obedience of Christ. Indeed it ought to be the aim of every ritual assembly to have people of the greatest possible diversity, humanly speaking, gathered together in love.

Ecclesial reassembly and human brotherhood

The Christian's role as reassembler in the People of God does not leave him indifferent to the ideal of a community of peoples on the secular level. The very virtue he has to exercise in order to fulfill his Christian role, love to the point of self-renunciation in acceptance of the creatural condition, renders him admirably suited for creatural love. He can accept the other in all his otherness, and thus is ready to promote what we call now the "encounter of cultures." The obstacles in the way of this are very formidable, because it requires dialogue between interlocutors who have really nothing in common. Nowhere is insecurity more evident: nowhere is self-interest liable to be more fatal. Social and economic inequalities add further aggravation, and constantly jeopardize the issue.

The close link with the ecclesial assembly in the Kingdom is the best hope for secular brotherhood. Love lies at the root of both, "filial" love for one, "creatural" love for the other. They are not different loves, but different dimensions of the same love, and that is the love that wells up in the heart of a man who becomes in Jesus Christ a child of God. The point is of importance in mission. In a world as concentrated as ours is on the need for secular transformation, evangelization will not be possible unless the Church is with humanity in the struggle. Efforts on her part to make the terrestrial city one of greater brotherhood can further her own particular mission too. It is a delicate area however, where she must move with circumspection, remembering the lessons of history. There are others besides Christians who work for human progress, and most often the Church will not be the controller of projects to this end. Her function is to be a leaven, but the leaven should be where the yeast is, not stored apart. Too often, even today, the organized Church will tend to regulate her proclamation of salvation according to the "opportunities" that arise, the "doors" that are opened, the "facilities" that are granted.

Ecclesial reassembly and eucharistic assembly

It is in the eucharistic celebration above all that the ecclesial reassembly in the Kingdom of the Father becomes a palpable reality. The whole purpose of the celebration is indicated by the explicit reference to the sacrifice of the Cross that should characterize both the liturgy of the Word and the liturgy of the Bread. Believers are brought together so that they will become reassemblers. The celebration builds them up in the charity of Christ, summons them to conversion of heart, and sends them forth as God's poor to be centers of gathering, cells of catholicity.

That is the ideal, but it does not of course come about automatically. Members do not always have the proper dispositions. Worse still, the conduct and structure of the celebration may be inadequate. It may not in fact be open to everyone, above all to the poor. It may be sociologically select, gathered on the basis of humanities, designed to be reassuring rather than a challenge to conversion of heart. Such an assembly will not prepare its members to be "reassemblers" in the Kingdom. Consequently the ecclesial Institution should be extremely careful about the composition and conduct of eucharistic assemblies. The Church is not, let us repeat, a terrestrial people. Her members are dispersed among humanity, and it is in this state of Diaspora that they are called to assemble the Fathers family. They do not lose this dimension when united for the Eucharist, but should actually deepen it. Then the eucharistic celebration will become truly a sign of ecclesial reassembly.

TWENTY-THIRD SUNDAY

A. THE WORD

I. Ezechiel
33:7-9
1st reading
1st cycle

The parable of the prophet-watchman (Ez 33:1-9) begins the second portion of Ezechiel's collection of oracles. Our reading today gives us only the last two verses, which are a sort of meditation on the responsibility of the prophet.

When the prophet evades responsibility, he lets himself be overcome by cloth, and does not redress the wrongs of his compatriots. He becomes responsible for their death indeed, because he does not warn them of the risks they run (v. 8). When he has the courage to protest against the pernicious atmosphere and negative thinking that surround him, the culprits may be lost, but he himself will be saved (v. 9).

The *responsibility of the prophet* then is that he must have the courage to challenge evil and sinners. He must do all he can to convert the latter, the threat of chastisement being his best weapon. His own salvation depends upon the zeal he shows in this task.

II. Isaiah
35:4-7a
1st reading
2nd cycle

These verses come from a poem about the return from Exile. It was inserted in the first part of the book of Isaiah, but was certainly written by a subsequent disciple.

The theme of our reading of the whole poem indeed, is the *return to Paradise*. The advent of God, Judge and Savior (v. 4), will transform the desert into a new paradise (vv. 6-7: cf. Is 41:17-20; 43:20; 48:21). Those incurably sick will be healed (vv. 5-6),

and fatigue itself will disappear (v. 3). What we have is an asser-
tion that the curses attributed to Adam's fall will soon be abolished. Fatigue (Gn 3:14), suffering (Gn 3:16), the brambles and
thistles of the desert (Gn 3:18), will be no more than a bad
memory.

The same theme is to be found in texts which describe the conquest of the Promised Land (Dt 8:7-10), but it is more prominent
in the accounts of restoration of the land after the exile (Is
43:18-21).

The theme of return to Paradise loses a good deal of its marvelous character in the New Testament. Thanks to his obedience
to the Father unto death, total fidelity that is to the human condition, Christ, the new Adam, returned to Paradise. Each time
that the people of God, following him, try to conquer war, hunger,
injustice and enslavement of labor, they are marking stages of
the road which will one day lead humanity back to Paradise.

III. Wisdom
9:13-18
1st reading
3rd cycle

This passage is the conclusion of a prayer for
wisdom, and the prayer itself concludes the
second portion of the book of Wisdom (Wi
6-9). Except for a few verses the prayer is undoubtedly older than the book, and probably
existed in the Hebrew before this Greek version was made. The
author himself adds verses 15-17.

His thinking is profoundly Jewish when he affirms that man is
made for immortality, and that God alone can grant this (v. 17).
He leans however to Greek philosophy when he tries to explain
man's trouble in acquiring the wisdom that would give him im-
morality. The incapacity is regularly laid in the Bible at the door
of sin, especially the sin of Adam. Our author attributes it to
man's state in the body (v. 15). The text is interesting in that we
have an inspired book reflecting about the *human predicament*

strictly speaking, in terms that are strikingly adapted to modern sensibility. It must be remembered however that the author is convinced that human happiness depends on God's antecedent initiative, and can only be attained through communion with his Wisdom and his Spirit (v. 17).

IV. Romans   Paul has just reminded his listeners that they
13:8-10   should obey the civil laws, even those of a
2nd reading   pagan and persecuting State. It is not only by
1st cycle   the sacred law of Sinai that God's will is mani-
                   fested, but by profane law as well.

There is no real conflict between the law of Moses and civil law, any more than there is between the principles of "rendering to Caesar what is Caesar's and to God what is God's" (Mt 22:21). The Sinai law is no more than civil law interpreted in the light of communion with God. When it commands believers to love one another, it also endorses the demands of civil law about adultery, theft and covetousness (v. 9). Its superiority to profane law consists in the fact that it makes *love of one's neighbor* the key to all human behavior.

When he makes the second table of the Decalogue (Ex 20: 13-17; Dt 5:17-21) the basis of the duty of charity towards the other, Paul is following a spiritual tradition that had already reduced all the law of Moses to the double commandment of love for God and one's neighbor (Mt 19:18-19; 22:34-40; Pss 14/15; 111/112; Ze 8:14-17).

Likewise, when he reduces all the commandments of civil law to the obligation of love for one's fellowmen, he is interpreting that law in the same way as the Jews interpreted the Mosaic.

Among Christians nowadays there is sometimes poor respect for civil laws, especially penal and fiscal laws. A certain moral casuistry maintains that it is not wrong to evade fiscal laws or purely penal enactments. Paul however rejects such a deformation when he asks the Christian to regard civil regulations as a way of loving the brethren.

In our socialized states of the twentieth century, taxes are in a sense the expression of love for one's neighbor. They will be expended largely on education, on caring for the sick, the aged and the disabled, on helping underdeveloped countries, scientific research, etc.

The Christian accordingly should see civil law as a means of extending Christ's loving lordship over humanity. He can only disobey insofar as these enactments contravene the law of love. It does not matter whether he approves or not of the political authority. They are not representatives of God and the Lord (Rm 13:4) by virtue of their origin, but because they are collaborating with the lordship of Christ in inculcating respect for the second table of the decalogue. That is why we pray for governments during eucharistic celebrations.

V. James
2:1-5
2nd reading
2nd cycle

The preceding portion of James' letter (1:27) had concluded with a summons to practice pure, unspoiled religion that aided the widow and the orphan. The author wants to find evidence of this attitude in the liturgical celebration itself.

Previously the prophets had condemned a cult that was pursued in the midst of social disorder (Am 2:6-7; Is 1:23; Ez 22:7). The God whom the people praise loves the poor with a love of predilection (Ho 14:4; Jr 5:28; 7:6), and his worship should manifest this. Christian assemblies however were reserving a privileged place for the rich and insulting the dignity of the poor (vv. 1 and 5). James condemns this attitude, which is contrary to the spirit of poverty of the original Jerusalem community. It is true that his concept of poverty is overly sociological. Subsequent generations will modify this: the Pauline churches will prefer having rich and poor live in harmony to insistence on poverty as the exclusive the same charity towards little ones in the name of God (vv. 5-7). road to salvation. The essential point of the teaching here however is not so much a defense of poverty, as the wish to have a proper link between true cult and the social attitude of the worshipers. Now that cult has become spiritual, the link between *rite and life* is closer than ever. It is firmly welded into the structure of the liturgy.

Later (2:14-16) he will return to this point. If one addresses the liturgical greeting "go in peace" to the poor, without doing anything to make that peace real, one is false to the principles of Christian worship. Since the event of the cross, the context of sacrifice is mercy and love. Generosity has more value than ritual offering (cf. Mt 15:1-10; 23:1-16). Our liturgical rites will not truly mirror the sacrifice of the Lord unless they have the dimension of service to others.

VI. Philemon
9-10, 12-17
2nd reading
3rd cycle

This is a letter that Paul wrote after his first captivity (61-63) to Philemon, a Christian of Colossae, who was his friend. Philemon had a runaway slave who had taken refuge with Paul's entourage.

The situation was embarrassing. It was strictly against the law for Paul to retain a fugitive slave in his service, and furthermore his friendship for Philemon made it impossible for him to conceal any longer the fact that Onesimus was living with him. Then there was the personal embarrassment. How could he adopt a purely legalist attitude to Onesimus, without taking account of the personal relationship that had grown between them?

a) Paul accepts the legal situation of his time without necessarily canonizing it. He sends Onesimus back to his master. He does so however in a fashion that indicates, from a Christian viewpoint, the inadequacies of the law.

A relationship has developed between Philemon and himself, because they share the same faith, and above all the exercise of Likewise a relationship has developed between Paul and Onesimus, so that Onesimus has become his very heart (vv. 10-12, 17). A similar relationship can grow between Onesimus and his master. It is true that the slave has given offense by his time of absence (vv. 11, 18). This however is a trivial matter when compared with the boon of brotherhood in Jesus Christ, and citizenship of the Kingdom (vv. 15-16).

b) In describing his relationship with Onesimus, he does not hesitate to use the image of *spiritual fatherhood*, which had been prominent in previous letters.

On Paul's lips, this is not merely a sentimental phrase. It describes accurately his whole apostolic mission; he regarded his ministry as a real transmission of life. His proclamation of the Gospel is not just the work of a propagandist. He is transmitting the message of God, and the Word of God is efficacious, bringing life and fecundity. The one who transmits it is a father in a certain sense (1 Co 4:14-21). And when, as well as giving the message, he lives it in his own person, to the point of suffering (Ga 4:19), the cross and prisons, it is clear that his fatherhood is instrumental, as Christ's life was the instrument of God's fatherhood for men (1 Co 4:15). He can demand filial affection from his disciples, which he is at pains to transmit to the Father, because his fatherhood is vicarious (1 Th 2:7-11).

Paul does not approve the laws about slavery, but he avails himself of them to make a loving gesture and lead men to a greater freedom in the Lord (cf. 1 Co 7:17-24; Rm 6:15-18). He accepts the master-slave relationship, but only to relativize it as against the relation of eternal brotherhood set up by the faith.

The Church was not founded in order to liberate slaves. That emancipation depends on the initiative of humanity itself, in the bosom of which Christians live and toil. When men fail in their responsibilities of course, the Church should remind them of that. But her real mission is to liberate man from himself by opening him to divine love. Imbued with that love, he is sent back to his terrestrial tasks and fulfills them by human means. Liberation of the poor and oppressed is one such task. When the Christian becomes involved in it, it is not for supernatural motives, but his faith does show him the deep meaning it can have. God himself is involved in the task, at a level far surpassing the human. The more fully the Christian accepts his purely human responsibilities, the more evident witness he will bear to the Father's love.

VII. Matthew 18:15-20
Gospel
1st cycle

This reading gives us part of Jesus' discourse about the proper attitude towards sin and scandal (Mt 18:5-11), and finally towards the sinner himself. The second portion stresses the mercy that the Church must show by recounting the parable of the lost sheep (Mt 18:12-14) and then giving details about the attitude of pardon. The sinner is first to be confronted alone (note that the formula "against you" is not found in the original text, which speaks of the sinner as such: v. 15). Then he is to be brought before two or three witnesses (v. 16). Finally he is to be questioned in full assembly (v. 17). So that the whole process will be effective, Jesus gives the apostles power in the matter (v. 18).

The third portion is concerned with the proper attitude of the injured party towards him who has given offense. Here the only rule is that of limitless pardon (vv. 21-22). Matthew reinforces this teaching with the parable of the unforgiving debtor (Mt 18:23-35).

Between the second and third portions (vv. 19-20) he inserts a *logion* of the Lord about the meeting of "two or three" in prayer. This is because there has just been question of the value in witness of "two or three" (v. 16). By taking something from a prayer context into one of victory over sin, he may have wished to indicate that prayer is a mighty weapon against sin (Jm 5:15-16; Mt 6:12).

a) The important theme of the passage is that of *pardon*. Jesus stresses the duty of pardon (vv. 21-23), and simultaneously transmits the power (vv. 15-18). The new age is one where the Lord makes it possible for man to escape from sin, not only by triumphing over his own personal sin, but by conquering the sin of others through pardon.

It is worth our while to examine the various stages in Jewish legislation that made this doctrine of pardon finally possible.

Primitive society in Israel was extremely harsh towards the fault of an individual. It had no means of pardoning him, and could only visit the offender with appropriate punishment, seventy-seven times more serious than the fault (Gn 4:24). The *lex talionis* was an important step forward (Ex 21:24).

Leviticus (19:13-17) goes further still. It does not of course institute an obligation of pardon strictly speaking (for the only Old Testament instances of pardon see 1 S 24 and 26); but it does insist on solidarity between brothers. It forbids them to have recourse to judicial procedure to settle their differences.

The decisive progress comes with the doctrine of Jesus. The New Testament provides constant evidence of his pardon. He pardons his own executioners (Lk 23:34); and Stephen (Ac 7:59-60), Paul (1 Co 4:12-13) and many others follow his example.

Generally the duty of pardon is associated with the imminence of the last judgment. If we ourselves are to be pardoned at this critical moment we must pardon our fellowmen as of now (partly the meaning of v. 35). And the measure of our pardon is to be none other than the primitive measure for vengeance (v. 22, cf. Gn 4:24).

This attitude, based as it is on the doctrine of retribution (Mt 6:14-15; Lk 11:4; Jm 2:13), is still quite Jewish. As time goes on the doctrine becomes more typically Christian. Pardon becomes a duty because one is oneself pardoned by God (Mt 18:23-35; Col 3:13). It is no longer just a moral obligation; it is the visible sign of God's reconciliation at work in each one of us (2 Co 5:18-20).

Such a concept could not flourish in a climate of thought which would see God's justice as distributive, with retribution always in the background. We are in a climate dominated by the mercy of God and justification for the sinner.

For all that its expression is still Jewish, Matthew 18: 15:22 echoes this concept. The evangelist is at least aware that the

Church is a community of the saved, which can only intend the salvation of the sinner. Should that not come to pass, it is because the sinner grows obdurate and refuses the pardon offered (v. 17). Thus the Christian community differs from the Jewish. It is only in pardoning the sinner that it judges him. Condemnation can only fall upon the sinner who refuses to live in the fold of the community.

b) Chapter 18 of Matthew was compiled fairly late. We see the primitive Church in the throes of trying to elaborate a discipline and construct a life. The Kingdom would not immediately present itself, and until it did some system was required. Probably the Church was inspired by the rules of Essene communities. These were professedly Zealot and easily condemned the sinner, even repeatedly: "let him be to you as the publican . . ." A Zealot community soon becomes sectarian. The primitive Church was more anxious to maintain dialogue than pronounce condemnations. Subsequently she was preserved from sectarianism, and able to fulfill her mission, insofar as she was ready to accept the "sociological Christian," and persevere in patience, pardon, and prayer in common.

The sinner will not come to realize God's pardon until he becomes aware of God's mercy at work in the Church and the eucharistic assembly. The solidarity between the members here is not that of a secular group who are obliged to pardon just their fellow members. They are part of a great history which is leading all men towards God's judgment. And God's judgment is his pardon offered throughout all time, until fulfillment comes.

VIII. Mark 7:31-37
Gospel
2nd cycle

The cure of the deaf and dumb man (*mogilalos*), as Mark relates it, has some remarkable features. He establishes a close parallel, for instance, between it and the cure of the blind man (Mk 8:22-26), which is already distinguished by its common inclusion in the so-called "section of breads" (Mk 6:30–8:26). We have the same "taking aside" of the sick man (7:33; 8:23), the insalivation (7:33; 8:23), the anxiety on the part of Jesus to enjoin silence (7:36; 8:26), the imposition of hands (7:32; 8:22-23), the same approach by friends who "bring" the invalid (7:32; 8:22).

Both pieces convey a single lesson. Inability to hear and see are signs of punishment (Mk 4:10-12; 8:18). The healing of these senses is a sign of salvation. God's gift of salvation however presupposes a breach with the world. When Jesus takes them aside, in order that they may see and hear, it is because the crowd cannot see or hear in the real sense.

a) The cure of the dumb man in the first place seems to be a replica of Isaiah 35:2-6. The prophet tells the people, who are exiled in Babylon, of a destiny they dare not dream of. They shall cry out for joy. In Mark we have Jesus in Gentile territory on the frontiers of Lebanon, and he makes a dumb man speak. The people are returning from exile, in transports of joy, rich with the renown of their foreign sojourn. The miracle is proclaiming the advent of the age of *salvation*. This salvation will be a judgment as well. The deaf shall hear (cf. Is 29:18-23); but others will become deaf to the Word.

b) It seems likely that Mark fitted this miracle into an already existing formulary for baptismal initiation. Christ's gesture of raising his eyes to heaven before curing the dumb man (v. 34) is only found elsewhere at the multiplication of bread (Mk 6:41). This seems to give the episode a liturgical structure.

Indeed we seem to have on the whole an echo of the primitive formula for *Christian initiation.** Our most ancient baptismal rituals suppose a rite for the senses (the eyes in Ac 9:18, the nose and ears in the Tradition of Hippolytus, no. 20; etc.). If we accept the view that spittle was believed by the Jews to be breath somehow materialized, it could signify the gift of the Spirit that

*See the doctrinal theme: *faith and the Word,* p. 43.

was characteristic of a new creation (Gn 2:7; 7:22; Wi 15:15-16). Mark probably retains the original Aramaic word spoken by Jesus, *Ephphata* (v. 34) because the ritual had retained it.

We can probably reconstruct the elements of the initiation rite as follows. There was an exorcism (Mk 7:29, the passage just preceding our Gospel); a sponsor ceremony, "those who bring"; a rite of imposition of hands (v. 32; a "taking aside" (v. 33. This is not the later *disciplina arcani,* but denotes an appreciation of the unique character of the faith); a rite for the senses (v. 34); three days of preparatory fast (Mk 8:3; Ac 9:9); and partaking of the Eucharist.

At the end of the passage Mark rejoins the synoptic tradition (vv. 36-37). He refers to the praise of the crowd who recognize in the miracle the advent of the messianic age (Mt 15:30-31), because it fulfills the oracle of Isaiah 61:1-2 that has been already interpreted by Jesus in this sense (Mt 11:5).

We have frequent instances in the Bible where initiation to faith is presented in the image of a cure from dumbness. Most accounts of the call of prophets, of people whose duty it will be to bear the Word of God, are examples (Ex 4:10-17; Is 6; Jr 1). What we have is a literary device meant to indicate that the prophet is incapable by natural faculty of even beginning to speak, that he receives the Word he transmits from another. The mute person who begins to proclaim the Word is a manifest sign of what the faith is, an infused virtue beyond human capability.

The image often has another important emphasis. During a period of divine chastisement the prophets are stricken dumb. The word of God is no longer proclaimed because the people have closed their ears so as not to hear (1 S 3:1; Is 28:7-13; Lm 2:9-10; Ez 3:22-27; Am 8:11-12; Gn 11:1-9). Dumbness then is associated with lack of faith, and the dumb man is frequently deaf.

On the other hand when prophets speak copiously, it is a sign of the advent of messianic times: God is present and faith is widespread (cf. Lk 1:65; 2:27, 38). In this context one prophetic text (Joel 3:1-2) is quite striking. It was fulfilled to the letter at Pentecost (Ac 2:1-3).

Christ's many cures of deaf-mutes are all signs of the advent of the messianic age (Lk 1:64-67; 11:14-28; Mt 9:32-34; 12:22-24; Mk 7:31-37; 9:16-28). The sending of the apostles, at the end of the Gospels, to bring the Word to the world, is also presented as a prophetic vocation. A new tongue is given to them (Mt 10:19-20; Rm 10:14-18) as if they too were emerging from dumbness.

Today's Gospel then teaches us that faith is a messianic blessing. But Mark is also anxious to stress the Old Testament theme which equated dumbness with lack of faith. On many occasions in his Gospel he points out that the crowd have ears that hear not and eyes that see not (Mk 4:10-12, again in 8:18). His whole "section of breads" (6:30–8:26) is a commentary on lack of understanding (6:52; 7:7, 18; 8:17, 21). When Jesus is about to cure the deaf-mute he withdraws him from the crowd (7:33), as if to indicate that dumbness is characteristic of the crowd and that he must leave them to become open to faith.

A filial relationship with God is characteristic of the final times. We become capable of hearing his word, responding to him and speaking of him to others. So that the Christian living in these times becomes as it were a prophet, a specialist of the Word, a confidant of God. But to hear this Word and proclaim it one needs the ears and lips of faith.

IX. Luke
14:25-33
Gospel
3rd cycle

This piece is made up of fairly disparate elements. For its proper understanding it is necessary to refer to verses 34-35 also. These parallel Matthew 5:13 and give us the *logion* about salt, the original context of which had been lost in the synoptic tradition. Luke makes it into a kind of parable in order to accommodate it to the lesson of verses 28-33, which are proper to him and concern the renouncement of all goods. Verses 26-27 are added as an introduction. They too belong to another context (cf. Mt 10:38; 16:24; Lk 9:23), and he gives another personal touch (the woman: v. 26) to reinforce the ascetic dimension.

a) The inauguration of the Kingdom is imminent. Consequently one must develop the necessary dispositions to surmount the obstacles that stand in the way of entry. The first one recommended is *prudence:* one must know what one wants. The man building the house without the wherewithal to complete it (v. 30), the soldier who goes to war without calculating the cost (v. 31), the salt which loses its savor (v. 34): all these symbolize the man who begins to believe in the Kingdom, but stops halfway. In Luke, it should be noted, salt is the symbol of prudence; whereas in Matthew it indicates the disciples' role in the world.

b) As Luke sees it elementary prudence consists in knowing how to renounce all one's goods (v. 23) and all human attachments (vv. 26-27). This *renouncement* must be total, and it is urgent in view of the imminence of the Kingdom. It also dispenses one from the normal responsibilities of terrestrial communities (1 Co 7).*

In reality of course the coming of the Kingdom did not change the face of the earth. Christian tension came to consist more in pilgrimage and delay. Was Luke then wrong in asking for total renouncement? The true lesson of this Gospel lies at a deeper level. The Kingdom is not "near" in a temporal sense: it is near in the sense that the Christian must utilize his goods or live with his fellow men through the mediation of Christ. This link is more "immediate" for a man than any one he can possibly have with persons or things. But such relations are not excluded; they are merely put in proper perspective.

*See doctrinal theme: *realism in the faith,* p. 48.

B. DOCTRINE

1. Theme of Faith and the Word

On many occasions in Scripture initiation to faith is described in terms of being cured from deafness and dumbness (Gospel, 3rd cycle). This is not accidental. Just as faith effectively lived will make a man attentive to God's Word and a proclaimer of it, so on the other hand lack of faith will make him deaf and mute. When we pass from unbelief to faith our senses really are opened. Basic in the symbolism is the idea that God only reveals himself to the believer, and that only the believer can convey the Word of God.

It is this intimate link between faith and the Word that we should try to analyze. A deeper understanding will be of immense value. Though Christians have always maintained indeed that faith was based on the Word, the implications of this are now being studied more deeply. For many centuries the Word of God was seen as a fairly objective reality, expressed in precise and determined formulas. To grow in the faith, the believer was simply asked to let himself be modeled by the numerous styles and propositions put forward by the Church. Being based on the Word amounted to acceptance of a certain order of things, imposed from the outside, and purporting to convey God's will for his people. Today however we begin to see that the Word of God is not really reducible to objective formulas. It is a living, mysterious reality which is revealed to the believer in proportion to the intensity with which he embraces his faith.

That leaves the Christian of today less comfortable than his predecessor was. The Church no longer leads him by the hand. Unless one's faith becomes more and more personal it is liable to disappear. The way to make it more personal is to adjust it more and more to the Word of God.

The Word of Yahweh and Israel's faith

Speech is the most precious gift man has. It enables him to

express what he is, and, more importantly, what he would wish to be. For himself and others he can formulate his ideas of the meaning of life and the hopes that he has. It is a faculty with a social and historic dimension. Each one must share it and it is the vehicle of tradition for all.

Its role in all religions is paramount, though there is a considerable difference between this in pagan religion, and in the religion of faith. The ancient pagan liturgies are concerned with man's human resources. Man is asked to communicate ritually with the sacral world. The language used is intangible, synonymous with security.

Under the regime of faith the word is different. It is only in the historical event that it is revealed, and it offers no security other than that of the Totally-Other God, master of human destiny. The Word in which man's ultimate destiny is expressed begins to require a capital, because it belongs to God.

The bearers of the Word are the prophets. The believer always sees it as a challenge to the securities round about him, and a challenge to cling more firmly to the Covenant. So much beyond human capability does it seem that its divine source is abundantly evident, and believers tend to forget that it is also the vehicle of faith. Yet when faith fails, Yahweh is silent. The true God only speaks through the mouth of the true believer; the history of his interventions is directly connected with the ebb and flow of faith.

But since this Word transcended him so completely, the believer under the old covenant had to face an ambiguity. It would not be resolved until a man arose who could speak the Word with absolute authority.

The Word of Jesus, the authentic Word of God, the norm of faith

Jesus, even more than the prophets, stressed the absolute transcendence of God's Word. Man could never appropriate it to himself. By his witness, absolute renunciation was the only road to salvation.

He called himself Messiah, and claimed to speak the saving

Word with authority. Yet he shared completely the human state. Here lay the utterly unexpected mystery; not only was he the bearer of Yahweh's Word, he was the Word of God incarnate. The human speech that was the expression of his human life was perfectly aligned to the divine salvific will. That is why John can say at the beginning of his first letter: "That which we have heard, that which we have seen with our eyes, that we have watched and touched with our hands: the Word who is life—this is our subject" (1 Jn 1:1, 3).

Jesus revealed the Word of God in concrete terms by a life of obedience to God's will, even to the death of the cross. The Word of salvation was delivered at that precise moment in history, where one was found who pushed to its utmost limit—acceptance of the human condition, and demonstrated by his life that man is born to love, with a limitless brotherly love. In Jesus this fidelity had an eternal value. Man was saved in him, and can share the life of God while in the human state.

Once we understand this link between the Word of God and Jesus' human life, it is clear that the Word cannot be anything static, imposed from the outside. He did not live a life that was previously planned by God and dictated to him. The truth is that he gradually came to realize that this life in which he was expressing his obedience to the Father would lead to the cross. He too had to search intensely for the Father's will, and when the cross confronted him, he had like any man his moment of recoil. But he said: "Thy will be done."

This connection of the Word of God with the supreme moment of acceptance carries with it no security. Acceptance, to be full, requires complete despoliation of the self, especially when the event has to be lived to the full. Conveyed in the event, the Word of God will often give scandal, and the only consolation a man will have is that of being true to himself.

The word of Jesus and Christian faith

The light of every man that comes into the world is the Word of Jesus. We have no other source of light; in his humanity God's revelation and man's response coincide. Each man's great task then must be to find on earth this Word of Jesus, which authoritatively conveys the Word of God. By having this shape our lives, we shall be saved.

His Word continues to reverberate in the Church which is his Body, and each man can reach it by entering the Church through baptism. This is a living Word which permeates the whole people of God. It is expressed with authority by those who have received this mission, the apostles and their successors. Each member of the Church should be modeled by it, not only at the times he comes together with others to hear it, but also more fully in the texture of a daily life where his communion with fellow members is deepened.

It is wrong to maintain that the Word of Jesus is to be found only in the Bible, and that one can reach it without benefit of the Church. Indeed we can only reach it through association with all the people who have carried it and lived it throughout twenty centuries. From the moment of Christ's own initiative, always under the living influence of the Spirit, a long, long path has been traced through history. Through all vicissitudes the Word has faithfully preserved according to the measure of people's fidelity to the human condition. It is this that governs its hearing and its proclamation. Once proclaimed it is its own witness.

Christian faith is not something to be lived vaguely, without precision. At all times it must be in process of alignment with the Word of Jesus living in his Church. The Christian is a man who has left all to follow Jesus. The Word that governs his life is that of him who is the Way, the Truth and the Life. He must search it out constantly, passionately, in his exchange with his brothers, and with all men.

Fidelity to the Word of Jesus in misson

Saint Paul is always reminding us that mission is a task of mystery, not policy. Before he is an organizer, the missionary must be a witness of the Spirit of Christ. It is true of course that missionary policy is necessary. The ecclesial institution must prepare and deploy the personnel at its disposal according to the actual needs of the world at any given time. But this should never be allowed to obscure the first essential. The men who really count in mission, who contribute to the building of the Kingdom, are those conspicuous by their fidelity to the word of Jesus. They are the men of faith who can say with Saint Paul: "for me, to live is Christ."

What does this mean? The Word of Jesus to which the missionary must cleave deracinates him doubly. In the first place there is that upheaval of the self which the Word of God must produce in any man. But more than that, for the missionary, there is an uprooting from origins and associations. He must enter the spiritual pilgrimage of the people he evangelizes. The Word of Jesus which must now shape his life emanates from a different culture. This is an extremely testing situation. He must find an identity when radically despoiled of all that is familiar. Only in the charity of Christ does such fidelity become possible.

There is still another consideration. The Word of Jesus that has to manifest itself in the country being evangelized is not yet expressed in a Church. It has to be planted as it were in new soil, that grace has been watering. An infant Church must be born, which will be the bearer of the Word. The missionary must carefully tend this growth. He must pour out the sort of life and energy that will nourish it to authentic stature. And this will require that he renounce the pattern of the Word of Jesus his previous surroundings had made familiar to him.

It is imperative in our time that these essential truths be remembered. The proclamation of the Good News for modern man must touch him at what for him is the center of gravity, his conviction that he must undertake the shaping of human destiny himself. Such a man must be brought to realize the decisive character of the Word of Jesus. Any diminution of the mystery in the missionary task would be particularly damaging at this time.

The eucharistic celebration and the Word

The eucharistic liturgy strictly speaking is always preceded by

a liturgy of the Word. This is not mere juxtaposition. The liturgy
of the Word really gives its full amplitude to the Word that accompanies the liturgy of the Bread. So essential indeed is the
Word that we might well describe the Mass as the eucharistic
celebration of the Word.

The Word proclaimed is always the word of Jesus, the perfect
expression of God's Word. It is based on Scripture, but above all
it is a celebration of Christ's today in the world. It reveals to the
faithful the paschal rhythm of their own lives and the life of
humanity as a whole. It touches the depths of their being and
summons them to renewal of faith. It initiates them into the way
of obedience unto death. Through it the thanksgiving of the
faithful gathered in memory of Jesus' passion and resurrection
gets actual expression, and the signs of the times are discerned.

Other symbols accompany the Word in the celebration, and
their meaning is obvious to the eye of faith. The very assembly
itself, insofar as it manifests the note of catholicity, is a visible
anticipation of the assembly in the Kingdom. The bonds of
brotherhood forged in the celebration are a sign of the love that
characterizes the Family of the Father.

2. The Theme of Realism in the Faith

At first sight, it might seem that the realism inculcated by the
biblical message is realism about means. To enter the Kingdom,
to become a disciple of Jesus, one must pay the price: "carry the
cross" "hate one's father, one's mother, one's wife, one's children,
one's brothers, one's sisters, and even one's own life" (Gospel, 3rd
cycle). But the serious challenge of Christianity goes much deeper
actually. It concerns the human condition itself, restored to its
proper dignity. The price one pays for entry to the Kingdom is
not arbitrarily fixed by God; it is a total fidelity to the human.
This sort of realism is by no means a spontaneous development;
nothing is more difficult for a man than full acceptance of his
human state.

The importance of the matter is obvious. If concern with the
human state itself is at the heart of Christianity, it is liable to be

considered in a new light by modern man. So that we need to say this with great emphasis, something that was not always done in the past, for the simple reason that the climate of thinking was otherwise. The principle indeed calls for the deepest study. If the believer is by right the most realist of all men where the human state is concerned, that should be made abundantly clear. Nor is it a matter only of the presentation of Christianity. Something deeper is at stake, because the whole concept formed of our religion flows from the Christian attitude to the human problem. In the past contorted views of it became prevalent as a result of shoddy presentation, and mission suffered.

Unrealistic is a term often applied to Christians by modern man. Nor is he always wrong. Yet it is true that were the situation reversed, the true nature of Christianity would be properly understood. Modern man does not try to evade the terrestrial state of course, but he does not really see it face to face as it is. He thinks he can dominate history and all that is, but in fact reality proves too much for him.

Israel and the terrestrial state

Like her neighboring peoples, Israel found the terrestrial condition an abnormal one. Man was originally made for paradise, but he lost it. He never had any doubt that because of sin man was expelled from paradise. Instead of awaiting from the hand of God the salvation that would bring fulfillment, he tried to divinize himself, and this was the source of his trouble.

The all-powerful Yahweh wills the happiness of man. He alone can save man in crisis, and he did so in marvelous fashion by liberating his people from Egyptian slavery. This intervention however requires in return man's fidelity to the Covenant. One day he shall lead his people into a land of plenty and endless joy, and here too the other nations will have their place.

In the last analysis it did not seem to the Jews that salvation was possible in the world as it was; they looked towards a new heaven and a new earth. But they did reflect on the terrestrial state. By contrast with the pagans who surrounded them, they assessed it with realism. They did not seek to cloak the pall of suffering and death that overhangs it, but to them it seemed a meaningless distortion. We have the witness of Job.

There was a continuous attempt to solve the mystery of suffering. The principle that sin was responsible for the actual situation of human kind sometimes, in fact, broke down. Suffering did not always correspond to sin. Gradually a glimmer of meaning began to be seen in suffering. It had a purifying value, and Yahweh could inflict his chosen ones with it. The terrestrial state must be one in which fidelity was tested. A further step is taken in some texts, which were put together during or immediately after the exile, those concerning the Servant of Yahweh. Suffering might even have an expiatory and redemptive value. Israel's insight about the terrestrial state was indeed quite remarkable, but there remained a decisive step.

The integral realism of Jesus

Jesus accepted the whole human state, the joys, the sufferings, the temptations, death. He was no Messiah "fallen from heaven," whose origin no one knew. He did however inaugurate the final times, but in the context of the terrestrial state. In everything he obeyed the will of his Father, and in his total acceptance of the terrestrial state he disclosed its true meaning.

The Kingdom he inaugurated is not of this world. Its members are children of God, and it has no terrestrial frontiers. But its roots are in this world. Jesus' terrestrial life is a Pasch from beginning to end, a passage from death to life. Fulfillment lies on the other side of death, but the growth takes place on this earth.

His attitude to suffering and death is characteristic. Wherever he went he healed, and sometimes he raised from the dead. It is as if he were anticipating in time the fulfillment that lay beyond time, in order to show the final goal of terrestrial growth. He also made it clear that in inaugurating the Kingdom he was planting the seed of the final and universal restoration. And all the time he was being meticulously faithful to the terrestrial state; he never wrought a miracle for personal advantage. Obeying the will of the Father, he himself confronted suffering and death without illusion. Before dying on the cross he could envisage the agony. He made suffering blessed in a real sense, because he showed it to be the vehicle of a love that could definitively triumph over hate.

So that the Jewish notion of the Kingdom, and of the terrestrial state, has to be totally revised. They thought the promulgation of the Kingdom would mean the end of the terrestrial state. He set up his Kingdom in that state, now restored to its proper dignity. They expected a Kingdom ready made, exclusively from the hand of God. He brought the seed of the Kingdom only, and revealed that it had to be built, that human cooperation, in the terrestrial state, was necessary for its growth. They had not discerned the true meaning of suffering and death. He showed that man's only way of fulfilling his role in the accomplishment of the divine plan was that of obedience unto death.

Christian acceptance of the human condition

The Christian, when he becomes a child of the Kingdom and a disciple of Christ, is not by any means removed from the terrestrial state. On the contrary he is now fully fitted to accept it. And when Jesus reiterates his appeals for renouncement in the gospels, and summons us to carry the cross in imitation of him, he does so in order to increase our fidelity to the human state.

The sinful world tries to gain happiness by cloaking all that is called suffering and death, and depending altogether on such security as this life offers. But the Christian is required by his faith to view this life altogether lucidly. He knows that the pall of death overhangs everything, even his encounters with his fellow men. His lucidity means that he must experience anguish and sometimes agony. He cannot avoid them. He must expect the day when the love of which he is a witness will encounter men's opposition, because their wisdom is of another brand. Perhaps, for having loved, he will be sentenced to death.

But, suffering as he does, confronting death as he does, the Christian makes a unique contribution to the human adventure. If he has to endure sorrow while the world rejoices, his sorrow is productive of life; it is not that of one who blinds himself to the realities of his state. His day of fulfillment will come, and his joy will be that of a mother who brings forth a child. The price to be paid for this joy, he realizes, is full acceptance, however painful, of the human predicament here below.

The human state, restored to its true dignity, is a paschal state. The Christian does not try to run away. His responsibilities lie on this earth; he must triumph over death wherever it manifests itself in the structure of human life. Such a task would be impossible without the leadership of Christ and the inspiration of the Spirit. Thus the mediation of Christ must permeate the texture of our existence. It will be there at every passage from death to life. The service to the world that the people of God are called on to render cannot be rendered by anyone else.

The realism of the faith and the building of the Kingdom

To Christians this universe seems rather like a gigantic workyard. All men are called, in Jesus Christ, to make their contribution to the building of the city of God. It is a colossal task that requires the cooperation of all peoples and all cultures. Christ once for all sowed the seed of true history, by his human life lived in absolute fidelity. Because he was the Son this had eternal dimensions. But from that beginning the building must go on, until all humanity attains in Jesus its perfect stature. This long growth, including not only all humanity but all creation, is conditional on the acceptance by men of the terrestrial state.

To the extent of his share in mission, his work for the reconciliation of peoples, the Christian is bound to encounter some of those "tribulations" of which Saint Paul is always talking. It could hardly be otherwise. The Kingdom cannot be built, nor can the human endeavor reach fulfillment, without constant passage from death to life. They are works of love which inevitably kindle opposition from the wisdom of the world. Its traces are found in the lives of us all. Yet, like Saint Paul, we "abound in joy through-out all tribulations" (2 Co 7:4) because we know that beyond them lies the definitive city.

Our hope is no longer that of the Jewish believer. He did not see the Kingdom as something that had to be built; it would manifest itself ready made. All our hope is concentrated on the task to be accomplished: mission. We have been told that this will not be complete until the Gospel is preached to all nations. The mystery of Christ must be rooted in time and space in such fashion that the paschal light will illumine the spiritual quest of every people and every culture. The task is exceedingly long. No sector of human life can be omitted from it, because its proper balance will depend on this illumination.

The Church today has a chance to see how closely mission and the whole human enterprise are linked. Saint Paul thought, or at least thought at one time, that universal mission was something within his own compass. We are only beginning now to see how vast the dimensions are.

Initiation to realism in the faith

We can never be proper disciples of Christ unless we share his realism about the terrestrial state. Such an attitude is so far from being the spontaneous human one however, that it can only be acquired and maintained by constant initiation. To this end all ecclesial assemblies are directed. When we are gathered together, we should find our acceptance of the creatural condition intensi-fied and deepened.

This is particularly true of the eucharistic assembly. Saint Paul for instance does not hesitate to say that, when Christians come together to share the body and blood of Christ, they are doing so to proclaim the Lord's death—to model their own lives, that is to say, after the pattern of his, a life where the challenge to the manifestations of death was always the decisive element.

We have to admit however that too often our eucharistic cele-brations fulfill this purpose inadequately. We must hope that as current liturgical reform continues to stress the importance of the

Word, the proclamation of the death of the Lord will become more evident. For that however it will be essential that the Word proclaimed be itself more dynamic and actual. Christians must find the actual tenor of their lives, and the whole pattern of their existence, permeated by it.

TWENTY-FOURTH SUNDAY

A. THE WORD

I. Sirach
27:30–28:7
1st reading
1st cycle

The good sense of Ben Sirach makes him very conscious of the importance of tact and harmony in social relationships. It is in this context that he discusses pardon and the way to combat anger and rancor.

Underlying the discussion in today's passage is the idea of immediate retribution. The reason for abstaining from vengeance is that we fear divine vengeance (vv. 1-3). The reason for pardoning is because we hope one day to have God's pardon (vv. 2, 5).

This is normal Jewish thinking. The *lex talionis* is likewise based on the principle of immediate retribution, and the first reaction against it is still in the context of the same doctrine. It was not until the New Testament that the doctrine of pardon was fully freed from such associations.

II. Isaiah
50:5-9
1st reading
2nd cycle

This reading is taken from the suffering Servant poems. There are four such poems, fairly awkwardly inserted among the most ancient texts of Second-Isaiah. This comes from the third, where the Servant speaks of himself. He compares his inadequate tongue (v. 4) to that of the great prophets of the people (Ex 4:10; Jr 1:6). Then he speaks of the affronts he has received during the course of his mission, using the phraseology of the ancient prophets to describe them. He "offers his back" (cf. Is 51:23); he "offers his cheeks to those who pierce them" (cf. Ez 21:14); he "does not cover his face" (cf. Ez 16:52; Jb 14:20; 30:10). Nevertheless, convinced that God will save him, he does not resent the insults (Jr 1:18).

Probably the figure of Jeremiah is partially the basis for these characteristics of the Servant. He was charged to "mime" the events of the exile (Jr 13:1-11; 16:1-13; 18) and became typical of the one who carries both the faults of the people and their chastisement.

Furthermore he is the only Old Testament prophet who is so concerned with his personal crisis. He, the mild and loving one, must undergo insults, persecution and injustice. In the midst of a sinful people he is innocent (comparison with the lamb in Jr 11:19; 15:10-21; 18:18-25; 20:7-18). By contrast with the superficial folk around him he is the man of interiorisation, conscious of his inner conflict. His oracles lay the basis of a new alliance, built on interior sacrifice, conversion of heart and personal responsibility.

The Servant in Second-Isaiah (Is 42:1-4; 49:1-7; 50:4-11; 52:13–53:12) has many of these traits. By his sufferings he substitutes himself for the great number who would have to suffer for their own sins. This enables him to contract a new alliance with God, of universal import.

However in the poems he is sometimes an individual (with Jeremiah's characteristics), sometimes collective (with the characteristics of the people who are persecuted by the Gentiles).

It is impossible to say which of these two images is the more ancient. Exegetes tend to favor the collective.

Christ himself referred explicitly to the Servant theme on one occasion only (Lk 22:37; Is 53:12), but primitive tradition frequently drew parallels. From the baptism onwards the Lord's messianic vocation is that of the "Servant Son" (Mk 1:1; Is 52:1). The miracles of healing are those of the Servant expiator (Mt 8:16; Is 53:4). His humility is that of the Servant (Mt 12:18-21; Is 42:1-3; Mk 9:31; Is 53:6, 12). The failure even of his preaching recalls that of the Servant and of Jeremiah (Jn 12:38; Is 53:1). It is clear that the theme was the best illustration of the fact that suffering and death were necessary in order that the plan of salvation should be realized (Ac 3:13-26; 4:25, 30; Is 53:5, 6, 9, 12; Mk 10:45; Is 53:5; 1 Co 11:24; Is 53:5).

III. Exodus   This is taken from the exchange between God
32:7-11, 13-14   and Moses after the golden calf episode. God
1st reading   denounces the prevarication of the stiff-necked
3rd cycle   people, decides to be rid of the Hebrews and
                form an alliance with another people with
Moses as patriarch (v. 10).

a) Despite the personal honor for him in this proposal, Moses
rejects it. God's promise, once given, cannot be withdrawn no
matter what the people do.

Moses certainly becomes a larger figure as a result of the
episode. Though he had the opportunity to begin again, he sub-
merges personal hopes and becomes the intercessor for his people
before God. Everything is subordinated, with overwhelming confidence, to the fulfillment of the promise to the Hebrew people
(Gn 15:5; 22:16-17; 35:11-12).

Moses' prayer of self-despoliation won him the support of the
people. They saw in him the ideal mediator, the *intercessor* who
was always heard (Jr 15:1; Pss 98/99:6, 105/106; 23 Si 45:3).

b) The episode reveals an essential law of prayer: it must be
theocentric. When the sinner approaches God he wants to excul-
pate himself. He seeks the pardon which will give him his previous state, and promises to do better in future. All this is really
egocentric; such a man makes himself the center of prayer and
wants to find inner peace and equilibrium. Moses' attitude is
altogether otherwise. He sees the benevolence of God, his patience
at all times, his fidelity to the covenant. A prayer such as his must
get heard; God must pursue the course of mercy. Prayer is really
alignment with the thought of God.

Moses was frequently put forward as the intercessor *par excellence* between God and man. He had this role at the time of the
plagues in Egypt (Ex 3:22-23; 8:4; 9:28; 10:17) and he continued
to have it throughout the vicissitudes of the desert sojourn (Ex
3:22-23; 32:11-32; Nb 14:13-19; 16:22; Dt 9:23-29).

The idea of such an intercessor was a natural growth among

a people who were weak and sinful, and who saw God as powerful and severe in his justice. They would choose as spokesman the one who seemed the most upright, and who seemed charged with divine power.

Here the traditional concept is altogether enriched by a decisive new dimension. God recognizes as intercessor only the one who embraces humanity however sinful, and stands in solidarity with it. His interlocutor is to be, not the "just" man in the legalistic sense, but the man who is totally given to the service of his people, even at the risk of his own downfall. He considers himself better represented among men by the servant who is ready to be deprived of all for the sake of men, than by a threatening witness of divine power and holiness.

IV. Romans
14:7-9
2nd reading
1st cycle

In this chapter Paul is dealing with the relations between Christians who have different attitudes on certain points of religious practice. These concern days of observance (of fast?), or abstinence from meat and wine. Some ("the strong") thought that their faith emancipated them from such practices. Others ("the weak") were more timid and felt they had to follow their religious scruples.

The verses in our reading state a principle that is quite fundamental. Each one, in every circumstance, must act for the Lord, who is Lord of the living and the dead. In the matter of life and death we all have a common attitude. Provided that the *service of the same Lord* is assured, minor differences about asceticism or religious practice do not matter.

He does not insist that the strong and the weak have identical attitudes. The unity required by charity is at a deeper level, where each one is aware that he serves the same God.

Our modern society tends to become more and more pluralist. Inevitably Christians will find themselves more and more frequently at odds, and not only on moral, religious or liturgical issues. There is no reason to lament this development, regard it with dismay, and consume ourselves with efforts to maintain uniformity at all costs. We should simply be losing sight of the fact that Christian unity is based only on the essential faith, and the glory of the one God that we all serve.

V. James
2:14-18
2nd reading
2nd cycle

This is one of the most important passages in James' letter. It is so in the first place because it is one of the most Christian passages in a letter otherwise strongly marked by Jewish culture. But the principal reason of course is that, on the matter of faith and works, it might seem to contradict Pauline teaching.

It is undeniable that James shows opposition to abuses that might seem traceable to some Pauline affirmations. The observers that he sometimes sent after Paul (Ga 2:12) may have reported to him not only what Paul thought and said, but the manner in which he was sometimes interpreted. Yet, despite numerous "clashes" and personal difficulties, the two apostles clearly share the same faith, and also take the same position about *faith and works.*

In the first place, James acknowledges the law of liberty (v. 12), understood in the sense Paul had given the expression (2 to 3:17; Ga 4:23-31; 5:1-13), a law that cancels the law of Moses.

Secondly, he shares with Paul the conviction that faith is not exterior conformity to the formulae of a *credo,* but something that transforms and permeates life (v. 14; cf. Ga 5:6). He is of course less mystic than Paul. He is more concerned with the practical, horizontal dimension of faith, Paul with the personal, vertical. The attitudes are complementary, not opposed. James does qualify the Pauline interpretation of Genesis 15:6 ("Abraham believed in God and that was accounted to him for justice," Jm 2:23; cf. Ga 3:5-7; Rm 4:2-3), by pointing out that Abraham's faith was expressed in a "work" of heroic dimension, the sacrifice of his son (Jm 2:21-22). Yet not even here are they opposed; they give very different meanings to the term "work." Paul sees "works" as the means of salvation which the law of Moses made available to the Jews (circumcision, temple, etc.). These he no longer sees to be necessary, because now he depends on a "law of liberty." James accepts this law too (v. 12) and does not deny him this right. But for him "works" mean activities springing from faith, which make faith efficacious (vv. 14-20, 26). No one could possibly maintain that Paul opposes this (Ep 2:8-10).*

VI. 1 Timothy Today we begin with the reading of Paul's
1:12-17 pastoral letters. Though they are addressed to
2nd reading his companions Timothy and Titus, they have
3rd cycle an ambit wider than personal relations. They
constitute a sort of general ecclesiastical instruction for the problems facing the Christian communities over the years 65-67. The main problem was syncretism and heretical gnosis. Paul provides a basis for solid refutation, and strengthens ministerial powers so that leaders of communities can meet their responsibilities.

a) He has recourse once more to a *personal apologia* (vv. 12-17). Heretics may develop attractive intellectual theories about salvation: he prefers to affirm that, sinner though he is, he has been saved by God's mercy (v. 16). He is maintaining that the minister of the gospel must have personal experience of the grace he is proclaiming. Otherwise his message becomes mere gnosis and theorizing. His outburst, when he calls himself the "greatest" of

*See the doctrinal theme: *faith and works,* p. 70.

sinners, suggests that he is thinking of his life as persecutor, and how through the power of God he was converted.

b) For the expression of his thought in verses 15-16 he turns to a hymn that must have been already classic among the primitive communities (he considers it a "word worthy of faith," v. 15a). An extract may be reconstructed thus:

> Christ Jesus has come into the world
> to save sinners
> Christ Jesus shows the magnitude of patience
> as example to those who believe in him
> for eternal life

The themes of the hymn: the coming of Jesus into the world (Jn 1:2; 6:14; 11:17); the mission of salvation (Jn 3:17; 12:47), and eternal life (Jn 3:15-16; 6:40-47; 20:31) are all Johannine.

As he cites the hymn Paul passes from his own personal case to a consideration of the broad lines of the salvation plan as willed by God: the patience and love of God, and life eternal for believers.

c) His contemplation of this gives rise to an act of thanksgiving (v. 17) in which he attributes a series of *titles* to God that are fairly unusual in the New Testament. Some are probably borrowed from old Jewish liturgical formulas (king, for example, which is found in the daily prayer), but others have a philosophical flavor which is quite striking: "incorruptible," "invisible," "unique."

We must remember that God's eternity (king "of the ages"), for Paul, is not just the philosophic concept, without beginning or end, but an eternity that governs events and molds them into salvation history. Likewise, when he speaks of the "invisible" God, he is not opposing a philosophic view to scriptural texts about desire to "see God" (1 Co 13:12; 1 Jn 3:2). He is merely affirming that God reveals himself precisely where human religion or philosophy would not expect him. He appears in folly, not in wisdom; in poverty, not in power. He, the incorruptible one, manifested himself in a flesh that is the prey of evil and sin.

VII. Matthew   The parable of the debtor belongs to the fourth
    18:21-35   discourse of Jesus, which concerns the rules
    Gospel   that ought to govern Christians' relations with
    1st cycle   one another. He has already spoken of the
    proper attitude to the sinner (Mt 18:15-22),
and of prayer in common (Mt 18:19-20). Now, in answer to a
question by Peter (Mt 18: 21-22), he considers the matter of
mutual pardon.

a) The duty of *pardon for offenses* was already familiar in
Judaism, but it was the result of a recent movement and could
only be maintained by a system of precise tariffs. Rabbinic schools
required their disciples to pardon so many times for a wife, for
children, for brothers, etc., the number of times varying from
school to school. Peter is anxious to know what Jesus' tariff is,
whether it is as severe as the school which requires pardon seven
times for a brother (Mt 18:21).

Christ replies with a parable which removes pardon from any
system of tariffs, and makes it the sign of God's pardon. The
primitive parable must have been quite simple. The servant of a
sheik has his debt remitted by his master, but he cannot bring
himself to remit a debt owed him by a comrade. The sheik re-
proaches him because he did not cancel the debt *just as* his own
had been canceled.

The hallmark of the Christian doctrine is this. One pardons as
one has been pardoned. One has mercy on a comrade because
one has obtained mercy (vv. 17 and 33; cf. Ho 6:6; Mt 9:13; 12:7).
It is no longer the Jewish doctrine of a graded moral obligation,
but a constant awareness that one has benefited by God's pardon.
It becomes a sort of theological virtue, which prolongs for the
benefit of others the pardon God has given (Col 3:13; Mt 6:14-15;
2 to 5:18-20).

b) Matthew allegorizes the basic parable. "Man" of the original
is fairly awkwardly changed to "king" (v. 23) so that readers will
immediately think of the king of heaven (the same procedure in

Mt 22:2). He fixes the debt at ten thousand talents to show the sinner's immeasurable weakness before God (v. 24). He heightens the religious atmosphere of the tribunal scene (falling at the king's feet, prostration, begging pity . . . v. 26) in order to suggest the last judgment. He emphasizes the difference between ten thousand talents and a hundred pence (like the plank and the splinter: Mt 7:1-5) to show the immense distance that divides human ideas of debt and justice from those of God. Finally, he enters into detail about the servant's punishment. It will continue until he pays back the wholly improbable sum, thus suggesting eternal punishment.

The effect of his manipulation is to set the duty of pardon in an *eschatological* context. The final times have come, in the form of a sabbatical year (Dt 15:1-15) during which God remits the immeasurable debt of humanity and offers justification. Some however refuse to avail themselves, and thus sentence themselves to endless misfortune.

c) Confronted by man's sin, Yahweh might at once have exacted vengeance, broken his covenant, and begun the eschatological judgment. The parable teaches that he substituted pardon for judgment, postponing the latter. The servant episode actually falls between two sessions (vv. 25-26 and 31-35) of divine judgment. The first brings acquittal; the second will depend on the use made of the time in between. Man will be definitively justified if he uses this to pardon and justify in turn. Christian life is a sort of probationary acquittal that will be ratified at the judgment. What we have is a theology of the *time of the Church,* the time allotted man for conversion (cf. Mt 13:24-30). The history of pardon will be continued throughout Church history, not only through the sacramental ministry of the apostles and their successors, but by the exercise of God's pardon each Christian can show in his love for others.

Our Sunday Eucharist has an obvious penitential dimension. God's pardon is proclaimed there, because the Church is just a

gathering of sinners who depend on God's mercy. The brotherhood however that we claim as pardoned sharers of the Eucharist
will have real meaning for the world only to the extent that we
cooperate in human enterprises of pardon, above all in working
for peace.

VIII. **Mark**   Mark sees Peter's confession at Caesarea as an
    8:27-35   important moment in Jesus' life. Prior to this
    Gospel   he has followed a policy of secrecy concerning
    2nd cycle   his messianic mission. People miraculously
                cured are forbidden to speak, and demons to
acknowledge their defeat. Suddeny now, not only does he abandon this attitude, but clearly asks his disciples for a confession of
faith (v. 29).

a) The apostles most often have had occasion to discuss the
personality of Jesus among themselves; and they were convinced
he was not a simple rabbi. This is what Peter expresses in his
profession; they now realize that they are linked with the Messiah
(v. 29).

In Mark's version Jesus does not seem to react to this profession
of messianic faith. He remains reserved and enjoins *silence* on the
apostles (v. 30, a detail peculiar to Mark). However the account
is followed by the first prediction of the sufferings of the Passion
(vv. 31-33), indicating the sort of Messiahship this is to be.

Here, in Mark, we have a decisive turning point. Jesus is no
longer just the rabbi and miracle worker. He accepts recognition
as Messiah, but he has yet to convince his followers that it is a
dolorous mission.

His account obliterates the ecclesial character of the primitive
confession in favor of this particular emphasis. He does not give
us for instance Peter's investiture (Mt 16:17-19). More than the
other synoptics he is preoccupied with the mystery of Jesus' personality, and the gradualness of its manifestation to his followers.

The importance of Peter's profession lies in the contrast with the crowd's reaction. For them Jesus is a precursor only; it is not he who will bring about the Kingdom. For Peter however, at least provisionally, Jesus *is* the Messiah and the architect of God's kingdom. He has yet, before his faith becomes adult, to learn to appreciate the humiliating aspects of this Messiahship, but his reaction is decisive.

The attitude of many Christians of course is closer to that of the crowd than to Peter's. Jesus is still a precursor. Because justice and peace have not been accomplished, because suffering and confusion still dominate humanity, it is thought that nothing has been done. They are unable to see the Messiahship of Jesus against such a background. But faith is only adult really when we see, as well as the Messiah, the crucified Lord (vv. 31-33). Until that moment it is better if we are silent and say nothing of Jesus (v. 30).

b) Jesus' own knowledge of the nature of his messianic role was progressive. It could not be realized in the role that he had at the beginning of the public life as missionary rabbi and miracle worker. He must become the suffering Messiah. One chain of events had convinced him, and his apostles too, of Messiahship, but there were other events, more menacing, that made it clear suffering and persecution lay ahead. The attachment of the crowd was too fickle for ultimate loyalty, and the establishment would not long now tolerate such an iconoclast rabbi. And so he foretells the *Passion*.

The text of this prediction is a product of careful editing. Either the primitive tradition, or the synoptic, recognized its importance. It is reproduced three times in the gospels, in rather stereotyped formula (Mk 8:31-33; 9:30-32; 10:32-34). So we have the detail of the three days, belonging probably to the primitive tradition. That Jesus however did actually foretell his resurrection at this stage in his career cannot be doubted. So conscious was he of the necessity to succeed in his mission that the only course that seemed open to him, with persecution looming, was a complete placing of his life in the Father's hands. The Father was capable of raising him up, and bringing the mission to successful issue.

c) Peter's insight falls far short of that of Jesus. It is still colored by the hope for a political Messiahship. The Twelve would no longer be simply disciples of a Master, as at the moment of their calling; they would be the collaborators of a King-Messiah. He does not hesitate to reprimand Jesus for pessimism. How could a Messiah have to encounter suffering (v. 32), especially in that Elias had already come before him to arrange everything (Mk 9:9-13). This Jesus regards as another satanic *temptation* (cf. Mk 1:13). It was jeopardizing his mission, and undermining the energies required, by purely human considerations.

d) The formula "he is destined" (v. 31) introduces the Passion prediction. This indicates generally in the gospels, above all in Saint Luke (2:49; 4:43; 9:22; 13:33; 17:25; Ac 1:16; 3:21), God's especial *will* for Christ. The formula is probably apocalyptic originally (Dn 2:28-29, 45 in LXX; Mt 24:6; Rev 4:1; 22:6) and refers to the inevitability of the final times. There is no question of course of blind fatalism; what is contemplated in God's plan in working out salvation history with man's free cooperation. "He is destined" here applies to the Passion of the Son of man, as that of someone on whom the eschatological future of humanity depends. The Father does not desire the death of his Son; his desire is that the Son should convey love to the world. This however cannot be accomplished without trial, without complete fidelity to man's mortal state. The love that will illuminate the final times has to come by the road of pain.

At each turning point in his mission Jesus encountered temptation. It assailed him when he began his career as rabbi in the wake of John the Baptist. It returned at the moment when he chose a Messiahship that would be one of suffering and death. It came again at Gethsemane when he was about to fulfill the destiny of the suffering Servant.

Temptation lies deep at the heart of those arguments we Christians tend to develop in justification of our worldliness. The arguments are not necessarily sinful. Indeed they are full of good intentions and good sense. Nevertheless they prevent a man who listens to them from plumbing the depths of his vocation, and fulfilling the role God has assigned him in the salvation of the world. The temptation is to weigh too reasonably the value of what one is abandoning. We must first bury our Father. We look for ways of escape. We debate about the meaning of the "neighbor" we are supposed to love. We tend to seek support from this or that compromising secular source, as if God by himself were powerless. The Eucharist, that great sacrament of Christ's complete victory over his own temptations, will be our sustenance when we have to combat ours.

IX. Luke
15:1-32
Gospel
3rd cycle

Luke devotes a complete chapter to the parables of mercy: the lost sheep (15:4-7), the lost drachma (15:8-10), the lost son (15:11-32). The whole piece might indeed be a midrash on Jeremiah 31. In the prophet we have the figure of the gathering of the sheep (Jr 31:10-12), of the woman who finds her lost children (31:16-17), and finally of God pardoning his favorite son Ephraim (31:18-20). It is noteworthy that in the parallel passage in Matthew (18:8-14) we have a further midrash on Jeremiah 31:8. The lame and the blind enter the Kingdom.

a) Severe pharisaic laws about purity and ablutions had excluded sinners and publicans from the sacred meals. To such ostracism Jesus opposed the *mercy* of God, who seeks always the salvation of the sinner. He is following the wishes of the Father when he carries to the limit the search for the sinner. We see this clearly in the parable of the lost sheep, where Luke, unlike Matthew 18:12-14, compares the shepherd's joy to that of God and the angels (vv. 6-7). It is not however stated that the sinner is more loved than the others; the joy over the recovered member is not to be confused with love for all men.

The parable of the lost drachma is identical in structure. This repetition is due doubtless to Jesus' wish to secure the attention of the women who surround him as well as the shepherds, but it is also a common procedure in Hebrew parallelism.

b) The parable of the prodigal son does seem to allude to Jeremiah 31. This was a text quite familiar to early Christians, in that it was the best Old Testament description of the new covenant (Jr 31:31-34). So it came about that the mercy parables constituted a commentary on Jeremiah 31, helping people to understand the new covenant, which was based on the love of God, something stronger than sin.

The younger son's motives for repentance are not particularly pure. His conversion is due to his needs for livelihood. But this does serve to set in prominence the magnitude, and gratuitousness, of the father's pardon.

However, precisely at the moment of highest expression of the Father's love, the elder son returns. In Jeremiah 31 we have at the end a description of reconciliation between Ephraim and Judah, the two tribes concerned with the covenant and the abundance that it brings (Jr 31:23-31). But in the parable the father does not have the joy of seeing the two brothers reconciled in his love at the banquet of abundance. Like the scribes and Pharisees (Lk 15:1-3), the jealous elder brother refuses to be confused with the sinner. His pride in vindicating himself is the same as that of the Pharisee in the temple (Lk 18:10-12). He shows the same contempt for the other (compare "this, your son" and "this publican"). The younger son's prayer is like that of the publican (cf. Lk 18:13). Thus the purpose of the parable, like that of the Pharisee and the publican, is to justify the welcome Jesus extends to all men, even sinners.

The elder son too is made aware that he will only be loved by his father if he in turn is prepared to receive the sinner. The loving father expects his love to be imitated. It is not he who excludes the elder son. He excludes himself by failing to love his brother (cf. 1 Jn 4:20-21).

So by the gratuitous love of God a new covenant is forged. It summons men to conversion and is sealed in the eucharistic banquet. It is a covenant where the ancient right of the first born becomes null, because the love of God is open to all.

This parable of the prodigal son is an excellent illustration of the whole procedure in penance.* Both sons are sinners: such is the human condition. One realizes this, and acts accordingly. The other refuses to realize it, and does not change his life in any way. God comes for both. He goes out to meet the prodigal, but he also goes out to meet the elder son (vv. 20 and 28). He comes for all men, for those who know they are sinners, and those who don't.

In the repentance of the younger son, we notice first of all the human initiative. We have mentioned his "imperfect contrition." He repents because he is miserable, because, everything considered, his father's house is better than the swinery where he lives. With these dispositions (v. 16) he proceeds to an examination of conscience ("entering into himself": v. 17), and even prepares the text of his avowal to his father (vv. 17-19). The essential discovery however of the penitent who begins his return to God is that God comes to meet him, and greets him with such generosity that he forgets the thread of his prepared statement (vv. 21-23). The roles are reversed. It is no longer the sorrow of the penitent that matters in the procedure, but God's love and pardon. Too often unfortunately the sacrament of penance suggests that the pardon is something conceded to an initiative of confession taken by the penitent. What it should suggest is the tremendous initiative of God and the celebration of his recreative love. Too seldom does the minister of penance give the impression of introducing someone to the joy of the Father.

*See also the doctrinal theme: *mercy,* p. 76.

B.   DOCTRINE

1. Theme of Faith and Works

Christians have always been concerned about the link between faith and "works." The practice of faith can never be reduced to acceptance of a creed-formula, nor to ritual performances. It must be a manner of action that conforms to the gospel, and it must permeate the whole life of the believer. No one has ever contravened the principle enunciated by Saint James (see 2nd reading, 2nd cycle): "if faith is without works, it is altogether dead" (2:17). On this point Paul is at one with James: his reservations about works have nothing to do with their necessity. His concern is about their relation to the salvation of Jesus Christ.

Make no mistake about it, we are dealing here with something essential to Christianity. And the matter is all the more important because just now we are in the throes of a profound change. It will not be sufficient to repeat what has been said previously on a theme that is as old as Christianity, more than that, as old as Judaism. Up to the present faith was the agreed basis for discussion of the problem, but today faith is no longer taken for granted. It used to be said that works were necessary to faith, because that was clearly God's will, but they had no justifying value. God alone justifies. Now it is works that are taken for granted. A man's activity is scrutinized in a climate where all men, Christians included, are trying to demonstrate their fidelity to the human vocation, and to themselves. The question that presents itself is not: is this work necessary? Nor, is this work justifying? It is rather: how far is this work, in which a Christian is fully plunged, rooted in faith as a source?

We have to ask ourselves whether the age-old principle that faith without works is dead, includes somehow the other affirmation that works without faith will never attain fruition. Does the

New Testament offer us any guidance on the problem as it presents itself in our day?

The works of the Law

Pagan man in history could not conceive happiness except in terms of sharing the sacral world. Thus he would be put in touch with stability, permanence, eternity, the absolute. Such a sharing however required from man a corresponding "work." Ritual works very soon came to be accepted as the means for men to reach this end. They were given value altogether independently of moral behavior otherwise.

Under the regime of faith in Israel this attitude was profoundly modified. Realism about the events of history led to a conviction that God intervenes in the daily life of his people, and hence to an awareness of the importance of moral behavior in the pursuit of happiness. The two insights were connected, and the second was affirmed by Israel to be the will of the God of the covenant. There was as yet no understanding of the fact that the new theology was really due to a fresh appraisal by man of the implications of existence. In any case, as we review the various stages of Jewish history, we can see that their estimate of the believer's "works" involved a gradual shift of emphasis from the liturgical to the moral. This had been begun in the desert with the law of Moses, and the subsequent rereadings of the law at moments of crisis served to accentuate the movement. There was frequent criticism by the prophets of a cult that did not express sacrifice of the heart. "Rite" that did not affect "life" was valueless. Worship of Yahweh implied imitation of his goodness, his mercy and his justice.

The recognition of a Totally-Other God led to the belief that human salvation depends altogether on that God's initiative. The "works" of the law could never merit it. Yet, at the same time, a deeper understanding of the Covenant made it clear that Yahweh would not save man without man's cooperation, without his contribution as partner. Hence came messianic hope, the search for a man who could provide the adequate response to God. Among the most fervent groups of the chosen people we find a very understandable hesitancy and ambiguity. There was no doubt about the importance of the works of the Law; there was however misgiving about their efficacy towards salvation. Only with the intervention by Jesus of Nazareth was this resolved.

The work of the Messiah and the salvation of the world

Where observance of the Law was concerned Jesus brought simplification. Jewish tradition had imposed innumerable works; he reduced the Law to the precept of love, a love which he showed to be limitless. In so doing he was affiming the importance of "life" as against "rite," the function of which is merely celebration. He was carrying further still the process of interiorization that the prophets had begun. If the great work of the Law was love, the expressions of that love were too numerous to be codified. They would only disclose themselves in the pattern of daily life to the person who was attentive to the others' needs. Jesus, in following the path of love, embarked on a course of obedience to the Father which culminated in his death on the cross.

Once it became clear that the will of God would not be fully codified, the danger of formalism was overcome, but man had once again to face the actuality of the human predicament. By proposing the new commandment of brotherly love without limits Jesus was inviting man to accept his humanity to the full. This could be done negatively, by absolute renunciation of self and of all attempts to achieve salvation by one's own resources. It could be done positively, by mustering every energy for the gospel task. Such a task of love however, while imminently necessary, still does not merit eternal destiny for men.

But Jesus, by engaging in it, put himself forward as Messiah, as God's true partner in the realization of the salvation plan. In him it acquires an eternal dimension, and produces salvation for all, because in him, and only in him, is this altogether human activity a divine activity as well. His work of love, culminating in the cross, shows men that he is not only Messiah, but Son of God.

Thus the Messiah's work, because he was without sin and able to use human resources without hindrance, was human in the fullest sense. But it engaged the full destiny of all humanity besides, and produced salvation, because he was the Son of God.

The works of faith

Among the convert Jews of the primitive Christian communities there was such attachment to the law of Moses, that the radical change introduced by the gospel tended to be obscured. This was the immense inportance of the personal work of Jesus. Believers who still clung to traditional legal observances were not yet properly initiated to the spirit of the new commandment. They continued to regard the Law as the perfect expression of God's will, and thought to acquire merit by its works.

It was this mentality that was countered by Saint Paul when he declared himself against legalism, or justification by works. Everything was contained within the gospel; people must concentrate absolutely on the salvation that had been acquired by Jesus Christ alone. There was one great area where sinful man had been most in need of liberation. That was in his encounter with the other. This encounter would have to be approached with full acceptance of the unforeseen and unpredictable dimension. It was God's summons to constantly new challenges, and to meet it properly one would have to feel free of observances. It was essential to realize that "one single precept contains all the law in its fullness" (Ga 5:14). Legalism was yielding place to the law of liberty, which was realized in one single work of the law: love. But this "labor of charity" was the "work of Jesus Christ" (1 Th 1:3) and could only be accomplished with his aid.

The followers of Christ then, now free of the law, must plunge into the great adventure of love. They must confront once more their own frailty and weakness, but also their creatural possibilities. They would come to realize that their human activity would only acquire full potential and authenticity if it was pursued in communion with the Church, where Christ was always actually present. Human works in other words could only be fully authentic through faith in Jesus Christ. This touches the heart of the problem we mentioned at the beginning of this meditation. It was only with the advent of the modern world, when man is really beginning to experience what freedom and mastery of human resources can mean, that the full applications of this principle began to manifest themselves.

Mission, the work par excellence of faith

Let us recall in this context the experience of the Antioch Church. It was the first time that conditions forced the disciples of the Risen Lord to realize actually how new the Gospel was. Convert Greeks and Jews met on an equal footing. They shared the same faith, and gradually came to realize how all-embracing the charity of Christ was. In the Jerusalem community works had been a very serious consideration, and the concept of them that prevailed was rather traditional and legalist. The last times were imminent, and it was clear what works were necessary. At Antioch on the other hand the overwhelming experience of brotherhood between Greeks and Jews made it clear that the work of faith that really mattered was universal brotherly love. This was a work that opened up avenues that were altogether new, and it could only be undertaken by depending on the liberating initiative of Christ. One such avenue, discovered by the Antioch community, was mission. This was the highest expression of love, the work *par excellence* of faith. We can only truly love all men by bringing them the Good News of universal reconciliation, by becoming somehow artisans of peace among all nations, that peace that Christ purchased on the cross.

Church history is full of lessons for us. Whenever there has been a tendency towards legalism mission has suffered. It became merely proselytism, a swelling of the ranks. Great heroism and great fidelity was displayed in such enterprises, but by and large there was no dialogue, no taking as well as giving. On the other hand when the pattern of events resembled the experience at Antioch, mission was always in terms of dialogue, exhibiting another dimension still of the Church's essential newness. Because the work of universal peace and reconciliation in Jesus Christ is endless, and a disconcerting one, it will inevitably take new shapes in different epochs. We may very well be on the threshold of some such development today.

Celebration of the works of faith

Because man by nature does not tend to appreciate the close connection between faith and works, some sort of constant initiation has always been thought necessary. The liturgy that provides this must be of a very specific kind, a liturgy of "faith" which issues in corresponding "works." Any eucharistic celebration worthy of the name should remind us that faith without works is a dead faith. The importance of the Word in it will be paramount, because it is always the proclamation of the Word that proves a continual reminder to the believer of the principle at stake. For some decades now a concerted effort has been made to induce the faithful to find in their liturgy the vital energy of their faith, instead of being passive participants. We are more aware of the necessity for a link between rite and life. In some instances people have been actually instructed that they must, by virtue of their faith, undertake certain responsibilities. They are asked, both individually and collectively, to become involved in movements for the construction of a world more habitable for men.

Today we should go one step further. Very many Christians find themselves associated in this domain with non-Christian brothers. The latter are sometimes more thoroughly involved than Christians themselves, and Christians are disconcerted to discover that faith does not seem to be necessary for a valid contribution. There should be some attempt in the eucharistic celebration not alone to induce the faithful to live a life in conformity with their belief, but to inculcate the all important principle we have discussed. They must be convinced that human activity itself, if it is to be an authentic expression of human liberty, needs faith as a source.

2. The Theme of Mercy

There are many avenues to the discovery of God; but one is very prominent: sinful man's experience of God's mercy. When we read the parable of the prodigal son each one of us can recognize himself in this son, who leaves his father's house to follow his own way, and dreams one day of returning there in a subordinate role. How many of us, like him, have been surprised on returning to find that we were long expected lovingly, that we are embraced as lost children.

And yet, we must admit, men today are somewhat unsympathetic to this theme of divine mercy. In most modern languages the word itself has fairly sentimental, paternalist overtones. We scarcely ever use it indeed, and if we do apply it to any Christian activity we do so rather pejoratively. Others among us go further still: they have a real fear that religion is alienating. Concerning a Christian who is rigorously loyal to religious practice, but not so ready to undertake his responsibilities as human being, one may hear the comment: "Is not this easy recourse to the outstretched arms of a merciful Father a way of evading conscience?" Or, concerning Christians who are engaged in works of mercy: "Are they not just salving their conscience and evading the real problems and responsibilities?"

The parables we find in today's Gospel of the 3rd cycle (the lost sheep, the lost drachma, the prodigal son) provide an opportunity for closer examination of this theme of mercy. The behavior they inculcate, the works of mercy they recommend, differ very much really from the procedures that modern man views as distastefully.

Yahweh, the God of Mercy

The word, mercy, in the Bible, is one of those that describe most accurately the relation between God and his people set up by the Covenant. It belongs to the vocabulary of faith, and gets its meaning from the revelation of the Totally-Other God, who lovingly intervenes in the life of his people. In Hebrew it has much richer associations than in our modern idioms. It suggests at once the loyalty of love and its tender aspect, as something that moves the heart and the entrails. An attitude of mercy is a disposition of the whole being.

The Jews, like any other people, had learned by experience the misery of man's lot here below. The pattern of events always had its share of misfortune and suffering, and this was intensified by hate and injustice arising from human sources. Uncertainty and insecurity was the whole lesson of history. To cope with this, pagan man took refuge in the security offered by his rites, seeking communion with the sacral world. Jewish man turned to Yahweh himself, begging him in his mercy to intervene in the event. He was capable of showering his believers with blessings; it was only infidelity that could thwart his benevolence.

But divine mercy, towards which Jewish man was turned by the human predicament itself, was more intensely realized through the experience of sin. Sin was a rejection of God's loving intervention, and Yahweh might have cancelled his covenant and abandoned his people. This he did not do. Why? The answer was to be found in the revelation of Sinai: "Yahweh is a God of tenderness and compassion, slow to anger, rich in kindness and faithfulness. For thousands he maintains his kindness, forgives faults, transgression, sin. But he lets nothing go unchecked, punishing faults . . . to the third and fourth generation" (Ex 34:6-7). This boundless mercy, it is clear, does not mean indifference to sin. When his people sin Yahweh is consumed with anger, it is something too serious to be overlooked. He shows his people mercy by summoning them to conversion, to return. And he invites them also to practice mercy. Man must realize that Yahweh is merciful to all flesh (see the book of Jonah), and he must learn, in practicing mercy, to overlook the barriers of race and belief. This ultimate dimension of Old Testament revelation we find in the later Wisdom texts (see, for instance, Si 28:7). Such is the lesson of God's love for his people.

Jesus-Christ, our High Priest of Mercy

With Jesus divine mercy is seen at its most intense, and the conditions for its authentic exercise become clear. One of the most striking things is the association, with Jesus, of divine and human mercy. The whole history of mercy is that of a relationship between God and man, and in the God-man it reaches fullest authenticity. In him we have the perfect encounter between God and man. We see in him the true countenance of the God of mercy, as he practices mercy, and as he summons men, now, in him, the children of the Father, to practice mercy also.

His whole life, above all his death on the cross, was an exercise of limitless mercy. Wherever he found himself he was always waiting for the prodigal son. He did not come for those who believed themselves to be just, but for repentant sinners. The latter, like the lost sheep or the lost drachma, he is continuously seeking. Some seemed to be favorite candidates for mercy, particularly in Saint Luke: the poor, women, strangers, all those who were excluded by one interdict or another, rejected by society.

Characteristic of his method of showing mercy was the absolute renunciation of self that was to culminate in the cross. Mercy is seen to be the true face of unselfish love, the love that conquers rejection and hate.

The Church of Mercy

What Jesus began the Church continues, and the mercy that he displayed in his love must go on being displayed by all the People of God.

Christians in the first place have experience of divine mercy towards themselves. They, like all men, are sinners, but they have found that, even in their sin, God's love reaches out to them. God takes us as he finds us, at each moment of existence, and, no matter what our infidelity, he never allows complete rupture. He is always near, ready to pardon, ready to give himself completely. We should not however make the mistake of thinking that this Christian recourse to divine mercy is merely a way of setting conscience at rest. Any procedure that withdraws a man from human responsibilities is certainly alienating, and cannot be that of a real believer. If he does not feel the urge to conversion, to shape himself for the future according to the true human standard, the penitent will not be experiencing divine mercy in the proper sense. Its proof is invariably the decision that a work has to be done, a challenge faced.

In a nutshell, the insight is imperative that we too must be merciful. Towards the other, whoever he be, we must show the attitude God has shown to us. Our reaction to all human misery, especially misery of the spirit, must be a loving one. We have to be loyal and tender, endlessly patient, and scrupulously respect the other's dignity. Above all we must never be condescending. Genuine mercy never hurts the recipient's dignity. It does not break the spirit, but begets on the contrary a surge of hope.

So that our own experience of mercy and the mercy we dispense are indissolubly linked. If we do not find ourselves anxious to show mercy, we shall have good reason to query the validity of our own experience of divine mercy. We cannot have one without the other.

The Good News of mercy

In our sort of world the poor really constitute a great anonymous mass. They are those who hunger for bread and justice. The small people of the universe. The Good News is meant for them. How are we to bring it?

In the first place it is becoming very urgent that we eradicate any obstacles that the ecclesial institution itself, or our actual conduct of missionary enterprise, are placing in the way. These would be, not only all exterior signs of wealth, but any power tactics to which we might be tempted to resort in order to get palpable results. The whole conduct of pastoral life should be designed to make the poor feel at home in the Church. This will require the adjustment of a great many details in the lives of both clergy and laity. We read for instance in the conciliar decree about priestly life: "Priests and bishops . . . should have their houses disposed in such fashion that they seem accessible to all, that no one, even the most humble, will be ashamed to come there" (no. 17).

Secondly, we must be careful that the dignity of the poor is never hurt by our manner of conducting works of mercy, whether individual or collective. Every procedure must be designed to bolster confidence, to induce people to plan their own lives and take their place with dignity in social life. This will require great tact and detachment on the part of those who conduct such works. We must remember that the poor are our masters.

Finally, because our world is extremely aware of the possibilities opened up by science and technology, the Church will be required to make judicious use of social and economic techniques in her works of mercy. In this context there are so many possibilities of error, of creating a wrong impression, in collective projects particularly. The absolute disinterest of the Church, and of Christians, must always be very evident. Any suggestion of a different motive is quickly discovered and proves fatal to our enterprise. Works of mercy are an integral part of the great task of evangelizing the poor, but only on the supposition that they are quite disinterested.

The exercise of mercy in the eucharistic celebration

The eucharistic celebration is basically a joyful family reunion of penitent prodigal sons. Nowhere is mercy more authentically evident. The Mass formularies are full of texts about the Father's benevolence and about repentant sinners. All those present realize that it is only by trusting his inexhaustible mercy that they can approach the Father. This is the whole meaning of the Mass.

It is also the memorial of the cross, the proclamation of Jesus' death until he comes. We are reminded that God's mercy is contagious. As he has been merciful to us, so must we be to our brothers. Only one man was merciful with the fullness of divine mercy. That was Jesus, and the Mass is the expression, not only of God's mercy, but of the mercy of the God-man, both indissolubly associated. When we Christians turn to God's mercy, we implicitly agree to follow Christ's example and show the mercy he showed. This cannot be described as a path of evasion, or a facile solution.

TWENTY-FIFTH SUNDAY

A. THE WORD

I. Isaiah
55:6-9
1st reading
1st cycle

This oracle comes from the final chapter of the Book of Consolation of Israel (Is 40-55). It expresses one of the prophet's dominant themes: a defense of God's unicity and transcendence.

Throughout all his work Second-Isaiah celebrates the transcendence of the God of history, the God of intervention, the God who is near (v. 6). All events, good and bad, are directed by Yahweh himself for the accomplishment of his plan. Because he is unique (Is 41:8-14, 17-20) he has no one to reckon with as Lord of history. He wills all the stages, and turns them ineluctably towards the eschatological future.

One of the signs of his transcendence, emphasized in our reading, is that his thoughts and his ways are not ours. So it is with divine mercy (v. 7). When the vicissitudes of life cause men to be disturbed and confused, we must always remember that Yahweh is ever-present, imperturbably carrying out his plan. When man feels his sin too great to be pardoned, a thought of God is revealed which transcends the limits of human justice. He is "generous in pardon" and can enable the worst sinner to be converted.

A belief then in God as unique and transcendent is the best anchor for hope in the fulfillment of the divine plan.

In the New Testament the full dimension of divine transcendence over history becomes clear. Man is actually invited to become God's partner in the accomplishment of his plan. History is no longer something to be undergone, but something to be constructed.

II. Wisdom   The Jews of the second century B.C. were still
2:17-20   dreaming of a political restoration. They
1st reading   thought a Messiah would come on the clouds
2nd cycle   to rescue them from the yoke of Gentile nations. Daniel's apocalyptic predictions were encouraging, and fostered this hope. A century later however, when the author of Wisdom compiled his book, the situation had worsened considerably, and the very existence of Jewish religion was threatened. Political restoration seemed infinitely remote.

Among the dispersed believers of this epoch, the just who claimed sufficient *knowledge* of God to call themselves his sons (v. 18) seem to have been exposed to severe challenge. There is even mention of "outrages and torments" (v. 19) which threaten them, of condemnation to an "infamous death" (v. 20).

Greeks of course, who were now so given to philosophy and science, would take very unkindly Jewish pretensions to wisdom and true knowledge of God. They were a people whose dietary and liturgical practices made them immediately "eccentric" (v. 15). But they were above all ridiculed for their beliefs: the final reward of the just (vv. 16 and 20), their concept of a covenant which set them apart and gave them a special knowledge of God.

Our passage, which refers principally to the situation of the Jews in Alexandria, is remarkably verified in Jesus' life. He too claimed to be son of God (Jn 5:16-18; Mt 27:43), to have a knowledge superior to that of the most learned among the scribes (Jn 8:55). He had to encounter the sarcastic challenge of men (Mt 27:39-44), and he was condemned to death in order that the divine promise of help should be verified.

III. Amos Amos delivers very many invectives against the
8:4-7 *injustices* of the wealthy (Am 5:7-13; 8:4-7;
1st reading 5:11-27; 6:17). The wars and social upheavals
3rd cycle of the 8th century led to the growth of a group
of unscrupulous merchants who trafficked in
the most necessary commodities. Not even religious cult proved
any protection against this: festival days were merely occasions
of further profit at the expense of the poor (v. 5). It was natural to
think of the tares in the wheat when the time of fulfillment came.
All the more so for Amos, who continued to live in a society that
was nomad and pastoral.

IV. Philippians For his beloved Philippians Paul provides
1:20-24, 27 news of his imprisonment. Our reading has
2nd reading some reflections on the fate that has become
1st cycle his lot.

For him, true life is *life with Christ* (v. 21). His thinking here
is really very traditionally Jewish, expressed in language that is
exceedingly emotional. Such a life means association with the
kingdom of the Messiah, sharing with the Messiah the eschatological banquet of the poor, sitting on thrones round about him,
judging the other members of the Kingdom, sharing his tent,
sharing with him the joys of Paradise.

Imagery like this is more or less explicit throughout all New
Testament writings. Paul, good Jew that he is, describes such
hopes at length in the letters to the Thessalonians. He wants this
life with Christ here and now, because the Lord's coming is at
hand. When he writes to the Philippians however there is a total
change. He is now seriously contemplating death. He compares
life and death, balancing the respective advantages (vv. 22-24).
To go or to stay, to be with Christ or to continue laboring for the
gospel. He makes his choice. To stay (v. 25), even though he is
persuaded of the advantages of death. It means being with

Christ. To share the messianic kingdom as envisioned by the Jews one must undergo the emptying that death means.

V. James   What James has said previously of good and
3:16–4:3   bad use of language he now repeats, in some-
2nd reading   what different terms, in discussing true and
2nd cycle   false wisdom. Realist that he is, he does not
                  concern himself overmuch with principles.
There are very concrete ways, as he sees it, of distinguishing the genuine sage from the false one. He proceeds to give us some.

a) The first essential for true *wisdom* is that it be "pure" (v. 17), without flaw, that is. There must be no jealousy or intrigue (v. 16; cf. 2 Co 12:20; Ga 5:20). This wisdom kindles a desire for peace (Pr 3:17; Rm 8:6) tolerance and docility, which enables "sages" to live in communion with their brothers, their adversaries and their superiors. It shows kindness towards the poor ("mercy", v. 17) and fairness to subordinates. It sets up an extremely varied set of interpersonal relationships, and charity is its basis.

b) Causes of *discord* that James denounces are first, the inordinate desire for material goods, and next envy of what our neighbor possesses (v. 2). Sometimes this envy even resorts to prayer, using God to acquire equal wealth with one's neighbor, as if prayer could be utilized for such ignoble ends (v. 3).

VI. 1. Timothy   Here Paul is concerned with the organization
2:1-8   of liturgy and the community as a whole. He
2nd reading   requires Timothy to make the decisions de-
3rd cycle   manded by his pastoral charge and the powers
                  he has received (1 Tm 1:18).

a) The first measures to be taken have to do with *universal prayer* (v. 1). In this context the apostle uses four terms: petitions, prayers, intercessions and thanksgiving. It is possible that he is thinking of the Aramaic terms used to describe the "eighteen prayers," a formula then much used in Israel. He would be recommending Christians to use a similar formula for their liturgical assembly.

The Christian prayer however would differ from the Jewish model in its frank universalism. It includes all men (v. 1), especially kings and governors (all pagan at the time), and is concerned with the maintenance of peace (v. 2). The prayer seems to be specifically for men (v. 8). It is to be pronounced, with hands lifted up to heaven, by people who live at peace with one another (cf. Mt 5:23-25; 6:14).

Gentiles addressed their prayers to the emperor himself, who was divinized and considered a savior. When Christians pray to God for him, they put him in his proper place, dependent upon the unique God.

b) The universal prayer is established on firm doctrinal bases. There are three reasons, as Paul sees it, for the Christian obligation to pray for the needs of all the world.

The first is God's *unicity*, and his will for universal salvation (vv. 4-5a). Since he is one, all the problems of humanity are his concern. Since he is the only creator he wills the salvation of all men, and the Christian who prays in these terms is cooperating with that salvific will.

c) The second reason is Christ's universal *mediation* (vv. 5b-6), which Paul associates with his humanity, or, more precisely, his absolute fidelity to the human condition. What he accomplished as the Messiah of his people is heavy with meaning for all mankind. He offered himself as ransom "for all" (v. 6), not "in place of" men, but "for" his brothers (cf. He 4).

d) The third reason is Paul's own universal *mission* (v. 7). Because he is "doctor of the nations," he feels he has the right to "demand" that Christians aid his ministry by the intensity and universality of their prayer.

The essential conditions for Christian prayer are that it be representative of humanity before God, and exhibit solidarity with the whole human race. Christ was the first to fulfill these, when he offered himself for the many in the sacrifice of the cross, that goes on reverberating in the Church's eucharistic prayer. The ministers of our universal prayer then must have a genuine interest in the problems of humanity, and look for means of associating all members of the assembly with these.

VII. Matthew This passage has certainly been subjected to
20:1-16 numerous revisions, each of which differed in
Gospel interpretation. To get at the original meaning
1st cycle it will be necessary to omit the conclusion
(v. 16b), which is probably an addition by the second century Church. It is missing in several manuscripts and is to be found in its correct place at Matthew 22:14, from where doubtless it was taken. The lesson of the parable according to this late tradition would be that "many people" are called to the Lord's vineyard. But it is not sufficient to be called: one must be "chosen." Only a small number has this privilege. This view is certainly a reaction by the Church of the second century against the naive belief of some Christians. Mere membership of the Church is not sufficient for salvation. The interpretation is in itself valid, but it imposes a meaning on the text that it does not seem to have had originally.

a) The conclusion in verse 16a (the first will be last and the last first) is from Matthew's hand. This does not prove however that Jesus uttered it on this occasion, or that its connection with the parable was established at this time of writing. The point of the parable is not the fact that the last shall be *before* the first (v. 8), but that the same treatment will be given all the groups. The sentiment itself "the last shall be first . . ." is not infrequent

in the synoptics. In Mark 10:31 and Matthew 20:16 we find it in
a different, and more natural, context. In Luke 13:30 it is softened:
there are "those" now first who shall be last, and "those" now last
who shall be first. What we have apparently is a saying of Jesus
that was delivered independently, but which the evangelists,
with more or less success, endeavored to fit into a different context. Matthew, whose gospel stresses the exaltation of Gentiles
over Jews, places it after the vineyard parable so that the first
Christians will understand the *reversal of situation* between Jews
and Gentiles, once Gentiles accept the faith. This was certainly
true in the first century and throughout all Church history, but
the emphasis given the parable is nevertheless a modification of
its original meaning. There was really no question of the last being
given priority over the first.

b) We have Christ's own conclusion to the parable in verse 15.
The basic complaint against the master of the vineyard (God)
is that he lacks "justice." It was a complaint already made by the
elder brother of the prodigal to his father (Lk 15:29-30). It is the
complaint of the "good" Jews when they hear the doctrine of
retribution (Ez 18:25-29), and it is the complaint of Jonah when
God pardons the pagan Ninevites (Jon 4:2). In each case we
have the human viewpoint about God's justice and his exercise
of mercy, which are so disconcerting (Lk 15:1-2). Jesus uses an
argumentum ad hominem. The master of the vineyard is "just"
(in the human fashion) with the first group, because he gives
them what was agreed. He is "just" after the divine pattern with
the last, because he is bound by no agreement in their regard.
The argument of course is weak, since God is not reproached in
respect of either group taken singly, but on the basis of comparison. For that reason Jesus turns to a different argument. He affirms
the primacy of God's goodness. His manner of acting is not to be
compared with human justice, so totally does it transcend this in
love. The contract between the master of the vineyard and the
workers seems to be an image of God's covenant with his people.
The covenant is not the *"do ut des"* contract the Jews wished to

make it, but a gratuitous act of God (Dt 7:7-10; 4:7). So is the new covenant a gift of the Father's *gratuitous love,* rooted in the absolute freedom of God and respecting man's freedom (Ga 3:16-22; 4:21-31). In the justice he dispenses to both groups God is indicating the love he has for both, with due regard for the situation in which he finds them.

The lesson conveyed then to Jesus' audience is the lesson of God's mercy. It transcends narrow human categories which attempt to project human views of justice and bilateral contract, that are altogether too prevalent in men's own relations with one another.*

VIII. **Mark**   For the second time, Jesus tells his disciples of
   9:30-37   his imminent passion (v. 31). Simultaneously
   Gospel   he deliberately ceases to preach to the crowds
   2nd cycle   (v. 30), and concentrates on the final training
                    of the disciples.

a) The apostles however are no more understanding than the crowds. Why must the Messiah suffer in order to gain the kingship? A few verses earlier (Mk 9:9-13) Mark has actually given us the echo of one of their discussions. It was the task of Elias to prepare everything so that the Messiah could mount his throne. Why then a suffering Messiah?

There was a way of dispelling their *incredulity.* It would be seen that Scripture had suggested the passion in a series of hints. Jesus' predictions of the passion indeed seem so thoroughly saturated with references to the Old Testament, that it is possible to discern the actual texts to which he may have been alluding. The verb "to be delivered" (v. 31) comes from Isaiah 53:6 and 12, supposing the whole doctrine of the suffering Servant. The phrase "into the hands of men" (v. 31) is from Jeremiah 33:24 (or 26:24) and associates Jesus with the first great prophet who was perse-

*See the doctrinal theme: *membership in the Church,* p. 93.

cuted. "Suffering much" (v. 31) is probably traceable to Isaiah 53:4 and 11 according to an Aramaic targum (to crush), recalling once more the suffering Servant. "To be rejected" (v. 31) suggests the stone rejected by the builders in Psalm 117/118:22 (cf. Ac 4:11; Mk 12:10).

The scriptural knowledge of the apostles must have been fairly considerable. It enabled them to see the meaning of the events that were to follow.

b) The second topic of the apostles' discussion arose from the imminence of the Kingdom. They were anxious to secure in advance their places as ministers and counselors of the Messiah (v. 34; cf. Mk 10:35-40). Jesus uses this to reveal the conditions for entry to the Kingdom. Not only must the Messiah go in by the gate of suffering, but his followers as well must become *servants* (v. 35) and poor (v. 36: the child at the time was not highly valued: the Aramaic word for child was the same as that for servant).

c) It is not to be thought of course that this network of motifs produces an artificial discourse. The underlying theme that gives unity to all the remarks of Jesus is that of conditions for *entry to the Kingdom*. For this, one must be as a child, modest, that is to say (v. 36), not seeking the best place (vv. 33-35). Once in the Kingdom one had to become the servant of all (v. 35), offering love to those most despised (v. 37, remembering that in Israel the child was not highly regarded). This charity would have a particular dimension in the leaders of the community. They would take care that the little ones were not scandalized. The little ones were those weaker Christians who were ignorant of casuistic subtleties in doctrine (v. 42). Their faith could be crushed by over elaborate theories (cf. Rm 14:1–15:8).

d) Possibly the reason why Jesus blessed the *children* was because those who were actually looked down upon were destined one day to be the beneficiaries of the Kingdom. This gives us a precious insight into the conditions for entry. We must be in the interval as simple as children, as open to the future, as unencumbered by systems and theories.

Jesus certainly did not intend to reduce the ethic of the Kingdom to an infantile standard. He has in mind a community that respects the little one and allows for his reactions, but he wants his disciples above all to be like children in being willing to depend on others. Man, and the Christian *a fortiori*, is incapable of saving himself.

The disciples are going to be looked down upon as feeble creatures, just as the child was in Jewish society. They will recall that acceptance of this disdain enabled them to follow Jesus as he went up to Jerusalem (Mk 9:29-32).

IX. Luke
16:1-13
Gospel
3rd cycle

This passage presents numerous problems. The words of Jesus recounted are certainly authentic, but we do not have the context that would clarify them. This was lost, and, in the primitive community, there were many different attempts at explanation.

Doubtless Jesus is referring to some cheating episode that would clarify matters if we knew about it (vv. 1-7). The context however eludes us. We just have verse 8 "and the master commended the unjust servant."

Who is this master? Not the master of the servant, but Jesus (*o kyrios*). We notice an identical change in the meaning of a word in Luke 18:6. There "Lord" indicates Jesus, not the judge.

a) Verse 8 then does not belong to the account of the cheating episode. It is Luke's addition. But why should the Lord commend this servant. Wherever we can penetrate, in the synoptic tradition, to the actual text of Jesus' sayings, we often find that he wants to convince his listeners that the judgment is inaugurated. This being so, there is no time to lose. One must foresee tomorrow (Lk 12:54-56), and be sufficiently *warned* to deal with one's adversary before the judge intervenes (Lk 12:58-59). The servant profited by the respite to make sure of his future and be among the survivors. For Luke apparently this is the primary lesson of the parable. One should make use of the short time remaining.

b) A second interpretation was developed in primitive Christian circles: "The children of this world are wiser than the children of light" (v.8b). This is a sad affirmation. In ordinary affairs (it is terrestrial affairs that are contemplated) Christians are always going to be at a disadvantage, because they cannot resort to the tactics others adopt. In this view the parable expresses Christian *resignation* when confronted by power tactics that are unlawful for them.

Other Christian circles provided yet another interpretation by discerning a lesson about the use of money (v. 9). The main point is not the ensuring of his future by the servant, but his example in *using the money*. Luke, who wanted only the poor in the Kingdom, was particularly open to this view. If the rich do manage to enter, it is because they have stripped themselves of money to purchase the blessings of the Kingdom. The servant is teaching us the correct use of money: it should be distributed in such manner as to assure us of heaven (Lk 6:29-30; 12:33; 6:34-35). So, to the basic eschatological lesson of Jesus himself, and the disconsolate one of verse 8b, Luke probably now adds a personal one (v. 9). It stems from his experience of the primitive community, and his personal predilection for poverty. He is the only evangelist to give us this difficult parable, doubtless because he feels he has the key to it.

Verses 10-12 bring us a final view. The servant is still an example, but an example of what not to do. The moral is that if one wishes to administer spiritual goods, one must have been *faithful* in the administration of material things as well.

Too often the "children of light" are overly concerned with intentions and principles. They run the risk of making Christianity an ideology and diminishing the real efficacity of the Kingdom of God.

B. DOCTRINE

1. Theme of Membership in the Church

Sometimes, throughout the Christian centuries, the idea put forward of Church membership has been a fairly distorted one. The Church is necessary for salvation of course and we become members through baptism, but baptism as such is no guarantee of attaining the Kingdom. Nor does the principle "outside the Church there is no salvation" indicate definitive reprobation of those who remain outside the visible Church.

Many Christians readily believe that practice of the sacraments gives some sort of assurance about the hereafter, provided they live lives in conformity with the moral law. Few on the other hand question themselves about the connection between the faith and natural reactions that are purely human, but often very noble. What is the real role of the Church in God's plan, and the real meaning of Church membership? Do we become members in order to gain our own salvation, or principally to cooperate with Christ in the salvation of humanity?

These are questions of very great importance just now. Everywhere at the moment the Church is called upon to be missionary. Christians and non-Christians are drawn into ever closer association. We Christians then need to be sure about the specific dimension that Church membership brings. What is at stake is universal salvation.

The assembly of the desert

In order to understand the divine purpose in assembling men, and what the response of faith is, we have to go back to the assembly of the chosen people, as it was in the desert after the delivery from Egyptian slavery.

When Yahweh convokes his people there, it is a purely gratuitous act. He is the Totally-Other, and need render account to no one. His gesture however is not ultimately reassuring. The promise of a land flowing with milk and honey does not dispense the people from encounter with the harsh reality of the desert, where day after day one must depend on divine benevolence. There was a temptation to regret the security of Egypt. This land of slavery had advantages which the desert could not provide.

Not alone is Yahweh's action not reassuring, but salvation itself is far from assured. It is not sufficient to undergo this trial from God's hand: Yahweh demands in addition the response of faith. One's thinking must be aligned to that of Yahweh, something that implies a permanent conversion. To this the people reacted badly, and Saint Paul tells us "with most of them God was not well pleased" (1 Co 10:3).

God's summons then in the desert was a sign of his benevolence, at once gratuitous and disconcerting. Those who responded to it formed of course an assembly of believers, of people who were ready to rest all their confidence in Yahweh and share his plan.

Once installed in Palestine, and throughout their long history, Jewish people were always tempted to give absolute value to membership of the chosen people and legal observance. The prophets were always reminding them that this did not avail for salvation. What Yahweh wanted was conversion of heart.

Christ as center of universal assembly

The first and only one to answer the desert convocation with full fidelity was Jesus of Nazareth. For him too God's action seemed far from reassuring. His "yes" to the Father's will led him to apparent failure in his work and to death on the cross. He came among his own, but his own received him not.

The first consequence of his fidelity was that the true nature of the divine summons to salvation was revealed, and the previous concept of the covenant dissipated. The true covenant, that which God had willed from all eternity, gave no precedence to any people whatsoever. It was a covenant with all humanity, who were invited to enter the Family of the Father.

Because it was based on love, love at once of the Father and of men, the man-God's "yes" had universal dimensions. It made him the center of universal reassembly, the first-born of the true humanity willed by God. To appreciate the nature of the work of Jesus Christ, we must never separate his personal fidelity to God's will from the role as savior of humanity. Each act involves the other.

The Church, the true desert assembly

The Church, because she is the Body of Christ, is the true desert assembly. In her the gratuitousness of divine choice is fully expressed. She is the only avenue of salvation, ensured always of God's fidelity. Here we have the mystery of the universal summons to salvation. In the person of Jesus God has made a covenant with all humanity. It is the task of the Church to carry this Good News everywhere and be a visible sign of it in her actual assembly. Wherever in space or time she finds herself, the universality of the summons to salvation must somehow be made evident. Otherwise the transcendent nature of the new covenant might get obscured.

Confronted by this constant summons, both baptized, and unbaptized, are always being spurred to conversion. Baptism is not properly speaking the goal; it is the point of departure. Throughout the pilgrimage we all have to discover for ourselves that God's great act gives no assurance or security, simply because it leads us into the precarious territory of love. Univeral love demands that we be stripped of self as Christ was. If we are journeying towards a deeper experience of the God of Jesus Christ we must face the disconcerting experience of the desert. We shall always like the Israelites hanker after the securities of Egyptian slavery.

So, because membership of the Church summons us to display the love Jesus displayed, the goal of individual salvation can never be the proper Christian goal. We are involved, with Christ, in the salvation of humanity.

The missionary's summons to conversion

The proclamation of the Good News always includes a summons to conversion. We should be very clear however that the conversion required is not confused with inessential elements. Otherwise the very idea of mission is likely to suffer. Conversion has nothing to do with cultural deracination in the first place. It is essential to the idea of the Church that all men should find themselves at home in her; she is not bound to any nation or any culture.

Before the missionary ever reaches them there is a sense in which all men are already in the bosom of the Church. And the missionary can never be proprietorial about the Church. For sociological reasons Christianity is sometimes regarded today as the white man's religion. The conversion of non-whites must never seem to suggest abandonment of their own religion for that of the whites. It must suggest fulfillment beyond expectation of their own spiritual pilgrimage, so that Christ may be all in all.

So that the requirement of conversion rests first of all on the missionary himself. The deeper his own conversion the nearer he will find himself to the non-Christian, and the more he will bear witness to the transcendence of the religion of love. He will seem the man who listens, who wants to accompany the other on his pilgrimage, to search out answers with him. He will never give the impression of having ready made answers. He, personally, has encountered Christ, but he realizes that this encounter must be an on-going one. From his sharing with the non-Christian he expects new purification and new deepening of his own awareness of the salvation mystery. He can find riches of which he was previously ignorant, give himself a new "catholic" dimension which will open up new vistas in universal love.

The Eucharist and the mystery of the universal Church

Between the Eucharist and the mystery of the univeral Church there is an intimate relation. Wherever it is celebrated it is at once a proclamation of the divine summons to universal salvation.

The celebration *par excellence* is that presided over by the bishop. Here the elements of summons and response by assembly become very visible. All the pastoral activities of the diocese: the various groupings of baptized and of catechumens, all the other masses, the whole ecclesial procedure, should be thought of as extensions of the episcopal Eucharist.

Its principal emphasis in catholicity. The universal convocation by the bishop is a summons to everyone in the district to gather, whatever their diversity, in brotherly union around Jesus Christ. When we share such a Eucharist, and all celebrations should be replicas of it, we should feel ourselves involved in God's great initiative. When we reflect on this project of the return of humanity to the Father, we begin to have some idea of the distance still to be traversed. The universal brotherhood we have now is still a far cry from the ultimate goal, and we feel once more what is demanded of us by the doctrine of limitless love.

2. The Theme of Efficacy

That one should get results is an extremely popular attitude in these days. Confronted by the great human problems of peace, development, social and international justice, good advice and high-sounding language win little attention. People expect action, and tangible results, at whatever cost. Political, social and economic structures have to be transformed; we are expected to take concrete measures and stop dreaming.

Many men are putting aside Christianity, convinced that it is basically futile, and some actually take the view that it, like other religions, has simply alienated people from their responsibilities. For some time now Christians have been extremely conscious of this, and have been concerned to show that their faith, far from alienating them from human responsibilities, actually proves an incentive in the search for peace, development and justice. Like their non-Christian brethren, they want concrete results. This sort of efficacy, now more than ever, requires cooperation and collective action, and in this context a particular problem arises for some Christians about involvement in various marxist movements. Avoiding such involvement seems like renouncing efficacity.

The preliminary question we should ask is whether Christian and non-Christian mean the same thing by efficacy. It is perhaps inevitable that a Marxist for instance must view a loyal Christian as inefficacious, when it comes to constructing the human city? And on the other hand, does efficacy on the Marxist pattern achieve everything that the Christian wants?

Efficacy in Jewish faith

Though it has sometimes seemed otherwise, mankind in fact has always made efficacy his goal, if not always in the same way. Pagan man in the past sought divinization in one way or another. If he could share the sacral world, he would find security, touch the absolute, be established in eternity, participate in divine privileges. His avenue to this communion was ritual, something that withdrew him from the insecurity of profane time and space, and offered, as he saw it, efficacy. If the ritual was scrupulously observed, it would automatically give results and lead to happiness. We know from the myth of Prometheus that gestures were made as mastery of natural forces. But these invariably provoked the anger of the gods.

Under the regime of faith in Israel there were profound changes. Realization of the Totally-Other God very quickly exposed the futility of the pagan search for efficacy by way of liturgies. It is true that originally the chosen people worshiped the golden calf and yearned for the security of pagan cults. But throughout all Jewish history the prophets were there to show how illusory this security was. No one but Yahweh had the power to save the people he had gratuitously chosen, and on Yahweh no one could lay hand. Happiness must come from him; to rely on pagan rites was to build upon sand.

Yahweh gives salvation, but not unconditionally. His people must be faithful to the Covenant. Fidelity leads them to find God in this history. It was reflection on this which deepened

Israel's awareness of the moral requirements of the covenant, and made her depend exclusively on Yahweh's gratuitous benevolence.

If she fulfilled the conditions of the covenant, the happiness in store was a new land free of the consequences of sin. Man would be overwhelmed with divine blessings; his work would produce fruit in abundance: peace and justice would flourish. In this new paradise people would enjoy the harmony that comes from friendship with God.

The efficacy of Christ's intervention

The Jewish outlook was altogether modified by Jesus. The absolute gratuitousness of salvation became clearer than ever before. But, on the other hand, man's own part in the work of salvation is more than ever emphasized.

In his action and in his teaching Jesus insisted constantly that human salvation was not within the compass of human resources. Men were called to be God's children, to live the life of his household, to enjoy his blessings. Their hopes would be fulfilled beyond expectation. But the realization of this was beyond their own capacity, any attempts at self-divinization were doomed to failure. By his emphasis on this Jesus gave scandal, because he was forcing sinful man to drop the scales from his eyes. He had to realize that he was but a creature, incapable of meriting divine salvation.

Yet, simultaneously, it was obvious that Jesus' coming in the flesh was overwhelmingly efficacious. Salvation was a gratuitous gift of God, but it was accomplished in the human state by the mediation of one who fully accepted humanity. A man had been found among men who could respond perfectly to the Father's initiative. He was the Son of God; no one lesser could have done what he did. In order that man might be able to reach up to God without forfeiting creaturehood, God had stooped down to him and pitched his tent among humanity. Such is the depth of salvific love; such was the divino-human work of salvation. God's initiative was total, but he summoned man to be his patrner.

There would be no alienation for man; in Jesus his contribution was fully effective.

Jesus loved the Father with the same intensity with which he was loved. And this love did not in any way diminish his humanity. On the contrary it developed that to its fullest perfection. Once the creatural state was established in proper relationship with God, it became clear that man too was made to love.

The Christian's efficacy in union with Christ

Jesus inaugurated salvation history and it is continued in the members of his body. "Without me you can do nothing," he said, but by him, with him and in him everything becomes possible even in the salvific order. All men are called in Jesus Christ to become God's partners in the building of his Kingdom, and each one plays a unique and irreplaceable role. Membership of Christ's Body gives a man the capacity to fulfill his role. He must live with Christ's life, drink the water of life that he offers, carry his yoke, follow him in every way. Christ is always the center and the source.

Following this model, we can all be efficacious, and get results from what we do. Insofar as we are "free from sin" we become "slaves of God," and enter upon that path of which "the culmination is life eternal" (Rm 6:22). In general, unfortunately, the grandeur of the Christian's mission is insufficiently emphasized. He is not just someone whom baptism has qualified to "receive" the gift of God. The gift of God is never received passively, because God gives himself to his partners only. True, the initiative is his, but it demands reciprocity. He gives himself to men so that men will give themselves to him, and in this mutual giving the Kingdom is constructed. For this reason the Christian's mission transcends the goal of individual salvation; it is always concerned with the salvation of humanity as a whole. Membership of Christ's Body involves us in the greatest human enterprise that can be conceived, the fulfillment of human destiny. It is in such terms that we must think about our efficacy. Such results are possible for us who have become adoptive children of the Father in Jesus Christ. Our achievement though in this context implies efficacy too in our creatural mission. Our creaturehood is not canceled by our sonship; on the contrary it is restored to its proper dignity, because the stranglehold of sin has been broken. And the great project of ultimate salvation for humanity is itself intimately connected with the project that must be carried forward on the natural level. That is the project of human betterment, for which we must rely on our own creatural resources.

Missionary witness to Christian efficacy

To evangelize the modern world the Church will be required to make common cause with the world in the area that concerns it most: that of human betterment. Modern man has carefully calculated the resources he can muster. He knows what he can do, and that what is at stake is human progress. There are many challenges to be faced, but he is determined to encounter them cost what it may. The task is immense. The earth must be made habitable for humanity. Peace and justice must be established, by gradually transforming political, social and economic structures. Modern man believes he has the tools to do the job, and he wants results.

The Christian's lucid view of man as revealed in Jesus Christ should not make him feel a stranger to these humanist ideals. He should realize that the construction of the Kingdom is inseparably associated with the betterment of humanity on the secular level. The quality of his contribution to salvation history will be influenced by the way in which he uses his energies for the advancement of peace and justice on earth. He will find himself at one with all men who labor for results, because he too wants to be efficacious. The efficacy that he envisions may out-strip by far the goal that modern man has set himself, but for that goal too it provides considerable thrust. Working for the natural goal, a Christian can lead his non-Christian brothers to some appreciation of the genuine horizons of Christianity. He will be setting up the "first signs" of evangelization in the modern world.

The challenge without doubt confronts him with a temptation to which it would be fatal to succumb, if he wants to keep his faith and be a true witness to Jesus Christ. Like his non-Christian brothers, he is a sinner here below. He will be always drawn towards efficacy in the secular sense, towards tangible results that seem so much more concrete than progress in the gospel sense. The temptation will be all the more agonizing in that, though he may be laboring exclusively for the gospel, he will run the risk of estrangement from Christian authority or establishment. Nor will he escape challenge from his non-Christian colleagues, even at the moment when he is expending all his energy in furthering their own project. Such is his lot, and such is the price of his witness. But all this must never deter him from involvement in secular programs. Inevitably, the tares will be mixed with the wheat. The main thing is that the Christian have the opportunity to manifest the wisdom that is his.

Christian efficacy in the eucharistic celebration

Because the Eucharist is the total act of Christ, it is the focal point of Christian efficacy. It has been well said that eucharistic celebrations mark the decisive stages in salvation history. Christ is always the principal agent, but, because it is the Eucharist that makes the Church, this is the moment when the members of his Body too can make their best concrete contribution. When we share the Eucharist, we cooperate actively in the work of human salvation. We intercede for the totality; we round out the sacrifice of Christ with the living and the toil of all humanity.

Yet our contribution here of course is of necessity a ritual one, and directly concerns the building of the Kingdom only. It would be absurd to expect concrete results in the secular domain from the mass. We do not celebrate it in order to resolve human problems, or supply inadequacies on the human plane. Efficacy in rite will not dispense us from seeking efficacy in life. All we know is that, because of the deep connection between rite and life, our performance in the first can be an earnest of what we will accomplish in the second. If we are to be efficacious at any level, we can rest assured that our eucharistic life will always be the great source.

TWENTY-SIXTH SUNDAY

A. THE WORD

I. Ezechiel
18:25-28
1st reading
1st cycle

Chapter 18 of Ezechiel is one of the more important ones in the collection (cf. Ez 14:12; 33:10-20; 34:16). Summoning the people to conversion, he inveighs against the fatalistic outlook. Where is the point in conversion, since we must pay for the sins of our fathers? This was a popular attitude, based on texts like Deuteronomy 5:9; 29:18-21; and Exodus 20:5, and on proverbs such as that refuted by Ezechiel in 18:1-4. In combating it, the prophet refers to a sort of decalogue that was common at the time (Ez 18:5-9, 11-13, 15-17), where personal responsibility was strongly emphasized.

The second portion (Ez 18:21-32) goes on to show that fatalism plays no part at the personal level. The individual will be judged by God only by personal justice or injustice. The sinner, if he is converted, can escape the threat of punishment; the just man, through weakness, can lose his claim to reward. Today's reading comes from the concluding part of this discussion.

For Ezechiel the fault of the people is collective and so is their punishment (Ez 16; 20; 23). He realizes also that even collective punishment is never final, and can be mended by a massive conversion (cf. Am 6:1-6). The essentially new insight that he brings is that God is preparing a *new covenant*. Into each man he will send a new heart and a new spirit (v. 31; cf. Ez 11:19), and this covenant will be open to both just and sinners.

God does not will death or punishment, but the life of the greatest number possible. His new covenant is designed to carry out this project, and the contribution by man is to be conversion. Each one of course will be individually engaged in the project

but in this context the prophet does not insist on individual interpretation of responsibility. The examples given in verses 26-28
are individual cases; but he is addressing himself to the whole
"house of Israel" (vv. 24, 29, 30 and 31) and envisaging the conversion of the whole people who are to begin a new life.

Today, as then, it is difficult to be free. The times confront us
with all sorts of challenges, and our freedom imposes personal
decisions. More often than not we choose the security of the
group, the party, the nation, the Church itself, and unload there
our personal responsibility.

We even tend to blame God for the situation. "If God be just,
how can he permit such things." Ezechiel's great achievement
was that he reminded man of the responsibility that freedom en-
tailed. He summons man to the challenge. The truth is that men
discover the true essence of their liberty only through crisis, anguish and revolt. If we are to avoid fatalism, or infantilism, it is
a discovery we must constantly be making.

II. Numbers   To the college of elders that surrounds him
    11:25-29   Moses imparts the Spirit of God that he pos-
    1st reading   sesses, so that they can lead the people and
    2nd cycle   interpret God's will. Two of the elders do not
    take part in the ceremony of investiture.
Nevertheless, though not legally commissioned, they prophesy.

The episode is all the more striking because we find it in a
book which is extremely concerned with protecting the establishment against any unrecognized activities (cf. Nb 12:1-10; 14:16,
etc.). Here, in a highly institutional climate, we have spontaneous prophecy tolerated. It is evidence that the Spirit is not
bound by the *institution,* that no one can claim monopoly of
charisms.

Those who exercise charisms in the Church are indeed required to exercise the greatest abnegation too. They are always
faced with the temptation of fixing a sphere for the Spirit's ac-

tion. The superior is never at ease when his subject embarks on projects that he cannot control. The hierarchy takes it ill when the laity exercise freedom of choice and action. In relationships between Churches we notice a similar tension, very often where collaboration is highly desirable.

III. Amos   Our prophet and his career in the Northern
   6:1, 4-7   kingdom under king Jeroboam II. The polit-
   1st reading   ical and economic conditions of the 8th cen-
   3rd cycle   tury, in both North and South, had brought
                  about a severe clash between rich and poor.
The former had derived much profit from the situation, whereas the poor were more deprived than ever.

Amos is a desert dweller, and consequently extremely conscious of social injustice in all its forms. He finds it unendurable that the oppressed in their misery should be so affronted by the *luxury* of the rich (vv. 4-6). In God's name, he roundly condemns those who revel in false security. Yahweh will not allow his people to live like this; his chastisement already looms on the horizon (v. 7). His strictures brought about his own banishment.

His message continues to be very relevant. In very many countries the luxury of the rich contrasts with the destitution of the poor, and very often poor nations continue to be exploited by wealthy ones. Oppressors will find no place in the people of God to whom the prophet addresses his warning.

IV. Philippians   The Philippians, among whom Paul sojourned
   2:1-11   during his second missionary journey (about
   2nd reading   the year 50; cf. Ac 16:11-40), were one of his
   1st cycle   favorite communities. Relations were always
                  cordial and affectionate, and the Philippians
showed great solicitude for Paul during his imprisonment (Ph 1:7, 13-14, 20; cf. 2:25; 4:18). He asks them now to crown his happiness by cementing yet more their brotherly ties, and giving

evidence of greater humility still in their relations with one another.

a) In his exhortation to unity, which is so pressing that it may very well indicate threatened factions in Philippi, Paul appeals to the basic values that he shares with his listeners. First, their "consolation" in Christ, the Lord's presence that is which strengthens their faith; the "persuasion" in love which is common to them both and which comes from God; the "communion" in the Spirit which enables them to share the graces of the new covenant; finally the "tenderness" and "compassion" of which all have had occasion to bear witness "in Christ."

Based on such principles the brotherly love which ought to unite the Philippians will express itself in "accord of sentiments" (v. 2). The phrase does not refer to unity of doctrine, but rather to the mutual sympathy and understanding that binds them, the readiness of each to give preference to the wishes of the other (v. 4).

b) The love and unity in question of course presuppose the sort of *humility* that "regards others as superior to ourselves" (v. 3), avoids vainglory (v. 3) and imitates the abregation of Jesus (v. 5). In the New Testament the theme of humility principally suggests man's humility before God (Ac 20:19; Ep 4:2; Col 2:18). Thus humility between brethren presupposes a spirit of faith. It is Jesus only who has given us the perfect example of this humility (vv. 6-11; see also Vol. III, p. 250, commentary on Ph 2:6-11). He can lead his followers to forget their titles to glory and superiority, and give themselves genuinely to brotherly union.

V. James
5:1-6
2nd reading
2nd cycle

James displays the same intensity as the ancient prophets when he attacks those who are so attached to their material goods (vv. 2-3) that they do not pay their workers properly (v. 4), and oppress those less fortunate than themselves.

He uses the language of prophetic *invective*. He tells the rich to howl, so great are the disasters that threaten them (v. 1). Doubtless it was a threat calculated to move even the hardest heart (cf. Am 8:3).

The chastisement is already here. James uses verbs in the perfect tense to describe it. But the rich alone fail to see it. They are altogether absorbed in the gold and silver (v. 3) that consumes them like a devouring fire.

The sin of such people consisted in failing to pay their workers (v. 4) in spite of the insistence by the law (Lv 19:13; Dt 24:15) and the prophets (Ml 3:5; Si 31:4; 34:21-27). This was at the time the quickest road to riches. Very often too judicial procedure (v. 6), because of chicanery and the venality of judges, allowed the just and innocent to be despoiled in favor of great fortunes (cf. the vineyard of Nabot: 1 K 21).

James does not hesitate to attack the rich violently. We find a similar attitude in the third gospel (Lk 6:24; 12:16-21; 16:19-31). The rich in our day are not very different; they still stand on the backs of the poor. Consequently the invective by James is still relevant. Perhaps however the number of rich among the people of God might conceivably prove embarrassing for anyone anxious to emulate James now.*

VI. 1 Timothy 6:11-16
2nd reading
3rd cycle

For Timothy's benefit Paul sketches here the portrait of the ideal pastor, as contrasted with false readers (1 Tm 1:18; 6:3-5).

a) He is above all someone who fights the battle of the faith (v. 12). The theme of *combat* is an important one in Pauline doctrine (cf. 1 Tm 1:18; 4:10; 2 Tm 4:7; 1 Co 9:25; Col 1:29) and here the combat is for the faith. The essential thing is not the struggle with enemies of the faith. The faith itself is a

*See the doctrinal theme: *riches,* p. 266.

combat, because the decision for the faith entails inevitably fidelity and constancy. There is the struggle with oneself as one strives for the incorruptible crown, and the concern about the salvation of others, especially if one be responsible for a Christian community.

b) In this context *baptism* is seen as the great moment. It is then that we are summoned by God (v. 12) to a life of communion with him, that we make our profession of faith (v. 12) before the assembled community and our guarantors, God and his Christ (v. 13). It is the moment when the "commandment" (v. 14) is formulated, the whole pattern of living, that is, which faith imposes on the believer. By this mention of God's call, the profession of faith and the commandment Paul is really recommending Timothy to preserve pure and intact the doctrine and the Spirit of the Lord until the day of his full manifestation (v. 14).

c) In the form of a doxology, Paul goes on to celebrate the *Lord's manifestation,* and uses language borrowed from the ritual of divinization for emperors and from synagogue prayers. To emphasize the distinction between the emperors and God, he uses substantives for God (king, lord, v. 15) while the former are designated by verbal clauses ("those who reign, who exercise sovereignty"), as if to indicate that their power is merely passing, by contrast with God's eternity (v. 16).

VII. Matthew
21:28-32
Gospel
1st cycle

The parable of the two sons is peculiar to Matthew. The first redaction of it ended with verse 31 "in truth I tell you." It then becomes an explanation to Jesus' adversaries of why the Gospel is eventually addressed to sinners, the "just" having rejected it.

However, prior to being chronicled by the synoptics, the gospel traditions were frequently grouped on a practical principle, according to key words for example. Thus to this parable, which ended with a mention of publicans and prostitutes (v. 31), an independent *logion* which also mentioned sinners was added (Luke 7:29-30 gives it as an isolated saying).

Matthew then revised verse 32 (mentioning the theme of justice, changing to the second person and introducing John the Baptist) and placed the whole passage 28-32 after another (vv. 23-27) which was concerned with the Baptist.

a) The parable is a justification of the direction of the Gospel now to those who are despised, a new category of poor. Jesus is actually addressing the high priests and elders (Mt 21:23), just as he had directed similar parables against the Pharisees (the Pharisee and the publican: Lk 18:9; the two debtors: Lk 7:40; the lost drachma: Lk 15:2). He wants to show those who are scandalized by his preference for *sinners* that these are actually closer to salvation if they do penance than the people who consider themselves just (cf. Mt 9:10-13). The sinners have opposed God's will, but they have repented like the prodigal son. The self-righteous have professed to serve God, but without really accepting his plan of love for men.

The targets of the parable then are those who close themselves against the Good News in the very name of justice. Jesus lets them know that God loves the rejected. They are capable of greater penance and obedience than the proud and self-sufficient.

b) The addition of verse 32 makes it an *allegory of salvation history*. John the Baptist, a prophetic envoy, like the messengers sent to the vineyard workers (Mt 21:33-38) or the wedding guests (Mt 22:1-9), clashed with the pride and hostility of his listeners, and was led to address himself to others (compare Mt 21:32 with Mt 21:41 and 22:8-10). The point is that the Church is not necessarily composed of members of the chosen people. Matthew is particularly prone to allegorization of the parables in the light of developments in the Church. By contrast with the structures and principles of historic Israel it was a new departure. John the Baptist was just another of God's envoys, but he was the one who foresaw most clearly that the chosen people would be deprived of their privileges in favor of "others," the Gentiles in particular.

God did not decide at a definite moment of history to reject the Jews and choose the Gentiles. His salvific will is at all times universal. Not even the scribes or Jewish leaders are excluded from salvation. Their treatment of the Messiah simply meant that they lost the role in mediation that was hitherto theirs. The character of their "yes" to the Law led them to say "no" to the gospel.

For Christians too there is a moral. A "yes" that is too much published, too much heralded, may conceal a large measure of refusal. Such people will tend to classify "others" as "no" sayers, when they really are not. Indeed the professional "yes" sayers are often so hide bound by system that "no" sayers feel no urge to join them. The Kingdom is made up of those who began by saying "no," but found one day they could say "yes" without being false to themselves.

VIII. Mark 9:38-43, 45, 47-48
Gospel 2nd cycle

These verses belong to a discourse, the original import of which has been lost in all of the synoptics. It has been possible however to restore the primitive version with some degree of certainty. Like the most ancient synoptic material, it is connected by certain key words. Mark's version, on many points, is undoubtedly the closest to the primitive:

Preamble (v. 30):
a) circumstances of the discourse (v. 33)
b) the first key word: *raba* (the greatest) (v. 34)

First article:
a) development about "the greatest" (*raba*) (v. 34)
b) second key word: the *raba* must be *talya* (servant) (v. 35)

Second article:

a) development about the *talya* (v. 36)
b) third key word: the *talya* should be received "in the name of Christ" (*bashma*) (v. 37)

Third article:

a) development about *bashma* (vv. 38-40)
b) fourth key word: the "little one" (*gatina*) (not in Mark) should be received in the name of Christ

Fourth article:

a) development about the *gatina* (not in Mark: reference to v. 41)
b) fifth key word: no *gatina* may be scandalized (*macsheka*) (v. 42)

Fifth article:

a) development about *macsheka* (vv. 43-47)
b) better to cut off the member that gives scandal than to be cast in the fire (*noura*) (v. 47)

Sixth article:

a) development about *noura* (v. 48)
b) seventh key word: everyone should be treated with fire and salt (*mehla*) (v. 49)

Seventh article:

a) development about *mehla* (v. 50a)
b) conclusion (v. 50b)

a) With regard to the *name of Jesus* (vv. 38-40) Mark's presentation of John's question indicates some sectarianism. How could someone use this name to expel demons without being a follower of Jesus? Jesus, in replying, uses a text from Numbers 11:26-29 (see, above, corresponding 1st reading, p. 105). He affirms that the Spirit (or in this instance his name) cannot be the monopoly of any single group or system. He is not restricted to the institutions or the persons he inspires.*

b) In a discourse where there is so little seeming unity, we find that the connecting idea concerns the *conditions of entry to*

*See the doctrinal theme: *the spirit and the institution,* p. 116.

the Kingdom. The verses which constitute today's gospel present
a number of them. One must show hospitality towards the disciples (v. 41). One must avoid at all costs scandalizing the little
ones, ordinary Christians, that is, who are ignorant of doctrinal
casuistry (v. 42). One must be drastic with oneself where moral
weakness is concerned (vv. 43-48). But, because the Spirit acts
with complete freedom, one should be extremely cautious about
determining criteria for the true disciple (vv. 38-40).

**IX. Luke
16:19-31
Gospel
3rd cycle**
It is only in Luke that we find the parable of
the wicked rich man and Lazarus. Rather
more than the other synoptics, he made use
of some source that was concerned with the
problems of riches and poverty (Lk 6:30-35;
16:12-14; 19:1-9; Ac 5:1-11). This parable however, at the stage
when he inserted it in his gospel, had undergone some modification of original meaning.

In the account as we have it there are two distinct parts. The
first (vv. 19-26) is the only gospel parable where a protagonist
is given a name: Lazarus ("God helps"). It could be a Christian
adaptation of an Egyptian story introduced into Palestine by
Alexandrian Jews. This tells of the different fates of the publican
Bar Majan and a poor scribe. The second portion (vv. 27-31) is
more original, but has a different purpose. Lazarus plays a sec-
ondary role only, and the chief interest is concentrated on the
fate of the five brothers of the rich man, who were not converted
by the threat of the Day of Yahweh (cf. Mt 24:37-39).

a) The first portion applies to poor and rich, the Jewish theory
of retribution by *reversal of situation,* just as in the beatitudes
(Lk 6:20-26; cf. further Lk 12:16-21).* The point is not whether
the rich man was good or bad, whether Lazarus, the poor man,
was good or bad. The parable is not really concerned with moral

*See the doctrinal theme: *faith and revolution,* p. 122.

performance, but with the proclamation of the imminent Kingdom in a climate that was sociologically established. What we
have actually is the ambience of the primitive community in
Jerusalem, which was made up of the poor and unsympathetic
towards the rich (Ac 4:36-37; 5:1-16). The latter seemed incapable of opting for the new dispensation, concerned as they were
with this world and their own possessions. The poor on the other
hand were more open, and consequently the Kingdom was more
accessible to them.

Subsequently other nuances were introduced. Matthew will
speak of poverty "in spirit," no longer taking the beatitude in
terms of economic poverty only, or pronouncing malediction on
the economic rich. The whole eschatological theme if reversal of
situation had to be handled more prudently, and its principal
emphasis became the proclamation of the final times.

b) The second portion of the parable is concerned even more
with *eschatological waiting*. It provides a striking corrective to
the overly sociological and materialist emphasis of the first part.
No longer is there question of wealth or poverty, but of irreligion
and selfishness on the part of people who are unable to read
God's signs. For them, death is the end (v. 28); they will not
even be convinced by the resurrection of the body, because they
are not accustomed to see in their own lives the signs of survival.
The search for signs is a pretext only. Man is saved by hearing
the Word (Moses and the prophets) and by vigilance, not by
apparitions and miracles.

The reversal of situation theme, the rich becoming poor and
vice versa, is a common literary cliché in the prophets and the
gospel. The figure perhaps has less importance than the fact. It
voices the revolt of so many human beings against essential
indignity, in a world where a man can often be mistreated by his
brother, the poor crushed by the rich, the just man persecuted by
the wicked.

Jesus himself endured maltreatment. He was taken for a madman or a malefactor, simply because this would prove more convenient for certain people: "it is expedient that one man die. . . ." (Jn 11:50). He made the cross the great testimony of love, and thus his revolt against indignity became supremely efficacious. It gave humanity the hope of a future where selfishness and hostility would have to make way for dignity and love. His disciples could only build that future by continuing in their turn the great movement of revolt by the poor.

B. DOCTRINE

1. Theme of the Spirit and the Institution

It is commonplace nowadays to say that all institutions are in crisis. This applies to all institutions, secular as well as religious. The crisis is acute in that it raises the question, a fundamental one, of the relationship of a man's conscience to the institutions and structures which shape his activity. The question is no longer one of determining how far present conditions in the world and in the Church require reform of institutions. People are beginning to query the very possibility for the modern conscience of performance within the framework of institution as we have it. It is a problem that is ubiquitous in our day, and it is constantly widening.

The Church, in particular the Catholic Church, is a glaring example. Up to recently its institutional facade seemed intransigent and fixed. It was often denounced indeed by other Christian confessions. The "system" seemed to be accorded value, not to say sacralized, in itself. Nothing more was required from conscience than free adherence to it. Since Vatican II, a movement has been started that is liable to have far-reaching results. The Council judged it imperative to reform institutions in such fundamental matters as liturgy and communications between central and outlying authorities. In the interval the progress of these movements has disclosed that the need for reform actually goes much deeper than was thought. Today's crisis of authority in the Church provides plenty of evidence.

Today's readings (first reading and Gospel, 2nd cycle) point out that the Spirit is free to act independently of established structures, and provide us with an opportunity of weighing the real significance of what is now happening in the Church. The crisis is a grave one, and its resolution in the future will depend on the accuracy of our analysis.

Prophecy and institution in Israel

Men have always attached great importance to their institutions. These form a secure background for action, and give man a tangible objective example of the sort of order he hankers after. Like man himself they carry the mark of history and geography. It is very easy to understand how they would tend to be absolutized, above all religious institutions. There would be concern to maintain them unchanged, to regard the gods as their authors.

With the regime of faith the process of desacralization began, though it was not to be properly completed until the advent of Jesus of Nazareth. From now on the believer's anchor in his quest for God is not security but the historical event. It was here that God came to be recognized as the Totally-Other, the Creator, and that man was forced to accept his creatural condition. No one could touch God. Consequently institutions begin to topple from the pedestal. The Jews did not doubt of course that Yahweh was their author; but the important thing was the use made of them by men. That Yahweh was absolutely free was the constant message of the prophets. He can dispense with the Temple if he does not receive proper worship there. The davidic dynasty can collapse if the kings are not faithful. Even outside the confines of Israel Yahweh can kindle faith: not even the Sinai convenant is absolutely eternal. The whole story indeed of Jewish prophecy is one of criticism of the most hallowed institutions.

One thing did withstand desacralization: the Jewish conviction that they were irrevocably the chosen people. The separateness and the privileges were unchallengeable. Nor did the prophets ever question this, even in their visions of the future. When the new heaven and the new earth would be a reality, a marvellously embellished Jerusalem would be the center of the universe. Israel would be the Elect of God, a nation of priests served by all the other nations.

Jesus of Nazareth and Jewish institutions

Jesus' attitude to the institutions of his people is characteristic. He accepts them with complete freedom, without ever letting himself become enslaved by them. All the evangelists stress the fact that he observed the Law faithfully. For the development of his messianic role and message he relied on the categories of thought and behavior that he found in his environment. But he was the prisoner of no category or institution. He stamped them with his message, and by that very action made them over new, or brought them inevitably to their end. Two examples will suffice. It was already realized that the whole Law was summed up in the precept of love for God and one's neighbor. But the commandment of love without limits transformed the ancient precept totally. The Sabbath was believed to be of divine institution. But, while observing it, Jesus showed himself to be its master. The Sabbath was made for man not man for the Sabbath.

In fact he brought the process of desacralization to its completion. No one had ever stressed, more than he, God's transcendence in the salvific initiative. The Spirit blows where he wills, unfettered by any human structure. But in all that he said and did, he was restoring man to his liberty. That could only flourish when man was ready to face the unpredictability of existence. He was also restoring institutions to their proper place, because institutions were made for man not man for institutions. Man sets up his institutions and reveres them. He remodels them and reinterprets them. In the process they are perceived to be either worthwhile or obsolete. They are all meant to contribute to man's destiny and growth. If they interfere with this they should be remodeled or abolished.

The great accomplishment of his people's hope lay in Jesus' transformation of religious institutions. All the Jewish particularism and exclusivism was made to yield place to the great event of the cross, which sealed the definitive covenant between God and all men. There was some sifting in consequence. Some institutions, like the paschal supper, survived the reevaluation.

Others, like circumcision, the Sabbath, temple worship, the Jerusalem pilgrimage, were phased out.

The work of the Spirit and ecclesial institutions

The first disciples of the Risen Lord were all Jewish converts. They continued to observe the law of Moses, though the faith they were living was something new and disconcerting, the fulfillment of the promises in Christ, crucified and risen.

New institutions were destined to develop, which would express the primitive Christian experience of the Risen Lord's presence with them through his Spirit. These would be the confession of Christ's Lordship, the Lord's supper, and the ministry of the Twelve. However it was only gradually that the full significance and richness of these became evident, due to the action of the Spirit in the early Church. His action was most evident in what early Christians came to see as the major ecclesial event: the entry of the Gentiles. This was of capital importance because it was directly concerned with fidelity to the new commandment. The disciples recognized that the Spirit was at work among the nations, and that the Church would find her true stature in this context. It was *the* Event. It gave real meaning to the institution, because this now became the expression of catholicity for the people of God. And side by side with this development, Jewish institutions began to wane, losing at least their obligatory force.

Ecclesial institutions however never became rigid in a pattern for all time. As time went by, often enough the faith led to face the danger of degradation. Whenever the faithful yielded in any measure to such temptations, the institutions that expressed the faith became deformed. Prophetic figures would arise, all through Church history, to disclose the message of the Spirit, and always it would be a renewed fidelity to the Event that would restore to the institution the visage of her youth. We have had evidence of that in our own day. At a time when the ecclesial institution seemed paralyzed, unable to engage in the sort of dialogue that modern man needed, a prophet arose: John XXIII. He convened the Council that forced the Church once again into reading the "signs of the times." In our world too the Spirit is at work. Discerned in the Event, he is summoning the Institution to a renewal of youth.

Crisis in ecclesial institutions

In apostolic times the Church was liberated from Jewish particularism and enabled to develop her own institutions by the mission, at the Spirit's summons, to the Gentiles. Today also it is the requirements of mission that impel us towards reform of our institutions.

Ever since the first World War there has been a growing awareness of one particular requirement of mission: the adaptation of ecclesial institutions to diverse cultures. We had been too often content with the establishment of ecclesial replicas of Western Christianity. It became clear that what was needed in the young Asian and African Churches was local liturgy, local law, local theology and local spirituality. In that way all peoples would begin to feel at home in the Church. Her very catholicity implies a great deal of diversity in her institutions.

There is another requirement that is engaging our attention here and now. It has to do with modern man's hopes for the future and the growth of human knowledge, something of which Christians too are now particularly conscious. Modern man is no longer willing to be shaped by ready made institutions that are imposed from the outside, that express nothing more than God's past intervention in human history. He is more fully cognizant of the possibilities of his liberty; and, in every domain, he wants the sort of institutions that will appeal to his responsibility. In religion, he wants those that are at once expressions of God's initiative and of man's, that express the actuality of the mystery of Christ for the secular future of humanity. Such a need makes a deep analysis of the current crisis in ecclesial institutions very imperative.

It is a crisis that could indeed be salutary. We must never forget that the modern world is in a way a product of Western Christianity. And the reaction of modern man in our day could have something in common with Jesus' saying about the sacrosanct Sabbath—that it was made for man. But of course it will be up to modern man too to acknowledge that he is someone who needs salvation. The Church could render great service in taking the initiative.

The great importance of the liturgical reform

In the eucharistic celebration we have conjoined the most basic institutions of Christianity. Believers are assembled for the Lord's supper; they listen to the Word; they confess their faith; and the presiding priest exercises apostolic ministry in a special way. The structure of the celebration is always a good index of the state of the people of God at any given time. We must always expect that liturgical reform will point the way for all ecclesial reform.

An increase in lay participation during the first half of the 20th century automatically brought about more active sharing in the liturgical celebrations. A more keen awareness of missionary responsibility brought about a greater emphasis on the liturgy of the Word and a better organization of the liturgical assembly itself. These were the main bases of the reform sanctioned by Vatican II, and set immediately in motion.

This, it might seem, was the essential measure. But it is not so. The very success of the liturgical movement has brought to the surface new problems, that were not foreseen but are certainly fundamental. Experience everywhere has shown that those priests and laity who contributed most to liturgical renewal still find that there is something lacking.

What is lacking is really, almost invariably, modernity. The reform took the direction of a vigorous "restoration." The liturgical heritage was purified, restored to its essential, stripped of excrescences. But it did not change structure, or provide sufficient openings for modern man to feel at ease there, to feel a direct link with his secular occupations. Thus, in default of institutional direction, we have seen modern Christians search out their own new ways, in domestic liturgies or the like. These experiments should not be allowed to remain peripheral; the needs they demonstrate are the needs of the whole body.

2. Theme of Faith and Revolution

The great change in thinking that has come about in our time is well instanced by the use of the word "revolution." It used to describe a sudden violent upheaval that disturbed the normal order, and could if it were not suppressed bring about a transformation of society. The French Revolution of 1789, for instance. It was as if order were regarded as of its nature perpetual. Revolution meant a violent interference with it. No one would have thought of associating the gospel with revolution. It was meant to transform persons, whereas revolution was a destruction of established system. Many sincere Christians would regard any revolution as a work of Satan, and the summons to conversion of heart was never seen as an eventual summons to substantial reform of structures.

Increased human knowledge has enabled us nowadays to analyze society more precisely, and many men have become convinced that existing social structures are alienating. We must, it is thought, envisage their thorough transformation, and take adequate measures towards that end. What is at stake is human progress. Consequently the word revolution has come to have wider applications, which would indeed be wider still were it not for the traditional associations of violence that frighten some. Revolution of course is really a political option, adopted with full lucidity concerning ends and means. It does not necessarily imply violence or lack of concern for human persons. We have now our explicit advocates of nonviolent revolution.

Our theme here raises a problem which we should try to pose correctly. The gospel (see, for example, today's gospel, 3rd cycle) treats of the oppression of the poor by the rich and does not foresee any reversal of situation on this side of the grave. The social structures of the time were apparently accepted in that way. Yet we have had many people point to Jesus as the greatest of all revolutionaries in the true sense of the term. What are we to say?

The struggle for justice in Israel

Members of all traditional religions have shown a natural tendency to support established order, even when it was manifestly unfair. The revolutionary mentality was foreign to them. There might be flagrant inequalities as between rich and poor, masters and slaves, but they would generally be attributed to chance or fate. No question of transforming social structures would arise. If occasionally the sheer misery of the oppressed drove them to revolt successfully, what came about was merely the substitution of one established order for another. The religious man's reaction to revolt would invariably be one of opposition, and he would require time to adjust to any new order.

Things were different in Israel under the regime of faith. Those intensely religious men, the prophets, were often social reformers. It is important however in this context to remember one fact. The prophets did indeed denounce vigorously the injustice of judges and kings, and in a larger sense any sort of exploitation of the poor by the rich and powerful. But they inveighed against persons, not structures. There may have been, with some, a nostalgic harking back to nomadism, an idealized nomadism, where the injustices consequent upon the installation in Palestine and the setting up of the kingdom were unknown.

The prophets' attitude can be very easily understood. Their quest of the living God is in fact closely associated with a deepening of their understanding of man. Once human beings are able to rise above notions of security that are bounded by human existence only, the mystery of human liberty begins really to be understood. When a man realizes his contingency and weakness before the Totally-Other God, he begins to feel the urge to love his neighbor, because such in fact is man's nature, once the scales fall from his eyes. Accordingly every form of racial injustice will be rejected as the result of sin.

By their vehement denunciations the prophets hoped to bring about a sensitivity of conscience and a conversion of heart. An immediate transformation was possible, but the great ideal was the day when genuine justice would reign and everyone would receive his proper due.

Jesus of Nazareth and the campaign for man

We do not find in the gospels that Jesus pronounced any revolutionary manifesto. Social and political programs did not seem to concern him, nor was he a member of any resistance group. Was he then less socially involved than the Old Testament prophets? The truth is that his campaign went deeper than theirs. If we compare the two types of preaching we see that, whereas the prophets were concerned with social injustice, he denounces pharisaism, with a growing intensity that was finally to bring him to the cross. A little reflection will show that the campaign of Jesus was far more crucial; it was a campaign for human dignity and liberty.

It was the legalism and particularism of the Pharisees that he opposed. These are in fact the two great pitfalls that stand in the way of human progress. Their legalism made the Pharisees faithful observers of the Law, of what in their estimation was the fixed and established divine will. But legalism of that intensity makes people incapable of standing outside themselves, of really understanding what human fidelity to God and to man means. Their particularism made them regard themselves as the privileged folk of God. They studiously maintained their distance from publicans and Gentiles. Such particularism is divisive and makes people incapable of true relationship with others, accepted in their otherness. In both cases we have the same sin, the same basic alienation: pride.

His denunciation of pharisaism in fact throws into relief the fulfillment he was putting forward: the new commandment of brotherly love without limits. Jesus was manifesting the true horizons of human liberty, and the dynamism that ought to inspire it. Legalism and particularism were to be left behind. When he summons us to accept the other for what he is, Jesus is drawing us into the high adventure of human liberty, which will always be unpredictable and disconcerting. If we are to embark upon that, we must be ready to strip away our pride. Such is the liberation that is given to us by Christ, when he makes us with him children of the Father. The great adventure of love is weighted with eternity.

Jesus' campaign for man continued in the Church

It was only after Jesus' death on the cross that his disciples began to see the dimensions of the work he had done for humanity. His life and his passion taken together disclose the secret of his personality and are a living commentary on his message. The great adventure of liberty to which he summons us was inaugurated in his own life. Since then, the avenue has been opened for every man who wishes to follow in his footsteps, and carry on the campaign for humanity. Such was the birth of the Church, and in such terms she is destined to grow, guided by the Spirit of the Father's Family and Christ's Body.

From the very beginnings of Christianity, we see the sort of difficulties that have to be surmounted before his disciples can carry out the project of the great Inaugurator. Only God knows how important all these years have been, and the future that will grow from them. When we review the history of the primitive Church, what strikes us is the extent to which development depended on an event and a person. The event then was the entry of the Gentiles into the Church. Could they be fully members at once, or was it necessary to be disciples of Moses first? The answer to this question was a test of the liberty inaugurated in Jesus Christ. A person had to intervene, who would brush away the obstacles, thoroughly complicated, that stood in the way of an affirmative answer. This was Saint Paul, a man of pharisaic training who had become a disciple of the Risen Lord. In combating legalism and particularism he was under no illusions. It was imperative that the work of Jesus should not be in vain. Love would have to have proper room for expansion.

Throughout all subsequent Church history the campaign went on. It is an exacting and difficult campaign that has to be taken up again after each new human experience. It continually encounters the very same obstacles that Jesus encountered for the first time, and after him Paul of Tarsus. From the 4th century onwards, when legalism and particularism began to influence, more or less profoundly, ecclesial institutions themselves, the difficulties were multiplied.

The campaign for man and revolution

The adventure of love inaugurated by Jesus invited men to accept the law of liberty. Gradually this brought about a transformation in human relationships. A system of values came into being, most often under the direct tutelage of the Church, which was destined to govern all relationships between Christians. It was the fruit of long experience of Christian living, and it inspired many initiatives in answer to the signs of the times. As time went on man became more and more responsible for his destiny, more and more aware of the prodigious possibilities, for better and for worse. It only needed the development of science and technology to do the rest.

Modern man then took the field. Relationships between men, between *all* men this time, have now taken on formidable complexity. Oppression of some by others has reached gigantic proportions. The traditional value system is incapable of controlling the situation. It has become imperative to forge a new one. For this the people of God are now at a disadvantage in a sense. The fact that in general they belong to the rich nations, and are very often in power in these nations, dissuades them. Meanwhile men are coming to see how alienating in fact for human beings are certain political, social and economic structures. The movement however to change all this, and bring about radical change, tends to shape itself outside the Church, among the poor of the universe. The moral force behind this movement is strangely similar to what we find in the gospel. Revolution has become a definite political option, but one, we must remember, that does not necessarily include violence.

The gospel gives us no theory of revolution, and, if we try to develop a theology of revolution in gospel terms, we are simply deluding ourselves, and running the risk of failing to see the wood for the trees. In this domain, the means that lie at hand for revolution, both Christians and non-Christians are dependent on exactly the same resources. What human reason can suggest, that is, socially, morally, scientifically. It is the business of both to search out solutions in these terms, and it may well be that something concrete will emerge. The most that can be said for Christian revolutionaries is that, living as they do after the example of Christ, caught up in the great adventure of love, they are liable to be more careful lest revolution become the occasion of another sort of oppression and a new legalism.

The Word of the Church and the word of revolution

The first reaction of a modern revolutionary to the Church is, very understandably, one of hostility. This particular political option was not developed in Christian circles for the very good reason, he feels, that Christians have a vested interest in established order. The Church was more concerned with preserving traditional values than with moving forward: her Word therefore was a reactionary Word. This basic misunderstanding runs so deep that genuine believers have a real obligation to dissipate it. And, so unthinkable is it for some Christians that the gospel be deprived of its power to challenge establishment, that faithful followers of the Word fail to challenge injustice and oppression, that they have gone the length of presenting the gospel as a charter for revolutionaries.

Now the gospel of course, which it is our mission to preach, can never be reduced to the dimensions of a secular manifesto, however revolutionary. In many contemporary environments, loyalty to the gospel may indeed impel believers to the option of revolution; but the gospel itself is neither the stuff of revolution nor its motive force. What then is it? It is an event in history above all, which opened a vista in the campaign for man that reaches down to our day. It summons us to do battle for man in the true sense, under the standard of Him who continues to be today the true Leader. We are challenged to the great adventure of Love, which requires that we be free of sin, which will never allow us to rest again, not even for the fulfillment of revolutionary projects.

Once this is understood, it still remains true that the Gospel will exercise its full influence only when its witnesses take the sort of options in secular life that command the attention of the world. It is through such dramatic witness that it speaks to men of good will.

TWENTY-SEVENTH SUNDAY

A. THE WORD

I. Isaiah
5:1-7
1st reading
1st cycle

In this allegory of the vine the prophet likens himself to the "friend of the bridegroom," whose task it is to guard the fiancee's virginity and lead her on the wedding day to the bridegroom. Verses 1-2 tell us of the bridegroom's care for the fiancee; verses 3-5 invite the crowd to understand the judgment he will exact by condemning the unfaithful spouse to barrenness (v. 6). Finally in verse 7, as a sort of gloss, we get the key to the allegory.

This allegory of the vine begins the theme of the *espousals* of Yahweh and Israel, which will recur often in biblical literature. Sometimes Israel is a vine (Jr 1:21; Ez 15:1-8; 17:3-10; 19:10-14; Ps 79/80:9-17), sometimes a spouse that has been chosen and then repudiated (Ez 16; Dt 22:2-14; 25:1-13). Here the two images coalesce perfectly. The prophet has the role of the bridegroom's friend. The care devoted to the vine (v. 2; cf. Mt 21: 33-44) is God's care for his spouse (Ez 16:1-14 or Ep 5:25-33). God's judgment on the vine is public (vv. 3-4), as the law required in the case of adultery. Finally the condemnation of the vine to barrenness (v. 6) is the threatened punishment of the unfaithful spouse. And the order to destroy the hedgerow and the wall (v. 5) recalls the precept of stripping the person guilty of adultery before the stoning (Ez 16:35-43; Ho 2:4-15).

Semitic religions had often used the image of God's wedding with humanity, but there had never been talk of mutual love. After Hosea, Isaiah was the first to describe God's passionate love, as evident in his attention for his fiancee as in his vengeance for her infidelity. His love is always dramatic. It is its own justification and manifestly it is lavished on a being that is unworthy of it.

So, throughout the ages, God was greeted by the weakness and fickleness of humanity. Until one day a vine grew in the midst of humanity, Jesus Christ, who was faithful and able to bear the fruit of divine life (cf. Jn 15).

II. Genesis 2:18-24
1st reading
2nd cycle

In Genesis 2 the creation of woman takes place in an essentially masculine world. Man had had time to know himself and give names to the things that surround him (vv. 18-20), before he discovers in woman the "help" he seeks. She is furthermore described only in terms of her relationship to man (v. 23; cf. 1 Co 11:9; 1 Tm 2:12).

Man's destiny is not fulfilled by mastering material creation and life: he has the inner need to encounter a being capable of communion with him. What he encounters in fact in woman is another self. She is not encountered in the mystery of otherness, but as bone of his bone and flesh of his flesh. Her very name (*ishsha*) is no more than the diminutive of man (*ish*) (v. 23). And the story of the birth of woman from man's side (v. 21) indicates the dependence of woman (v. 22). Man estimates her by the standards of his own self awareness. He is the center, and his partner is merely a "helpmeet" destined to help him realize his project. She has her own personality and we see her break down man's isolation by offering him communion (v. 18); but the author is not interested in considering whether this also breaks *her* isolation.

Thus the primitive tradition recounted in versus 18-23 is highly masculine in emphasis. It reflects contemporary social structure, where woman was subordinate to man.

The last verse however, which was doubtless added by a

Yahwist editor, indicates the beginnings of another emphasis. Woman is drawn from man, but she has her own individual excellence. To attain her, man does not hesitate to abandon his family, just as Abraham abandoned his country for the land of Promise. The verse (24) accords the initiative in love to man only of course; but already we see signs of the mystery of otherness. Man is beginning to see the value of two in one.

This particular biblical tradition calls for modification. Genesis 2-3 envisages a couple that is isolated, at the mercy of forces that it cannot control (cf. v. 25; Gn 3:10-16). Genesis 1 on the contrary envisages the couple that is blessed and concerned with the mastery of creation (Gn 1:27-28).

Yet throughout biblical history it was the former, misogynist, tradition that determined the *female status*. She came as "the other" into the masculine world, not fitting the predetermined masculine standards. She was regarded as foolish or senseless, or even possessed, and was alienated by male attitudes. We find the influence of this tradition still in Saint Paul's letters (1 Co 11:7-9), though he did make important correctives.

It was Jesus who liberated woman from her alienation, not in a sociological sense, but by the revelation of the mystery of his person as New Adam and first born of creation. Man would no longer exercise any office of mediation where woman was concerned; he alone is the one mediator for reconciled humanity (1 Tm 2:5).

III. Habakkuk   The book of Habakkuk is really the liturgical
   1:2-3, 2:2-4   formulary of one of the last great ceremonies
   1st reading   of the old temple before the fall of Jerusalem
   3rd cycle   in 586. Habakkuk was an official prophet in the
temple service. The Chaldeans were threatening the city, and King Joachim was maintaining a tyrranical reign over Judah. The people assembled in the temple ask the

prophet to formulate their complaint to Yahweh (1:2-4). Yahweh responds with an oracle (1:5-10), but it is too general in content for the people. Consequently they request Habakkuk to address a second complaint (1:12-17). There is a second oracle in response (2:1-4).

The liturgy then continues with five prophetic imprecations (2:6-20), followed by a psalm (Ha 3), where the people express their hope for an early intervention by God to liberate them from the tyrant.

a) The first *complaint* (1:2-4) is formulated in the first person. The prophet alone speaks, but he stands for all the community, according to normal usage in such prayers. We have all the usual elements of the genre: an initial invocation, the avoidance of any epithet for Yahweh (v. 2; cf. Ps 11/12:2; 43/44:2; 59/60:3), a lament for the people's misfortunes and a request for deliverance (vv. 3-4; cf. Ps 7:15; 27/28:2; 54/55: 10-11; Jr 20:8, etc.) with the "how long" formula and the "why" of despair (vv. 2-3; cf. Ps 41/42:10; 42/43:2; 12/13:2-3, etc.).

Habakkuk uses established formulae. He is a professional and cultic prophet, without originality or inspiration. His courage is nevertheless considerable. He dares to assemble the people in the temple to complain about the reigning king before God himself (cf. Ha 1:12).

b) The culminating point of the liturgy comes in Yahweh's second oracle (2:1-4). Doubtless the prophet remained all night in vigil (v. 1) awaiting this response. Once God manifests himself, he realizes that before the fulfillment of the oracle there will be some interval. Thus he must write it down so that it will be preserved until accomplishment (vv. 2-3). God's desire to have the oracle graven on a tablet, which was the traditional style in the temples of the time, is a sign of fidelity. He will certainly fulfill it.

The oracle itself is quite brief. The impious one (the king) will fall, and the just one (the people), who was remained *faithful* to God, will be saved (v. 4). It has all the characteristics of the oracle genre: mysterious tone, anonymity of persons, and brevity.

The liturgy, which began with the complaints, is concluded with the certainty of God's proximate intervention. The Chaldeans are now near Jerusalem and will put an end to the king's despotism. If the people are patient and bow for a while longer to the royal tyranny, the injustices, the acts of violence, the unfortunate diplomatic alliances; if they remain firmly faithful to God (cf. Rm 1:17; Ga 3:11; He 10:38), their fidelity will save them from the coming disaster.

IV. Philippians   Paul's final recommendations to his beloved
4:6-9   Philippians are more than exhortations. There
2nd reading   is a missionary urgency underlying them. If
1st cycle   they are followed, Christians will be signs of
Christ in the world.

a) The list of qualities in verse is borrowed from some stoic catalogue of virtues. The terms themselves are rarely found in Scripture, and when they are, the meaning is different. "Truth" for instance here does not mean conformity to revelation, as in John, but uprightness in relations with the other (2 Co 6:8). "Nobility" describes the good reputation of the Christian in his environment (1 Tm 3:8-11; Tt 3:2). "Justice" is not so much that which is approved by God (this would be the biblical sense: Rm 2:13; 3:10) but fairness in human relations (Ph 1:7; Ep 6:1). "Purity" of course designates the virtue of purity, but "lovability" and "honorability" are qualities that Paul is mentioning for the first time. Likewise the word *virtue,* which is found nowhere else in the New Testament, clearly emanates from Greek ethical theory (cf. however, after Paul, 1 P 2:9; 2 P 1:3).

b) Paul's concern then is really the *sign* that Christian behavior can provide. The majority of the virtues he catalogues have to do with relationships between people: justice, lovability, honorability, praise, loyalty, purity.

V. Hebrews
2:9-11
2nd reading
2nd cycle

The author of Hebrews, in 1:5-13, used scriptural arguments to show the superiority of Christ to the angels. It should be noted that, after the exile, Jewish speculations about the angels took on considerable importance. We are told much in the book of Tobias, the book of Daniel, and the first two chapters of Luke, but with regard to gnostic speculations discretion is exercised. The whole climate of speculation allows the author to develop his thesis of Christ's exclusive mediation.

a) In today's passage he adds a new theme to those he has considered earlier: the *lowering* of Christ beneath the angels during his earthly life (v. 9, note in vv. 6-8 the citation of Ps 8:5-7 according to the Septuagint). What is meant is not the obedience to God of Philippians 2:5-10, but submission to the laws of human existence, death included (cf. 1 Co 2:8). It was precisely these laws that the angels were thought to control (Col 2:15; Rm 8:38-39; Ga 4:3-9). Once glorified however, Christ escapes these laws, as do his disciples. Henceforth there is only one law: the life of the Risen Lord which radiates throughout the universe.

b) The author then stresses the *solidarity* of Christ with humanity (vv. 10-11) in this submission to natural laws, as in the liberation from their dominance by the victory over sin. This bond is the one that is forged between a people and the priest that issues from their ranks (He 2:14-18). Such a relationship in the order of salvation would never be possible between angels and men, because angels could never exercise priesthood in the name of men.

Modern man no longer gives any place to angels in his concept of natural laws. He is however convinced that a particular view of these laws can keep humanity in a state of alienation. In this context the hope put forward by the author of Hebrews is not perhaps so irrelevant now. When he makes Christ Lord of the laws that were hitherto controlled by angels, he is implicitly affirming that man is greater than such laws, and has a mission to humanize the cosmos. A universe shaped by technology might in the end of a better reflection of God that one altogether shaped by nature.

VI. 2 Timothy The second letter to Timothy is a composition
1:6-8, 13-14 of Paul's last years, doubtless during the sec-
2nd reading ond captivity at Rome (cf. 2 Tm 1:12-17; 2:9)
3rd cycle which was to end in martyrdom about 67 A.D.

Paul is certainly over sixty, and with age comes the inclination to counsel the young. His tendency toward personal apologia has increased, and turns him to thoughts of the future and the destiny of the communities he has founded.

Apostolic preaching was at this very time encountering a series of obstacles. Persecution, for the first time, is not confined to Jewish opponents, but comes from the Roman authorities themselves. Timothy, who was timid by nature, may have been overly affected by Paul's imprisonment (v. 8). The message of the cross, this infamous death, may have been somehow acceptable among Jewish people, for whom the cross was the sign of foreign domination. But how was it possible to convince people of genuine Roman stock that a crucified person could be Lord? The temptation to discouragement was strong.

To renew his courage and fidelity Paul recalls to Timothy the grace of his *ordination* (vv. 6-8).

This was given by imposition of hands on the part of Paul (v. 6) and the presbyterate (1 Tm 1:14). Generally in the New Testament the rite conveys the charisms of which the recipient had need for the exercise of certain functions in the Church (Ac

6:6; 13:3; 14:23; 1 Tm 5:22). It is accompanied by prayers, "prophecies" (1 Tm 1:18; Ac 13:3) and fasts (lest it seem to be magic), and apostolic intervention is always presumed. The Word expresses God's will, the gesture transmits the grace; and by this grace Paul and his disciple are henceforward united in the same destiny and the same responsibilities.

There is little point in attempting to give a modern theological analysis of Timothy's ordination. It is more than a simple blessing because it has permanent effects. It is distinct from baptism because of the special functions to which it is an initiation, and which will enable Timothy to succeed Paul in the apostolate (1 Tm 1:18).

A gift of God is transmitted, a "charism," a grace that is to say which is for the benefit of the community, not for personal salvation (1 Co 12:7; 14:12). The ordinand receives the strength not to be ashamed of the gospel of the cross (v. 7), a charity that makes him zealous for the proclamation of the Word to all men, the prudence needed by a leader of the community and a doctor of truth, and daily solicitude for the "deposit" of doctrine (v. 14).

When the apostle requires Timothy to be faithful to his state and his function, he shows great psychological insight. He does not ask for fidelity to a past decision, for passive resignation. The fidelity is to be based on present motives, which probably are not those of the original decision but spring from a more adult awareness of responsibilities. If the Spirit has sustained the imperfect motives of the original decision, how much more will be the present ones. They are to be found in the meaning of the service undertaken, and in the lucidity of one's vision of the accomplishment of salvation.

VII. Matthew	The primitive version of the parable of the
21:33-43	vineyard workers appears to have been more
Gospel	sober in tone. Doubtless we can determine the
1st cycle	actual words of Jesus by comparing the synop-
	tic accounts with the apocryphal gospel of

Thomas. The piece was subsequently allegorized to represent the history of Israel and provide a basic christology.

a) In the original we have the owner of a vineyard (v. 33), who, because he is far away, is obliged to deal with the workers by means of his servants or his son.

The circumstances are those of the contemporary economy. The country was divided into huge *latifundia* which belonged for the most part to foreigners. The Galilean and Judaean peasants who rented these lands, displayed, under the influence of zealot propaganda, a lively opposition towards such owners. It is improbable that Jesus had the vine of Isaiah 5 in mind.

Killing the heir was a way of getting possession of the land. Land left vacant in such a way became by law the property of the first occupant. In the parable though the workers make a mistake. The owner will return to take possession of the vineyard and he will entrust it to others (v. 41).

What was Jesus' purpose in recounting the parable? Conceivably he may have wished to distinguish himself from the Zealots. Injustice might indeed reign in the world; but the kingdom of God would not come through violence and hate. But he was addressing himself principally to the leaders of the people, who readily identified themselves with "vineyard workers." He is telling them that they have not been faithful to their task, that the land in consequence will now be given to others, to the poor above all (cf. Mt 5:4). He has often asserted that the Good News, because it is rejected by the leaders and notables, will be given to the little ones and the forsaken (Lk 14:16-24; Mk 12:41-44).

b) The primitive Church very quickly allegorized the parable. To verse 33 was added an allusion to Isaiah 5:1-5, and to verse 42 reference to 2 Chronicles 24:20-22. The idea was to read into it the *history of the vine-Israel,* her constant rejection of the Messiah (the meaning of "Son" in verse 6; cf. Ps 2:7; Mk 1:11; 9:7), and finally the transference to the apostles of the workers' prerogatives (not now to the poor, as in the primitive version).

Matthew's version allegorizes the primitive parable (which probably ended at v. 39) with the purpose of explaining the reasons for *Christ's death* and its consequences. He quotes verses 22-23 of Psalm 117/118 which the crowd had used a few hours earlier (vv. 25-26, quoted in Mt 21:1-10) to acclaim Jesus. This recalls that Christ is glorified by means of suffering and death. Psalm 117/118 was in fact considered messianic by the primitive community (cf. Ac 4:11; Mt 21:9; 23:39; Lk 13:35; Jn 12:13; He 13:16).

The death of Christ then leads to the building of a new Kingdom: the rejected stone has become the cornerstone of the definitive temple. Note how Matthew, with an eschatological purpose, associates the image of the rejected stone particularly with death outside the city (v. 39; cf. He 13:12-13). He wants to show that the new vine workers depend upon a new sacrifice.

VIII. Mark
10:2-16
Gospel
2nd cycle

Mark's version of the discussion between Jesus and the Pharisees concerning divorce is slightly different from Matthew 19:1-9. Conscious as he is of an audience less familiar with the niceties of Jewish Law, and less sensitive to the value of the Word, he is more insistent on the law of nature. He says that "God *made* them man and wife" (v. 6) whereas Matthew refers to a "word" of God to Adam and Eve (Mt 19:5). And where Matthew draws a distinction between the law of Moses and what it merely tolerates (Mt 19:7-8), he refers directly to God's will (v. 9). Finally, by dropping the precision of Mt 19:9, he avoids a serious difficulty in the interpretation of Jesus' thought. As he sees it, man cannot destroy a unity that is engraved in nature.

a) In commenting on Deuteronomy 24:1 the Pharisees had considerably widened the reasons for separation, but they were not in agreement about the list of reasons (cf. Mt 19:3). Mark does not give us the discussion. He simply supposes that the

Pharisees approached Jesus with a question: whether it was permitted to divorce one's wife. The question in itself is surprising on the part of the Pharisees, in view of the fact that Deuteronomy 24:1 allowed the possibility. The truth is that Mark did not have the primitive version on this point.

He supposes that the Pharisees are referring to the law itself (v. 4). Jesus tells them that this precept should be abolished and a solution sought on the basis of God's law of nature (Gn 1:27; 2:24). No one, not even Moses, has the right to interfere with the basic *oneness of the couple* (vv. 11-12).

b) For the proper understanding of the passage it is well to remember that its message is part of the proclamation of the Kingdom, which comes in the guise of a recovered *paradise*. Mark has already shown that the Kingdom is a victory over original sin (Mk 2:1-10), and a victory over disease and death (Mk 5:21-43). Here he is showing that it is a restoration of the original enterprise of a couple united in love. From now on the conjugal state, provided it is lived in fidelity to God's original plan, will become one of the chief manifestations of the Kingdom.

The teaching of the evangelist is clear. Marriage is more than a contract between two people: it involves God's own will, expressed in the complementarity of sexes. It is not limited to the wish of the contracting pair. For that reason divorce is an injustice not only to the abandoned partner, but to God himself. Of course the question still remains whether the consent between the human partners is always sufficiently lucid to set up a valid natural union, and consequently engage God's will.*

IX. Luke   Luke shows most originality in that section of
17:5-10   his gospel which describes the journey to
Gospel   Jerusalem (9:51–19:28). Many items here are
3rd cycle   peculiar to him; others have been clearly reworked. From chapter 14 onwards he is warning his readers against the Pharisees particularly, and against

*See the doctrinal theme: *indissolubility*, p. 142.

riches. He wants to turn their attention to the feeble and the poor.

The parable of the worthless servant (vv. 7-10) was perhaps originally delivered by Jesus in order to castigate the Pharisees, who believed they had rights before God. Luke suggests that it was addressed to the apostles (v. 5) to teach them modesty. The transference however is somewhat awkward, because no apostle seems to fit the description of verse 7 ("who among you . . .").

a) The master-slave image is often used in the gospels to describe the relation between God and his servants, the scribes and Pharisees (Mt 25:14-30). God is represented as a demanding master, little concerned with the wishes or well-being of his slave. But the parable stresses above all the fact that the Pharisees, those believers who measured their merits and rights against God, are in fact servants incapable of rendering proper service. To their assurance and calculation of merits is opposed the pure and simple faith (v. 6) of the poor and the little ones. An attitude of *unconditional confidence* in the Lord is contrasted with the murmuring of those whose concept of religion is confined to merits and a right to reward (cf. Mt 20:13).

b) Transferred to the other context, where the apostles are addressed (v. 5), their *ministry* is represented as *worthless* (v. 10). It would be wrong to regard this as Jesus' intention. God has need of men, and Christ has need of his Church. The lesson concerns the element of Pharisee and authoritarian that is in all of us. When we are given credit for something that could only come from God, we should beware of regarding the function we exercise as a right of life eternal, of glorifying ourselves instead of "glorifying in the Lord" (1 Co 9:16; 1:31; 2 Co 10:17; Ph 3:3; Ga 6:14).

Luke has an obvious purpose in juxtaposing the two passages of this gospel (vv. 5-6 concerning the power of faith and vv. 7-10 concerning worthless service). He is giving us a short treatise on faith and works. For this reason he introduces sayings that do not belong in the context, and are partially inadequate. Faith does not give us power to plant a mulberry tree in the ocean, nor does it on the other hand tell us to regard our efforts as worthless. The general lesson is clear. Man cannot accomplish his project alone; he needs communion with God and his brothers.

B. DOCTRINE

1. Theme of Indissolubility in Marriage

A factual analysis of history shows that moral attitudes among men gradually evolve towards monogamous marriage. This tendency is even more pronounced as peoples approach modern standards of living. There are a number of factors which contribute to this. Men, and above all women, begin to have more control over their persons. Marriage becomes less of a group institution and depends on the partners' individual choice. Economic considerations, and the needs of children in nutrition and education, make anything other than monogamy practically impossible. Polygamy, even in areas where up to recently it was common, has in fact diminished. Most modern states have made monogamy mandatory in their civil codes.

But the more monogamy gains respect, the more indissolubility in the marriage contract seems to be questioned. A greater appreciation of marriage as a free agreement between two individuals does not at all entail assent to the law of indissolubility in groups where it is part of religious, or even civil, legislation. Monogamy has seemed to reinforce individual choice, particularly for the woman concerned with her "recognition" by man; but indissolubility has seemed to restrict that choice. Young peop'e indeed who set up a household continue to do so in terms of a love that is indissoluble. But they see little point in legislating this. Experience shows that marital love often fails. Are we so certain that divorce is always a bad solution. Is there any good reason, in any case, for having a law against it?

What are we to say? As we survey the great stages of salvation history, we can see the real requirements for conjugal love gradually being manifested. We shall then have a better understanding of indissolubility, and be in a better position to further it in the world in which we live.

Conjugal mores in Israel

The most ancient Jewish texts that we have reflect an attitude towards marriage which closely resembles that of neighboring countries. The institution is regulated strictly because on it depends the survival of the community. Social needs take precedence over individual ones, over the personal love that unites person to person. The desire for numerous progeny, which was regarded as a sign of power, favored polygamy, and it was thought normal for the king to have a harem of some kind. Barrenness in a woman was universally regarded as a curse, and reason for repudiation. Lastly, the man was master of the woman and had rights over her that were guaranteed by law. The woman caught in adultery was punished severely, because of the injustice to her husband.

But, under the regime of faith, there was a gradual change. Custom ceased to be the norm, and interiorization brought the real values of conjugal love into focus. We have only to look at the Canticle of Canticles, this marvelous celebration of love between two free agents. A composition of this quality presupposes some development. Conjugal love had to be lived under much constraint, but it was becoming more and more personalized. The woman was coming to be viewed more and more as man's partner, no longer as just the "woman thou hast given me" according to the most ancient account of creation (Gn 2:18. This should be compared with Gn 1:27: "God created man in his image, in the image of God he created him, male and female he created them"). This development explains the gradual disappearance of polygamy; in New Testament times monogamy was the norm for Jewish marriages. It also explains why conjugal fidelity was more and more extolled by prophets and sages. Indissolubility soon became a normal dimension of conjugal love, though it is to be noted that as late as the time of Christ the possibility of divorce is still admitted.

Summing up, what we find in the Old Testament is a long cultural development, influenced by the regime of faith. It would be wrong to regard polygamy, or divorce, as declensions, due to sin, from an original monogamy. It is perfectly in accord with salvation history to suppose some development that culminated in monogamy and indissolubility.

The prophetic witness of Christ for indissolubility

If we are to understand the attitude of Jesus in this matter, we must recall the general environment in which the Good News was preached. The gospel is new because it is a fulfillment. The message of Jesus summons us to pursue fidelity to the utmost human limit, because this is also the ultimate limit in the search for God. It clarifies the conditions under which we must encounter the other. We must love him in his otherness, recognizing him as the always possible enemy. This is the greatest spiritual adventure that is, one without limits. The obstacle that we have to overcome, with the aid of the Liberator, is the sin of pride. Man will always be trying to absolutize his own existence by reducing the other to his own dimensions. That is why Jesus denounces with such vigor all forms of legalism and particularism. He wants to safeguard at all costs a full ambit for the operation of love.

Conjugal love is an especial case in point. A man and a woman only begin to love properly, when they come to recognize their differences, and realize that acceptance of the other means death to oneself. This view of conjugal love makes indissolubility the great means to victory over the divisive elements that militate against real encounter between spouses. Neither has to succumb to annexation by the other. Indissolubility is the sign of love's victory over hate.

We can see then the reasons for Jesus' opposition to Jewish legislation about divorce. We are dealing, it must be remembered, with the law of Moses, which purported to be the expression of the order of faith. What Jesus is denouncing, once more, is legalism. He opposes the law because it is liable to obscure the genuine reality of marriage. Marriage is anterior to law, nor can it ever be properly safeguarded by any law. Jesus is concerned to liberate it from all legal constraints or limitations. When he insists on indissolubility, it is clear that he is not propounding a law, but restoring the reality of marriage.

The ecclesial interpretation of the Lord's "Precept"

In the New Testament itself we find evidence that the primitive Church was obliged to interpret Jesus' teaching on divorce according to practical circumstances. Indissolubility was indeed immediately accepted as the norm in this domain, and there was a very early attempt to provide theological basis by associating the Lord's precept with God's creative act: "that which God has joined let no man put asunder." However, we have two main indications that, in actual practice, indissolubility was something that had to be verified in men's actual experience. Often, because of human weakness, experience failed to correspond with it. The first is in Matthew. It seems clear that, in spite of his ardent defense of indissolubility as against Jewish divorce "for whatever reason," he admits divorce if there be adultery by one of the partners (Mt 19:9). There is in fact no contradiction here, because marital unity has been so destroyed that it no longer exists, in practice. The second is in Saint Paul. He took the view that in marriages between pagans and Christians, if the pagan partner wanted a divorce, the Christian was no longer bound (1 Co 7:15). He was in a new situation, not of his seeking, where liberty and peace were being offered.

We realize that Christian churches, in the past and now, have taken different views of the Lord's statement on divorce. Their reading of the New Testament has been inevitably affected accordingly. The Catholic Church in particular has been distinguished for its intransigence, and hitherto one could not contemplate the sort of exegesis that Catholics now are ready to give the texts we have discussed. Yet, whether they are intransigent or not, Catholics generally view the positions of other churches as a compromise. An ecumenical exchange would enable all of us to penetrate the meaning of the Lord's precept, and understand the dangers of presenting it in legal terms only. Legal intransigence can lead to considerable laxity in practice (a civil marriage for instance, null in the eyes of the Church, may in fact be valid). There are other cases where an insupportable burden is laid on the partners, because they did not realize the real meaning of God's summons to liberty and peace.

Evangelization of the nations and indissolubility

The affirmation by Jesus of indissolubility was not made haphazardly in time or place. It came at a certain moment in Jewish religious history, in a particular cultural context, that was quite sophisticated and deeply influenced by faith. Indissolubility is a very elevated human value which requires a long period of preparation during which man has confronted the mystery of his liberty. Marriage also is an extremely complex social institution, that varies considerably between one culture and another.

The Church is charged with the mission of proclaiming the Good News to all peoples, and must also convey the doctrine of Jesus concerning indissolubility. She must however be constantly mindful of the two great principles of evangelization in everything that concerns the realities of daily living. In the first place the summons by Jesus Christ to salvation must encounter people, individually and collectively, where they find themselves. It is by joining people as they find themselves that the Church can draw them into the adventure of faith, and let them see how Christ brings fulfillment to every spiritual search. Secondly, the proclamation of the Good News does not necessarily include cultural elements that are nonessential, even though centuries of living have conjoined them.

When we consider the history of mission, we realize that these considerations have not in fact been kept in mind. Too often the indissolubility of marriage was imposed as a prerequisite, and consequently as a law. Furthermore the notion propounded of Christian marriage was identified with what the institution had become in the West, influenced by Roman law. Today we realize that all this has done more harm than good, and that a revision of pastoral attitudes is highly desirable.

The Eucharist and indissolubility

There is actually a close connection between what takes place, or ought to take place, during a eucharistic celebration and the attempt of a married couple to achieve indissolubility. The encounter with the other is predominant. A person is challenged towards that realism which accepts otherness. And he becomes aware that in the order of true love the sinner can accomplish nothing without his Liberator. The horizon in the Eucharist is brotherly love between all men. It is a perfectly possible ideal that is already being celebrated in anticipation; the obstacles are swallowed in the believer's hope. In marriage the horizon is the greatest possible union between man and woman. This is to be achieved with full respect for the individuality of each, and in spite of everything that throughout the years makes for division.

At the eucharistic celebration which makes its ideal very evident, husband and wife who are daily struggling to find the true meaning of marriage will be at one. They will also be constantly reminded that the indissoluble union they seek cannot be isolated from responsibility for others, for all humanity. The adventure of love, inaugurated by Jesus, is one whole. It cannot be lived conjugally without being simultaneously extended to other fields. The couple who attempt to confine the horizon of love to their own marriage will quickly discover that this is doomed to inevitable failure. For this reason they will always find the Eucharist a source of valid insight.

2. Theme of Ministry in the Church

It had been customary to divide the people of God into three classes: clerics, religious and laity. For centuries the two former groups have been asked to play an active role in the Church. The third on the other hand (consider the canon law still in vogue) would speak of the Church in the third person, as if it were something distinct from them. All that is changing over recent decades. The laity are becoming aware that their role, far from being passive, is one of contributing, each his unique and irreplaceable stone, to the building of the Kingdom. We have had theologies of clerics and religious. Now we have one of the laity. The output of books and articles in this vein is vast. There is a concerted effort to demonstrate the great significance of the laity in the accomplishment of God's plan for the Church and the world.

It might seem that this was sufficient to redress the balance. However, quite recently, another aspect is being canvassed with some rigor. Theologically speaking, what is the basis for this classification? Are these not merely sociojuridical categories that developed during the history of the Church? It is beyond doubt that there is a specific theological basis, at least where the first two classes are concerned, but have we not perhaps "theologized" over much in this matter? The primitive communities did not have such groupings, and we can very easily see how history explains their development. By developing a theology for each group, do we not run the risk of perpetuating an ecclesial structure that is no more than contingent?

In any case, nowadays, all groups are undergoing crisis. We might resolve this better by returning to our origins, and neglecting for the moment the tripartition. The primitive Church was not concerned with clerics, religious or laity (in the sense we use the term), but with "ministries." If we begin with that, we shall be able to determine whether a solution lies there to our difficulties.

Segregation from the general group in Israel

As with other peoples, in Israel the exercise of an important function led to segregation from the group. In the case of the king or the priest we can easily see why. The case of the prophet is more interesting.

The king, like all kings, was the incarnation of the security towards which the people yearned. His very existence was a guarantee of power and dignity. Royalty for that reason had a sacral aura. Generally the king had a special relationship with Yahweh. He was in a fashion the mediator between Yahweh and his people: his destiny involved the whole community. He is then by definition someone set apart. With regard to the priestly institution, it is clear that from the time it became a specialized function it is reserved to a certain caste, the tribe of Levi and some great priestly families. The conduct of worship, especially in the Jerusalem temple, was something which set apart as well.

The prophet however, at first glance, does not seem to be apart in the same way. Unlike the king and the priest, his function is not hereditary, or reserved to a specialist caste. He is not segregated; he is merely a man of faith who one day receives from Yahweh the unenviable mission of recalling all the people, including the king and the priests, to the exigencies of the covenant. He is a man of the people only distinguished from his fellows by the call of God. Yet, strikingly enough, this prophetic function too became a reason for segregation. Not, in this instance, on the basis of social class, but based on a certain concept of holiness and fidelity to Yahweh. The spiritual elite among the chosen people, those who called themselves the "poor of Yahweh," saw themselves as a community apart. They avoided association with other members of the community, and *a fortiori* with Gentiles. Eventually they sought fulfillment with one another only; some took to the desert to live with God in asceticism and contemplation. They felt at any rate that they could no longer share ordinary life.

Attitudes to segregation in the primitive Christian community

The summons to the Kingdom, proclaimed by Jesus, was a very demanding one. To enter it one had to renounce everything, because everything else was subordinate. "Seek ye first the Kingdom of God, and everything else will be added unto you." Yet the call was addressed to everyone, in whatever condition they found themselves. It was even addressed to sinners by choice. Jesus actually encountered people of all kinds: men and women, Pharisees and publicans, rich and poor, healthy and incurably sick. He deliberately disregarded the numerous intredicts maintained by society or the spiritual elite against certain classes. For him, all were brothers. No one was without sin. The important thing was to repent. Those who regarded themselves as just had already received their reward.

Thus there was no need to leave the ordinary human state, or be segregated, in order to respond to the call of the gospel. Indeed this would have been a falsification of grace. God exercises mercy without acceptance of persons, and segregation would have rendered universal brotherhood impossible. There was then a complete reversal of traditional Jewish attitudes. We have only to compare the ministry of the Baptist with that of Jesus. He is an ascetic, a poor man of Yahweh who lives as a solitary in the desert in fidelity to the best Jewish tradition. Jesus on the other hand lives the life of an ordinary Jew of his time. John does not hesitate to have his public ministry begin with the wedding of Cana. So unusual is all this that the poor of Yahweh find it material for scandal.

Lest there be any distinction, any divisiveness, among his disciples, so that they be brothers to one another and to all men, Jesus recommends each to be the slave of the others. He gave the example: he came not to be served, but to serve. The image he uses is that of serving at table (see the doctrinal theme: *service*, p. 243). It is by service of the other, whoever he be, that we come to realize how in fact all men are brothers, and how encounter in brotherhood is also encounter with God. If we are in search of the Father of all, we need never go apart from others.

Charisms and ministries in a Church of brothers

The dominant note that strikes us as we study the New Testament descriptions of the primitive community is brotherhood. To restore the reality, Vatican II had but to look to our origins. The Church is indeed a community of brothers, all basically equal, all responsible, and all called to make their contribution to the Kingdom.

Such a community of brothers is at once unified and diverse. Each must, under the inspiration of the Spirit, give of his best. It is a charismatic community, and the genuine charism always contributes to unity. The work of the Spirit is love; the best element in every man always works towards love. Consequently all charisms are basically deaconships, that is to say service of others.

Because the community is diverse too, there are diversities of charisms. These answer not alone to the difference between persons, but to the diverse needs of the group. Official charisms, we should give them the name of ministries (in the sense of service), varied as between one community and another. Saint Paul's lists make this clear. And they did not all have the same importance. For Paul service of the Word in particular has first importance: apostles, prophets, doctors.

One particular ministry has a privileged place: the apostolic ministry. Like other ministries, it can only be exercised by gift of the Spirit and it fulfills a need of the community of believers. The need is a very fundamental one. From Pentecost onwards one intense conviction overshadows everything else among the disciples; the people of the New Covenant depend for their existence and their performance on the intervention among them of the Risen Lord. There had to be concrete expression of this. Thus very soon among the group "certain ones" were set apart whose service indicated the Risen Lord's personal intervention. For such service there had to be evidence of choice by Christ himself. So important was this apostolic ministry that the term ministry began to be reserved for it. It was thence forward exercised by bishops, and in a subordinate way by priests.

Grandeur and decadence in a Church of clergy and religious

A decisive turning point was reached with the official "conversion" of the Roman Empire. There was a massive intake of man and woman, who were altogether ignorant of the responsibilities of baptism. Soon, under political pressure, the whole of European society was to become Christian. During this period the Church took on the semblance of a great religious complex. Two dominant groups seemed active: "clergy" and "religious." The first monopolized authority and responsibility; the second directed the quest for Christian perfection. The Church gradually came to be identified with them. The idea grew, a rather extraordinary idea by the standards of primitive Christianity, that in order to answer the call of the gospel, or exercise a role in the Church, one had to leave the ranks of the laity. Yet, throughout these Christian centuries, the segregation of clergy and religious did not at all entail separation from secular affairs. On the contrary this Church of clergy and religious was exceedingly present in the world.

Furthermore, the Church stepped in to fill the void created by the decay in the West of the institutions of the Roman Empire. Clergy and religious felt themselves responsible for a world that was totally Christian and needed secular as well as religious direction. Ecclesial institutions were developed on an unprecedented scale that governed all aspects of life, individual and collective. The ecclesial institution itself became a great, complex organization where positions of power were multiplied. Very understandably, clergy and religious formed the staff of full time personnel that was needed. They were an efficient corps of dedicated men and women who gave their lives to the multifarious tasks of this enormous enterprise. Very understandably also, the charismatic dimension of such service tended to disappear in a context that was altogether institutional and predictable.

Since the Renaissance there has been a gradual change. As the world of modern man and profane civilization began to dawn, and the tutelage of the Church was gradually shuffled off, segregation of clergy and religious in the Church became sociological. They were actually cut off from the secular stream of life. Their predecessors in the Middle Ages had exercised a profound influence on secular life. Now, their very association with the ecclesial institution was proving a barrier between them and the world. People were beginning to savor their liberty and withdrawing further and further from any sort of ecclesiastical tutelage. The divorce between the Church and modern man, whom she had done so much to bring into being, was complete.

Vatican II and the current crisis

Over half a century there have been attempts to bridge the divorce. One of them was the appeal to the laity to be active in Church mission, and other such enterprises have been multiplied in our day. However, as long as the Church continued to preserve her traditional structure, the laity found that her manner of apostolate did not answer the missionary needs of the actual world they lived in. It became clear that the gap could not be bridged until a page of history opened in the 4th century was closed once for all. The great insight of John XXIII was that nothing short of an ecumenical council would provide the necessary impetus. The page of history in any case had been for all practical purposes closed. It was no longer possible to see the Church as a Church of clergy and religious. If it meant anything, it was a community of brothers, where all were called, precisely as they were, to give of their best for the common good. The Council of course did reaffirm the importance of the apostolic ministry, but in terms of service according to the Gospel. Bishop and priest were restored to the ranks of the people of God. The value of religious life was also reaffirmed, but in terms of a general summons to holiness.

As the Council gathered momentum, inevitably, among clergy and religious, a crisis developed. How could dialogue be resumed with the humanity of our time? It was evident very early that the problem could not be resolved on the individual basis only. The institution had been the product of particular historical circumstances. It could well be that our circumstances now called for something other than this Church of three classes, clergy, religious and laity. The real problem was not the reintegration into the modern world of clergy and religious. It had become one of determining the charisms actually present among the people of God (above all, who were the actual bearers of the apostolic charism). How could these be translated into the ministries required by the Church for the fulfillment of her mission?

TWENTY-EIGHTH SUNDAY

A. THE WORD

I. Isaiah   Chapters 24-27 of Isaiah, a postexilic collec-
    25:6-10   tion, had long been regarded as an interpola-
    1st reading   tion. Recent commentaries however, based on
    1st cycle   discoveries like the Qumran manuscript of
                   Isaiah, defend the unity of the passage and
suggest the 5th or 6th century B.C. as a date of redaction. The
most likely hypothesis put forward is that we have here the
formula for three liturgies of the Word. The second would be
composed of a prophetic proclamation (24:21-23) followed by
an acclamation (25:1-5); then a second prophetic proclamation
(25:6-8) closed by the classical prophetic readings "Yahweh has
said" (cf. Is 1:20; 21:17; 22:25; 24:3; 40:5; 58:14) and a thanksgiving (25:9-10). The whole piece is a celebration of Yahweh's
royalty. The first liturgy, a reading with acclamation, celebrates
his victory over his enemies; the second (our reading) the banquet for Yahweh's enthronement (vv. 6-8) and the crowd's acclamations (vv. 9-10).

a) Eastern custom, and biblical usage in particular, made the
banquet part of ritual enthronement. It was a public manifestation of the king's power (Est 1:1-4; 1 K 10:5; 1 S 16:11; Dt 5,
etc.). It is also a banquet of alliance to which only allies and
friends are invited. It sets up obligations for host and guests that
nothing can change (1 K 2:7; 2 S 9:6-8). Such sumptuous banquets were sometimes celebrations of victory over an enemy, and
live captives would form part of the menu.

Here however the prophet is celebrating the *kingship of
Yahweh*. God is not inferior to earthly kings, and the magnifi-
cence of his table eclipses anything contemporary (v. 6). He is

certainly put forward as a king of future times. The banquet that he gives is a victory banquet and the enemy is none other than death (vv. 7-8; cf. Rev 21:4; 1 Co 15:26). In this context of course it is no more than a symbol. But the day will come when the eucharistic banquet, which celebrates the enthronement of Christ, will be a real victory over death, and entry to immortality (Jn 6:51).

b) The banquet of Yahweh's investiture is one of alliance and friendship. The glory of Yahweh and the splendor of his banquet already invest the royal city (theme of the mountain, vv. 6, 7, 10), but king Yahweh wants to contract alliance with all the peoples of the world (vv. 6-7). The author certainly could not have imagined this universal alliance, were it not for the reflections of Third-Isaiah about the role of Sion (Is 56:6-8; 66:18-21). When we remember the conditions of ritual purity imposed on the banqueters, which excluded all Gentiles, we can conjecture the extent to which Isaiah had to violate interdicts in his vision of a messianic abundance that would include all the nations.

Despite the barbaric background, we can trace the features of the Eucharist in this victory banquet. In the Eucharist God shares his friendship; the victory over death is celebrated, and above all the victory of Christ and the Christian over self is commemorated.

II. Wisdom 7:7-11
1st reading
2nd cycle

Remembering that the young King Solomon had asked God for Wisdom (political *savoir-faire*, at that epoch), the author imagines his representations before God, and he takes some liberties with history (1 K 3:6-12; 5:9-14). He will return later to the subject in Wisdom 9:1-18 (cf. further Si 47:12-17).

Unlike his predecessors in Wisdom writing, the author does not confine himself to the horizon of the family. The ideal is not now the father who transmits his experience to his children, but the king who procures the good of his people by having divine *wisdom* influence his life. This is the guarantee of happiness for all. Thanks to the king's wisdom the people can attain blessings they have not even contemplated (v. 11).

The lesson is that knowledge and conquest of the visible world can only be properly attained with the help of divine wisdom. It is this that shows man his place in the universe, and renders him sufficiently open and pliant to further the human project. There can be no proper relation between man and the universe, unless there is a proper relation between him and God.

III. 2 Kings 5:14-17
1st reading
3rd cycle

Naaman the Gentile was cured in the Jordan of a malady which the waters of his own country had failed to cure. Efficacity of waters was, according to the ideas of the time, linked with the divinities who brought them forth.

a) Thus, for Naaman, Yahweh becomes a divinity more potent than others. Ideas of divinity were also territorial; gods exercised sway over carefully defined areas. When one left the territory of a god, one abandoned the god. For this reason Naaman signifies his conversion to Yahweh by bringing sufficient soil from Israel (v. 17) on which to stand and worship.

The background is rather primitive; but the account is highly interesting in that it opens the door to *universalism*. It also indicates that Yahweh can exercise his influence outside the confines of Israel. We have the first results of monotheistic belief among the elite of the people.

b) The *detachment* of the prophet (vv. 15-16) is likewise a result of monotheism. If God is not linked with nature, then neither is he with men's thaumaturgic or prophetic powers. In any case, God's servant cannot claim proprietorship of such powers.

c) The main lesson however is certainly that of *gratuity*. Naaman is a Syrian, from a country that had tense relations with Israel then as now. He is afflicted with leprosy, and the physicians and magicians of his own country are powerless. A poor slave suggests that he entrust himself to a Hebrew prophet. Following such menial advice and dealing with an enemy are extraordinary enough. He was ready to do and pay what was necessary. Eliseus however refuses to accept anything from his client, and merely suggests that he plunge himself a few times in the waters of the Jordan.

The requirements of true religion are not harsh; one must just learn to receive. The hardest lesson is one of unlearning. One must forget about heroic struggles and great sacrifices. God does not want payment; he wants to be accepted.

IV. Philippians 4:12-14, 19-20 *2nd reading 1st cycle* These verses are among Paul's final remarks to his correspondents at Philippi. The community had probably helped him during his imprisonment.

For the help that they have given him, a real sacrifice for them as he sees it (v. 18), he gives thanks to God; but affirms at the same time his *detachment*. He is not grasping (cf. 1 Tm 6:6-10); but he does not refuse the gifts he is offered or practice asceticism. The essential thing is that his heart is not given to abundance, or penury, but rather to the fulfillment of God's plan and the exercise of his apostolic mission.

Penury has perhaps one advantage over abundance. It reveals to us who are our genuine friends.

V. Hebrews 4:12-13 *2nd reading 2nd cycle* The author of Hebrews has just been meditating on God's revelation by means of the prophets and his own Son (He 2:1-4). All this revelation is a promise of salvation and of "rest" (He 3); but it cannot be accomplished without the faith of the hearers. Without faith it becomes a threat and a chastisement (He 4:2). The two verses of today's reading form the conclusion of this meditation.

The Hebrews were wont to measure the *efficacy of God's Word* (cf. Is 55:11). It is first of all manifested in those who proclaim it. The prophet is transformed, sometimes after a violent struggle (Jr 20:7; Ez 3:26-27), into an authentic witness, or sometimes indeed into a living parable of the Word (Is 8:1-17; Ho 1-3; Ps 68/69:12). The Word's power in this sense is more than ever evident in Jesus. He was so dominated by the Word that it became his life, the sign of salvation for all men (He 1:1-2).

What the Word became in the prophets and in Jesus, it can accomplish also in the life of each Christian. It can help him to penetrate his most secret motives and make the decisions he needs. In this sense the Word is judgment, not alone because it judges man's exterior conduct like a legislative precept, but at a deeper level, because it forces him to choose between his own wishes and what the Word requires. The Word is indeed a sword (Lk 2:35), which requires the most radical detachment in the Christian.

This Word is efficacious when it kindles faith and penetrates the conscience of the believer. It is so also when it accompanies the sacramental act. When we share the bread and wine, the Word we hear is the very Word of God. It is sharpened like a sword to elicit from each of us our profession of faith, and the sort of decision that fruitful reception of the sacrament demands.

VI. 2 Timothy 2:8-13
2nd reading
3rd cycle

For Timothy's benefit, Paul has just sketched a tableau of the apostolic life. It is a life of struggle and frequently agonizing toil; he himself has to endure the restraints of captivity (2 Tm 2:1-7). Yet the minister of God should be encouraged by the glorious passion of Christ (vv. 8-10), and the certainty that his own life will be transformed (vv. 11-12, using a primitive Christian hymn).

a) The basic doctrine in Paul's Gospel is *Christ's resurrection*. He had encountered the Risen Lord on the road to Damascus, and made this the foundation of his preaching. He adds a mention of the davidic filiation of Jesus (v. 8), showing that as well as being heavenly he is completely human, sharing the state of apostles.

b) Paul sees a connection between the *suffering* of Christ and that of the apostle. Both are fulfilling the plan of God, who destines men to salvation and glory (v. 10). Suffering cements the union between Christ and men. It enables us to imitate Christ and work for the glorification of the elect.

c) The principal theme of the hymn that Paul uses (vv. 11-13) is the connection between suffering and Christ's glory on the one hand, and the glory of men on the other. This is the fruit of *baptism*, the mystery of life and death with Christ (v. 11b). Following baptism, there are three stages in Christian life: death already experienced (aorist verb), actual suffering (verbs in present tense: v. 12), the coming kingdom (verbs in future). But this development depends on Christian loyalty to baptismal faith (vv. 12b-13). Christ remains loyal because he cannot deny his word.

VII. Matthew 22:1-14
Gospel
1st cycle

There is an obvious difference between this text of Matthew and the parallel account in Luke (14:16-24). The principal addition is the reference to the wedding garment (vv. 11-14). Matthew makes the banquet a wedding banquet (v. 2) which is shared by "bad and good" (v. 10).

If we compare the two accounts we can reconstruct the words of Jesus, as he described the eschatological era in terms of a messianic banquet (cf. Pr 9:1-5).

Luke relates the message of Christ to the problems of early Christian assemblies, how open they were to the poor and to sinners. Still under the influence of judaism, throughout his Gospel

find" (Mt 22:9-10), a totality including the good and the bad, the chaff with the wheat, the bad fish with the good (Mt 13: 24-30, 36-43, 47-50). We have the same outlook in chapter 24, where Matthew describes the gathering of all humanity after the fall of Jerusalem (Mt 24:30-31).

The parable might have ended here. It would have clearly demonstrated the salvation plan. Christ comes to bring Israel a message that is not heard. But God cannot be foiled in his plan. If it be necessary, his envoys will go again to present his message.

e) At the time of redaction of this account, Christians were despised and persecuted by the Jews. It was necessary to help them persevere in the faith, by showing how their present misfortune was merely tolerated by God as a prelude to the proximate punishment of the persecuting Jews. For that reason Matthew adds to the parable the episode of the *wedding garment*. It is just possible that the juxtaposition is suggested by Zephaniah 1. His seventh verse could have inspired the first parable, and verses 8-9 the second. The verb "enter" (v. 11) actually has an eschatological flavor (Mt 25:10, 21, 23; 7:13) and the place of darkness and gnashing of teeth traditionally indicates hell (Mt 8:12; 13:42, 50; 24:51; 25:30).

Placed side by side the two parables describe the position as God's plan unfolds of the time of the Church. A first stage has been completed with the rejection of the Jews and the call to the Gentiles. Now however a long period must elapse during which the behavior of each is to be confirmed. Mere exterior membership of the Church will not be sufficient, unless it includes the sort of moral preparation that the wedding garment indicates.

The theme of the garment is highly symbolic in salvation history. Clothing humanizes the body, takes away anonymity and enables a man to take his place among his peers. Very naturally it becomes a sign of the covenant between Yahweh and Israel. God extends the fold of his mantle over his spouse like a bridegroom (Ez 16). She becomes unfaithful and exhibits herself to every passerby. Her garment gets worn or is withdrawn by God, and he relegates her to anonymity and nakedness.

On the cross Jesus is deprived of his garment in order to join the ranks of sinful humanity in face of death, that destroyer of all false appearances and securities. But, at the resurrection, he is quickly clad in divine glory.

"Putting on Christ" or "putting on the new man" (Ga 3:27-28; Ep 4:24; Col 3:10-11) means sharing the salvation brought about by Christ's stripping and resurrection. The fullness of sharing is reserved for the consummation, where all humanity will put on incorruptibility, and be arrayed for the eternal Spouse (Rev 21:2).

But the wedding garment must be put on before sharing the eucharistic banquet. Such sharing has moral demands that must be honored by the guest.

VIII. Mark   The previous history of this passage saw many
   10:17-30   changes, but it is easy to reconstruct. Only at
   Gospel   the final redaction were the two sections that
   2nd cycle   form it brought together. The primitive first
                   section was an account of vocation (vv. 17-22),
which made no mention, or a very slight one, of the candidate's wealth (v. 22).

The second section was limited to verses 24b, 25 (with no mention of "a rich man") 26 and 27. It was concerned with entry to the Kingdom without any reference to wealth. Jesus and his disciples, observing the incredulity of the crowds, were asking themselves how many of the chosen people would be saved. Jesus leaves everything to God "to whom nothing is impossible," a reference to Genesis 18:14 and the promise made to Abraham. This is an implied affirmation that God is well able to raise up a new people (Mt 3:9; cf. Rm 11:11-32).

At this stage, Jesus and the disciples, experiencing the first formal rebuffs from the Jews, were disturbed about the outcome of the messianic mission (cf. Mt 22:14). Subsequent handling of the tradition, that is already evident in Mark, transformed these accounts into lessons concerning poverty, thus reflecting the pre-occupations of the primitive community. Verses 23 and 24, which are merely doublets of 24b and 26, were added. Jesus is made to repeat exactly what he has said in verse 24b, with a reference now to riches. The disturbance of the disciples in verse 26, when they worry that few people will be saved, is hard to reconcile with their disturbance at verse 24, because the rich will have difficulty in entering the Kingdom. They themselves were in fact poor (cf. v. 28), and Jesus' normal audience was composed of simple folk. Why then this "consternation"?

It was because of their desire to intimidate those who were overly attached to material goods (cf. Ac 4:36–5:14) that the primitive community took the accounts in this sense. Material poverty was made almost an essential requirement for sharing the Kingdom (Lk 6:20-24). Unlike Matthew and Luke, Mark has not obliterated the traces of this rehandling, and consequently provides an opportunity of reconstructing the prior development.

We have two themes interwoven in the passage: the primitive theme which is concentrated on Jewish incredulity, and the second one, added, which stresses the difficulty of entering the Kingdom with riches.

a) Jesus concluded his mission as itinerant rabbi without attaining the hoped-for success. The chosen people rebuffed their Messiah and his death began to be a probability. It was clear that those entering the Kingdom would not be numerous (v. 24).

His reaction to this challenge in Matthew and Luke is sharp. He curses this hard-hearted people and predicts for them the fate of Sodom (Mt 11:20-24). But with Mark it is otherwise; he is more concerned with Jesus' own psychological evolution. He and his disciples did not encounter the failure of their mission without profound emotion; they were "more than ever astonished"

(v. 26; cf. further the allusion, particular to Mark, in v. 21, to the unavailing love of Jesus). Verse 27 goes on to describe Jesus' *abandonment* to God's will. It is only he who saves, he who brought people from the sterile loins of Abraham. In the same way he will be able to make his kingdom emanate from a mission that has been apparently a failure. God's servant bears witness to his plan; but he is not necessarily the executor of the plan. To God himself are reserved the ultimate means of execution; he is the only one who knows (cf. Mk 13:32).

b) Jesus however cannot refrain from making precise the reasons for the people's *incredulity,* and here the episode of the young man is particularly revealing.

The young man straightway raises the only important question, what one must do to be saved (v. 17). He does so in the wrong fashion, addressing Jesus as "good master," one rabbi among many (v. 17). He is simply looking for the opinion of a school as among other schools. He is reserving to himself the right to choose one, or not to choose at all. Jesus at once rejects this attitude by reminding him that there is but one good God (v. 28). He implies that his answer is not going to be that of a school, but a divine command that demands action rather than endless discussion.

He recalls to the young man the essential core of the law (v. 19); but the young man raises a new question, not with a view towards proper obedience, but in order to prolong the discussion, and delay the moment of decision (same attitude in Lk 10:29). His good pharisaic conscience manifests itself; he obeys, he thinks, all of the law (v. 20). What more need he do to be saved?

This sort of legalism is quashed by Jesus. It is merely another pretext for not believing, and he formulates a precise precept: "follow me" (v. 21). At this stage the young man makes it clear that his earlier questions were no more than a screen. Faced with the challenge of faith he admits that he cannot face it. When invited to throw aside ethical and legalist questions, to encounter and follow Jesus, he withdraws. In the end, believing and being saved means attaching oneself to Jesus' person.

c) The rehandling by the primitive community added a new obstacle to salvation. It is not only pharisaic ethical and legalist discussions that preclude one from the Kingdom, but *wealth* as well (vv. 22, 23, and the word rich in v. 25). The Jerusalem community in particular sometimes tended to identify the Kingdom with the sociologically poor, though the assembly brought about in Christ actually takes no account of social, cultural or national allegiance. Saint Matthew modifies this detail by speaking of the "poor in spirit" (Mt 5:3) and suppressing the malediction on the rich that Luke 6:24 retains.

If we maintain that the rich have to become materially poor to share the Kingdom, this is just another sort of legalism; and it is equally ridiculous to regard poverty as blessed, because the poor one day will share a kingdom of prosperity.

A rich man acquires poverty not by "having nothing," but by involving himself with the poor, especially those who have no means of organizing, defending or liberating themselves. Such an engagement is especially required from those Christians who freely renounce material goods and take a vow of poverty.

The way of poverty in our day requires that we be ready to analyze the causes of misery, take the class struggle seriously, and take the necessary means to ameliorate the lot of each person. Poverty then will have some claims to be described as evangelic.

IX. Luke 17:11-19
Gospel
3rd cycle

This account of the cure of the ten lepers is set against the background of the leper legislation in Leviticus 13:45-46 and 14:2-7. When Jesus tells the lepers to show themselves to the priest, he is obeying the requirements of law. Nine of them do go to the priests. The tenth, a Samaritan, is not liable for inspection by priests in Judaea. Consequently he is free to return and express all his gratitude to Jesus.*

a) This passage also belongs to the dossier of early Christian polemic against Jews. The law impedes liberty of expression. The non-Jew is in fact closer to true religion because he is free of the law, and thus closer to the only true liberation, that of the cross (Ga 2:19-20; 5:11-16; 2 Co 3:15-18) and gratuitous grace (Rm 5:12-17; 6:14-15). The spontaneous expression of thanks on the part of the delivered man corresponds to the gratuity of grace. Such an exchange would be impossible in the framework of a law where everything is on a "give-and-take" basis. In the order of *faith* it becomes possible "Go, your faith has delivered you."

b) Leprosy, in the Bible, is often a symbol of sin. Thus Christ's miracle has more signification than that of a simple cure. It suggests the *salvation* that liberates a man from sin.

We still meet Christians who resemble the nine Jewish lepers. They practive assiduously, but are incapable of contemplation. They take communion frequently, but cannot give thanks. Their ethic is narrow, turned inward; scrupulosity and detail bedevil their moral performance. Their God is a bookkeeper. They become incapable of openness to the Other, to gratuity.

The Jewish priests were wont to shut up the healed lepers in the temple, because they alone had the right to declare the disease healed. Our clergy likewise have tended to train the laity in the narrow limits of a legalism that is altogether foreign to true thanksgiving and genuine personal communion with God. These are the people who today find in themselves a growing distaste for the sacraments.

*See the doctrinal theme: *universalism of the faith,* p. 176.

B. DOCTRINE

1. Theme of Convocation and Reassembly

One of the major achievements of Vatican II was certainly the Dogmatic Constitution on the Church. The Christian becomes an active member of Christ's Body, the Church, by means of baptism. He is summoned to play a unique and irreplaceable role in the salvation of humanity, and this he can only do properly in the Church. What does all this mean?

When we Christians come together for the Eucharist, do we realize what the assembly means? Church membership is not a boon conferred once for all by baptism. Our initiation should be something constant, something progressive, something that engrafts us ever deeper into ecclesial relationships and bond, above all in the eucharistic assembly. Yet very many Christians take the composition of the assembly as a mere detail of administration. For them the essential thing in the celebration is the re-enactment of the sacrifice of the cross to be shared by each member. They participate, without seeing any great significance in the assembly itself. And because the official eucharistic assembly does not mean very much to them, in daily life, the ecclesial coexistence that ought to be the leaven in the bread fails to manifest itself properly.

Hence the real need for a theology of assembly that will deepen the ecclesial awareness of each Christian. That should extend to the official ecclesial assemblies where the faithful are progressively initiated into the mystery of Christ. It should also extend to the whole arena of nonecclesial life where the faithful are dispersed among other men.

Formerly, during what we call the Christian centuries, the Church administered a great deal more than eucharistic assemblies. She controlled a great many areas in people's lives, and consequently no very special ecclesial awareness was needed. Today however, in a profane culture, ecclesial influence tends to recede more and more. Christians for that reason have to be especially careful not to be isolated, not to have their witness to Christ altogether obscured.

Israel, a people gathered at Yahweh's summons

The primitive social structure of the Jews was built around concentric groups: the family, the clan, the tribe. The further they developed from the family, the less important was the role of blood in community. On a national scale unity did not depend on political organization, but on acknowledgment of the same God. It was in the name of Yahweh that the federation of tribes was formed.

This unity was seen in terms of assembly, an assembly that was constantly being convoked by Yahweh. Consequently the focus of unity was the actual, cultic assembly. From the desert sojourn onwards we see Moses, the bearer of God's message, convoking such assemblies. The convenant which conveyed the Law was ratified on such a cultic, even sacrificial occasion, in the presence of the assembled people.

Thus at all turning points in Israel's history, when circumstances made this possible, such assemblies would be repeated. The idea formed about them, and the shape they took, indicate progressive deepening of the faith. Little by little a theology of assembly was elaborated. Yahweh, and only Yahweh can convoke the assembly, because only he has the initiative of salvation. The assembly is always essentially ecumenical, because salvation lies in unity, and thus all the people, even when divided or dispersed, are represented. Finally it is always regarded as a service of the Word, because only the proclamation of the Word can convert the people and restore them to fidelity.

When the prophets foresee the messianic future they naturally turn to the theme of assembly, and they give special characteristics to denote the final times. This final assembly will gather, under Yahweh's initiative, all the tribes of Israel who have been dislocated by schism or exile. It will also concern all the nations. This wider ecumenism will have greater or less intensity according to particular epochs and particular authors. For some, the nations will be present to be judged. For others, their intervention will be a means of restoring Israel's unity. For others still, they will be actual sharers in the assembly and exercise a role, because Yahweh's salvation extends to all nations.

It is evident then that the Old Testament theology of assembly has the first rudiments of New Testament ecclesiology. But Jesus of Nazareth was to modify it radically.

The Risen Lord, assembler of all humanity

The divine plan of reassembly was accomplished in Jesus. To begin with, he thought that the chosen people, being first assembled themselves, would become the privileged instrument of universal reassembly. Israel's refusal however deprived her of her privilege: the great reassembly would take place around the Crucified One whom God had raised up from the dead. Numerous New Testament parables present the accomplishment of Jesus in terms of "convocation" and "reassembly" (those of the banquet, the net, etc.).

Certain things should be noted about this messianic reassembly of Jesus. In the first place the Messiah himself makes an active contribution in its construction. God's plan cannot succeed unless man cooperates. It does not come down like lightning from heaven; it confronts man with a task, a program, the fulfillment of which is part of salvation history. Jesus places the cornerstone of the edifice, and under this Head everything must be recapitulated. All men are called to cooperate.

Secondly, neither at the accomplishment of the reassembly nor during its accomplishment, is there any allowance for Jewish privilege. Absolute universalism has come into being. All men are precisely on the same level where the assembly is concerned.

They are all creatures and poor sinners. But they are all, of whatever kind, invited to join the Family of the Father. And they can all in Jesus Christ actively cooperate in the work of reassembly.

Finally, love itself is the ultimate basis. God summons all men to salvation because he loves them, because he loved them first. The Father's love was expressed in the sending of the Son, who, in his very humanity, becomes God's partner in the realization of the plan. Incarnate in Christ, this love becomes universal brotherly love, love that makes the total gift of self in obedience to the Father unto death on the cross. In the resurrection accordingly Christ fully enters into his role as reassembler of all humanity.

The Church, the sacrament of universal reassembly

On Pentecost Day the tiny apostolic community realized that it itself was the assembly of the final times, foretold by the prophets. It was the result of divine initiative, an assembly gathered around the Risen Lord, and the miracle of tongues indicated that it fulfilled the requirement of universal convocation. As mission to the Gentiles gathered momentum, their assembly took root in different locations. The scope of the universal summons to salvation in Jesus Christ became wider and wider.

The mystery of the Church can be expressed in terms of convocation and assembly, and her real quality, wherever she is implanted, can be measured thus. The universal Church is not the sum of local Churches; she is the communion of these Churches, because all of them have the mission to convey her mystery and her universalism.

Wherever the universal summons is heard, God's initiative is its ultimate source, but it is the act also of Christ, and the Church which is his Body. This active function of the Church entails the individual contribution of each member. The priest of course, because he is the minister of Christ as Head, acts to convoke in a particular way, but every member has his part in the summons.

The summons is essentially universal. No one, of whatever provenance, is excluded on the basis of sex, social situation, cultural allegiance or moral performance. It is the Church's mission to encounter all men, precisely where they are, in the state that they are. This requires wide-ranging adaptability. Precaution must always be taken, as historical circumstances change, to make the universality of principle a universality of fact.

Finally, the universal summons should produce a universal assembly. The way to which the Church introduces all her members is that of love without limits, of which the exemplar is Christ's pilgrimage of obedience even to death on the cross. This love will radiate from the assembly principally because of the presence there of Jesus Christ, but each of us has the responsibility to see that it is manifested before men.

Mission as the instrument of universal convocation

During the years immediately following Pentecost the apostolic witness to Christ's resurrection took final shape in the mission to the Gentiles. It was the accomplishment of Saint Paul's career, and has deep meaning in the understanding of Christianity. The divine act of universal convocation will only become real for men by means of specific action on the part of the Church. This specific action, which is mission, is so very essential that a nonmissionary Church would not be the Church of Jesus Christ.

In our modern world mission has so changed aspect that we almost need a redefinition of the terms "convocation" and "assembly." Mission is actually carried on where Christians and non-Christians find themselves side by side in daily life, where Christians have an opportunity to convey to the others the hope that animates them. Obviously this today is an environment cut off from the direct influence of religion. It is the environment where modern man has become more and more aware of the need to depend on his own resources for what he wants to do. He must take his destiny in hand and construct the terrestrial city. He does not want interference from the institutional Church; and in such an environment the Church does not in fact act to assemble.

Later on (first doctrinal theme, 29th Sunday) we shall be pointing out how mission as addressed to modern man must be concerned with the issue that might be described as the center of gravity: human progress. The question we have to consider in this context is: what real meaning in the circumstances can terms like ecclesial "convocation" and "assembly" have? If we take them in the traditional mold of "word explicitly proclaimed" and "community actually assembled," have they not ceased to exist?

We, for our part, take the view that the terms ought to be retained, but that we have to borrow for deeper meaning. Indeed the correct direction of mission may well depend on this. It is true that mission in our day must be carried on in an environment where the Church cannot assemble. It is also true that Christians in this environment are "dispersed people." Yet we maintain that they are not "isolated." They remain living members of a Church that has now become the leaven in the mass. If witness to the resurrection of Christ is to be borne in this secular environment, we Christians need our ecclesial "supports." These are none other than our fellow Christians, priests and laity, who are involved, like us, in the secular stream. It will be our business to be aware of one another, to be supported by one another, and to share experiences.

So that in fact the terms "convocation" and "assembly" do retain their essential meaning. The Church is always the "convoker," because the individual Christian only bears witness in communion with her, "assembled" by her. The non-Christian will perceive that the summons to salvation, which reaches him through the Christian life of a fellowman, comes ultimately from a far deeper source.

Importance for the institution of the eucharistic assembly

All activity on the part of the ecclesial institution is directed towards the proclamation of the Church as the mystery of convocation and assembly. Its terrain then is essentially that of "rite" (in the widest sense of the term). The area of man's relation with God. In this domain there will be an explicit summons to salvation and an explicit response by assembly. Today, for the very reason that mission has to be exercised in an environment where the Church does not actually assemble people, the importance of the assemblies she actually does gather is heightened. A Church that we have described as the leaven in the mass will be effective only if the institution plays its role properly.

The organism that the institution administers is based, it must be remembered, on religious, not administrative criteria. All members are to be initiated to the mystery of Christ by means of a constant network of assemblies that make their meaning clear. Central among these is the eucharistic assembly, whether at the bishop's convocation, or in the centers of evangelization we call "parishes" (the majority of these do not answer to the primitive definition of the term). Here it is essential that the convocation to salvation be fully an expression of catholicity. The word proclaimed must emphasize that the assembled faithful are being confirmed in universal brotherly love. And the actual organization of the assembly must make it possible for all, whatever their differences, to feel at home there. Any eucharistic assembly should try to be an instrument in the universal call to salvation.

The whole of ecclesial life, according to the needs of mission at any particular time, should radiate from this essential assembly. The convocation should reach various key points in the social organism itself. For instance there ought to be provision for the welcome and weaning to the faith of non-Christians, a dimension we very much need to restore today. Among Christians themselves there are various key points too. The sociological circumstances and apostolic needs of different groups ought to be remembered.

In general the Word should be made to reach men precisely where they find themselves, so that their initiation into Christ's mystery can be furthered by more and more "catholic" assemblies.

We very much need an "aggiornamento" in these terms, according to the norms of Vatican II, if the ecclesial Institution is to have full vigor again. The administrative emphasis that is still too evident ought to be softened in favor of emphasis on manifesting catholicity. Christians who are "dispersed" in the secular world must be constantly made more conscious of catholicity, if they are to be living examples of it in their daily avocations.

2. Universalism of the Faith

This meditation (see Gospel, 3rd cycle) will be concerned with universalism as an essential trait of faith in Jesus Christ. We shall be considering how this characteristic is translated into a missionary project directed towards all humanity. We shall then be in a better position to understand why the project is so overwhelmingly complicated and long.

Universal ideologies are always common of course, and Christians frequently, under their influence, have tailored Christian universalism into some sort of ideal about world brotherhood. Non-Christians like Gandhi have made it clear that Christianity lends itself to this interpretation. Yet that view falls short of the essential thing: the mystery of Jesus Christ, the man-God. The real secret is left out: the sharing with men of divine life.

The particularism of Jewish faith

The spiritual insight of the Jews was that they acknowledge God as the Totally-Other, the universal Creator, the absolute Master of human destiny. All nations were included in Yahweh's plan, and none of them could escape his intervention. It was an insight that was developed only gradually. One can say that after the Babylonian exile it becomes common. From now on universalism is part of Jewish faith.

This however is, so to speak, as seen with God's eyes. From man's point of view, acknowledgment of the saving God requires fidelity on the part of Israel. The covenant calls for a response that mere membership of the chosen people cannot provide. What could that be? Led by the prophets, here began a great process of interiorization that was destined gradually to clarify the moral demands of the covenant. Few indeed met the demands. The small Remnant came into being, the Poor of Yahweh, those who would reap the reward of the promises because they depended on God for everything and observed the law with love. True, Yahweh's plan was universal, but only the small Remnant would be saved. Other men would undergo the judgment.

Naturally then, practice of faith in Israel did not issue in mission. This is the great evidence of particularism. After the exile indeed, the Jews of the Diaspora did make a great effort to be open to the world around them, and win adherents. But this was never more than proselytism, swelling the ranks of the chosen people. There was no question of leading Gentiles to the living God by means that did not entail membership of this people.

Christ and universalism in faith

When Christ intervenes in human history the deep relation between faith and universalism becomes clear. His response of faith to God's loving initiative is that of one whom the hypostatic union rendered ontologically a "son." His response was efficacious because he was the only Son, not because he was a creature. It was based not on any moral achievement, however remarkable, but on the actuality of Sonship. His moral performance of course corresponded to his perfect "yes," but it was not the source of the "yes."

Salvation in Jesus Christ allows no privilege of race, culture, intelligence, or moral performance. All men are called to share his "yes" to the Father, no matter what their state or situation, by virtue of adoptive sonship. No one is excluded, which is to say that love is all-embracing.

His life was a constant testimony to this universalism. He was obviously one of the Poor of Yahweh; but he did not hesitate to oppose particularism of any kind. He consorted with publicans and sinners, and rejected all tabus about social categories. When he encountered Gentiles, he was always ready to commend the faith they manifested.

The universal Church of believers

Any meditation about universalism in faith must take account of the catholicity of the Church. Catholicity is not satisfied by an affirmation that the Church is open to all peoples, that she can adapt herself to all cultures without being bound to any. We must go further and assert that all men have a right to feel at home in the Church. And we must determine concrete means of bringing this about.

As we have just seen, acknowledgment of the Savior of mankind does not of itself entail any cultural uprooting. It requires conversion, which in fact means the rejection of any particularist bias in the religious tradition to which one happens to belong. When the mystery of Christ is implanted it brings accomplishment, not destruction. Every kind of human group is summoned to fulfillment in the Church; nor is there any conceivable religious tradition that cannot lead there, once the necessary purgings have taken place of unacceptable elements.

The more profound the sense of universalism among the people of God, the more likely they will be to welcome all religious searches that lead to God. When our faith is universalist it means that we are being as faithful as possible to the commandment of brotherly love without limits. Love of this quality means more than acceptance of difference in the other: it actually means promotion of the other in the mystery of his otherness, and a renunciation of any attempt to annex. True Christian love and universalism go hand in hand. Catholicity comes to be seen as the communion of those who are different. An exchange of life and energy between a multiplicity of religious traditions leads to convergence finally in the unique mystery of Jesus Christ.

Universalism of faith and the missionary task

Invariably we have great lessons to learn from the experience of the primitive community. From the moment when events compelled them to relinquish Jewish particularism, mission became an essential duty. Antioch was the decisive turning point. Prior to that most Christians were converted Jews, and there were misgivings, if prospective Gentile converts failed first to submit to the mosaic law. But at Antioch, the third city of the Empire, Gentile converts came in sufficient numbers to pose a problem to the local community. The Church was encountering a world that differed from the Jewish one, and the meaning of universalism began to be evident. Barnabas and Paul maintained that it was not necessary to become a Jew in order to be a Christian, and they obtained the support of the apostolic Church of Jerusalem. This led to an event in the Antioch Church that was destined to have incalculable consequences. They despatched their leaders on a mission. Thenceforward missionary activity became the mark of authentic faith, a faith shorn of all particularism. The true way of expressing it was the promotion among others of the new commandment of love.

Mutatis mutandis, the Church of our day finds herself in a similar situation. She is always encountering men and women who belong to a different cultural universe. The young Churches of Asia and Africa are a case in point. Furthermore, just now, all cultures are undergoing the profound mutation brought by science and technology. A new world is taking shape, and the Christians who are being shaped by it seem to be a new breed in our Churches. It is high time that the modern Church emulate the Church of Antioch, relinquish all particularism and let her universalism be evident. The change will not indeed be easy because the Greco-Roman heritage has become a sort of second nature for us.

However, Vatican II has pointed the way. The Council very deliberately accepted the principle of large diversity among the people of God. But, if all the diverse elements are to coexist in one Church, if each member is to bring his irreplaceable stone to the building, there must be constant communication between them. The Council spoke of dialogue, a dialogue based on completely lucid charity. It will have to take place in the concrete framework of daily life, accepting all the challenges this imposes. It will have to be something more than exchange between churches: the mission of the Church is to promote peace among all men. Unity in diversity can become our great ecclesial sign, letting the world know that Jesus has in fact destroyed the walls of separation between peoples. If we understand the missionary task to be something of this kind, it can be the expression in a new way of universalism in the faith. It can promote dialogue among all men, dialogue based on the charity of Christ. Once our missionary enterprise is linked in this way with the total human adventure, we begin to appreciate its scope and its urgency.

The Eucharist as inspiration of universalism

In the eucharist celebration believers are put into the most intimate contact with the mystery of Christ. Consequently they learn to believe in the most universal dimension conceivable. It is only the adoptive son of the Father who can follow the First-Born into those limitless horizons.

But we must never take such possibilities as automatic, or for granted. The actual structure of the celebration, and the intensity of our participation, have great importance. It should always be very evident that the Kingdom to which we are being initiated is one of universal brotherhood, made possible through Jesus Christ. We should always be learning the lesson that what remains to be accomplished is an ideal infinitely greater than what has been already done.

As we emerge, the uppermost thought in our minds should be this: how far the actuality lags behind the universal brotherhood Jesus envisaged. It is a tension that must be experienced with courage and lucidity, and it will spur us to further effort to make the ideal real. In this way we can make our daily lives the theater of the Good News of salvation.

TWENTY-NINTH SUNDAY

A. THE WORD

I. Isaiah
45:1, 4-6
1st reading
1st cycle

The Persian king, Cyrus, is engaged in overthrowing the Babylonian empire. In 539 his armies will enter the capital. To win their favor, he will set free captives of a great many nations, among them the Hebrews, who have been enslaved by Babylon. The prophet is foretelling this liberation. It will restore to the people their land and their temple. He does not hesitate to attribute to Cyrus a vocation similar to that of the Israelite kings and prophets.

In this passage Cyrus is even regarded as "the Anointed" of Yahweh, a title originally given to the King (1 S 9:26), later a messianic title ("Anointed" = "Messiah"). The attribution to a foreign king may seem surprising; but it is explained by the clear affirmation of *monotheism* (vv. 5-6). Yahweh is unique and therefore master of all men and all events. He can direct them as he will, to manifest himself to the world. Why then should not a foreigner be the instrument of God's plan?

Our faith in God tells us that he is present everywhere in the world, and acts as he considers fit. To accomplish his plan for humanity he can raise up instruments, outside the Church, who "without knowing it" (vv. 4-5) carry out his purpose. Today we can see this in the multitudinous challenges which undermine the illusory securities of believers, and summon them to purify their faith.

II. Isaiah   These two verses of the fourth Servant poem
   53:10-11   emphasize the expiatory value of suffering,
   1st reading   when accepted unto death in obedience to
   2nd cycle   God. The whole poem is commented upon at
          Good Friday, Lent/Easter volume, p. 293.

The Jews, like other peoples, had expiatory rites. They realized
that salvation was linked to the redemptive initiative of Yahweh,
of which the first manifestation was the liberation from Egypt.
From the desert experience onwards however God's initiative
met with the people's infidelity, and we have Moses and Aaron
constantly interceding for the people's faults (Ex 32:30; Nb
17:11-13). Their prayer arrests the anger of Yahweh.

Jeremiah's experience (Jr 11:19) is a good indication of the
manner in which the people's faults are *expiated* by the sufferings
of the persecuted just man. While the old expiatory liturgies
were going on, in some prophetic circles Jewish religious thought
was reaching remarkable degrees of insight. The great weight of
death brought about by infidelity was a more and more overwhelming burden, but some were beginning to see that intercession, in expiation of the people's sins, would entail the suffering
and death of the intercessor. Today's reading indicates this unmistakably.

Expiation of this order opens the way to God's salvation (v.
10). The suffering Servant will himself be crowned (v. 11) and
see posterity (v. 10).

III. Exodus   The Amalekites, with whom Moses does bat-
   17:8-13   tle here, are a very ancient tribe whom David
   1st reading   subsequently will have to confront. They were
   3rd cycle   enemies of the Israelites, of Judah above all,
          for several centuries (Nb 13-14; Ps 83/84:8).

The episode of today's reading emphasizes the importance of

Moses' *mediation* in the war, and provides, with slightly magical nuances, a lesson about perseverance in prayer.

IV. 1 Thessa-	It seems certain that this letter was composed
lonians	at Corinth in 51. Timothy had been sent by
1:1-5	Paul to Thessalonia, and had now returned
2nd reading	with a rather favorable report about the faith,
1st cycle	hope and charity of the community (v. 3).

The address of the letter and the opening sentiments reflect Timothy's good news.

a) In stressing the remarkable progress in the faith of the Thessalonians (v. 3) and the marvellous nature of their evangelization (v. 5) Paul gives the credit not to human eloquence, but to the *power of God*. He frequently contrasts human language with this power of God (1 Co 2:4; 4:19-20). It is only the word of the apostles that can borrow strength from the Spirit who raised up Christ (Rm 8:11; 1 Co 6:14). This takes up where the miraculous word of Jesus left off.

b) It is because it has Christ as object that this apostolic word is charged with the power of the Spirit. The kerygma is accompanied by miracles like those of Christ (v. 5), while the catechesis and paraenesis (v. 3) kindle faith, hope and charity, of which Jesus is the only source.

Faith in this letter indicates above all a man's basic attitude to the revelation of salvation. This distinguishes him from unbelievers. It means fidelity (1 Th 3:2-6; 5:24; 1:8) and adhesion to truths like Christ's resurrection (1 Th 4:14), the resurrection of all men (1 Th 4:13-18) and the unity of a history which God directs toward fulfillment (the subject of the whole letter).

c) *Love* is placed in our hearts by God himself (2 Th 3:5); and if Paul does not actually speak at length of it in this letter, it is because his audience does not need this (1 Th 4:9). He does insist that they should not confine their interest to their own community. They should extend it to the world (1 Th 3:12; 1:15).

d) Three stages of *hope* are distinguished. It is the expectation of a marvelous future (2 Th 3:16); confidence in God throughout the earthly pilgrimage (1 Th 2:9); and patience (v. 3; 1 Th 5:8) under trial. But in sum the object of hope is always the same: access to God's glory (1 Th 5:10; 1:11).

The triad of faith, hope and charity was probably formulated among Christians before this letter was written. It is a Jewish literary technique to use the triad whenever something sacred is being described. Paul may have found it in use among primitive communities, as a designation of the fundamental Christian attitude toward God and his Messiah.

V. Hebrews
4:14-16
2nd reading
2nd cycle

For these Jewish converts who remained faithful to the temple, but who were obliged by persecution to leave Jerusalem, the author of Hebrews has some reassurances. They have not lost contact with the priesthood or sacrifice. The true High Priest is not the one who celebrates in the Holy of Holies, but Jesus Christ who, as the unique mediator, has celebrated once for all.

From verse 14 onward people are reminded of the content of their profession of faith. Christ is "heir of all things" and he is united to the Father ("seated on his right": He 1:2-3). The author then goes on to show that he is priest and mediator (He 4:15–5:10).

The argument has two facets. Christ represents humanity on the one hand because he became man (vv. 15-16). But he also represents the divine world (v. 1) because as Son of God he is seated on the Father's right hand. Thus he is the perfect *mediator*.

He stands for humanity because he assumed the totality: the failures, the limitations, the temptations all these he transformed to accomplish his priesthood. Why should not his faithful too enjoy this privilege?

The conclusion follows. Let us go forward confidently to the "throne of grace" (v. 16; cf. He 10:22), to the all-good king, that is, who shows grace even to the guilty and benevolence to those who ask (cf. Est 4:11; 5:1-2).

VI. 2 Timothy
3:14-4:2
2nd reading
3rd cycle

Having reminded Timothy of the past marvels of evangelization (2 Tm 1) and described the present difficulties (2 Tm 2), Paul goes on to consider dangers in the future: heresies and corruption of doctrine, apostasies and perse-cutions, forerunners as he sees it of the decisive struggle between good and evil. Anxious to equip his disciple for the coming strug-gles, he tells him to avoid heretics (2 Tm 3:1-9), to imitate his ex-ample and follow his doctrine (2 Tm 3:10-14). He should there-fore instruct himself in Holy Scripture (vv. 15-16). Thus armed (v. 17), he should speak "in season and out of season" (v. 2).

Here we have the most explicit text in the New Testament con-cerning the meaning and value of *Scripture*. Paul reminds Tim-othy first of all that his whole formation has been in the Jewish manner, based on holy writings (v. 15). It does not rest, like that of the heresiarchs, on theories or magical formulae, but on docu-ments and "scriptures."

These have an efficacy in themselves. They provide not alone philosophical and cosmic knowledge, but a "wisdom" that is none other than that of "faith." Consequently those whose profession it is to instruct others should depend on them (v. 16) whether it be for formal teaching, apologetic, or moral training. The man of God (v. 17) who depends on the multiple values of the Scriptures and relies on their efficacy is an "accomplished man," fully fitted for the ministry.

Paul emphasizes that the Scriptures are inspired (v. 16). The words there have a value that distinguishes them from human words. They have been formulated under the power of the Spirit that guided the prophets. It is this quality that makes the Scriptures useful to the preacher, and makes it imperative that he be impregnated with them.

The biblical movement in our day finds good support in this affirmation by the apostle of the priority of Scripture. God's presence in the salvation history which found fulfillment in Jesus Christ is the subject of the Scriptures; and this is the fundamental basis of Christian faith and hope. The Christian however who is also sensitive to the presence of God in the actual world about him will have the best appreciation of Scripture. The Scriptures are our rule of faith, but it is the "signs of the times" that reveal their full message.

VII. Matthew 22:15-21
Gospel
1st cycle

This passage is part of Matthew's account of the "temptations" of Christ by the Pharisees and Sadducees. The partisans of Herod make the first effort, hoping that Jesus will be led to say something damaging concerning Caesar.

a) To their question "Is it lawful to pay tribute to Caesar," Caesar having no divine right over the people because he is not of David's line, Jesus replies with an argument *ad hominem*. If the Pharisees themselves and their followers are ready to accept the authority and advantages of the Roman empire, then let them accept the responsibilities and obligations. He avoids any opinion about legitimacy, and simply states that what is accepted should be obeyed.

But because his questioners have to accept this in silence and might consider their pro-Romanism confirmed, he adds "And render to God what is God's." Civil obedience is no obstacle to fulfillment of our duties to God.

There is then a double lesson. *Civil authority* should be obeyed, particularly by those who derive advantage from it (Rm 13:1-8; Tt 3:1-3; 1 P 2:13-14). But this should not be allowed to interfere with one's obligations to God.

b) By placing the incident in this particular context, following the parable of the banquet, Matthew gives a further precision. In the parable we were told of those who refused God's convocation. Here, in the triple opposition of Herodians, Pharisees and Sadducees, we have the three types of *refusal* which confront the ecclesial assembly. Some are so bound to a particular "Caesar" that it is impossible for them to acknowledge the Lord, others cannot accept the idea of an afterlife. Others still, like the Pharisees, are so intransigent, so preoccupied with ritual purity, that they cannot conceive a Church open to all. Matthew is actually leading up to his twenty-third chapter, where Christ curses his opponents, and the twenty-fourth where the new assembly is proclaimed. The "blessing" of the new assembly (Mt 24:34) is contrasted with the "malediction" upon those who refused both convocation (Mt 23) and the title of assembly (Mt 25).

There is then no opposition in our passage between what is Caesar's and what is God's. Earthly kingdoms are not in fact outside the ambit of the Kingdom of God, because in Jesus Christ they too are taken up by God. Rendering to God what is God's entails indeed rendering to Caesar what is Caesar's. The Kingdom of God is not of this world in the sense that it is not just another earthly kingdom. But it is very much of this world in the sense that it embraces all earthly kingdoms. Being Christian does not mean that we stop short of reality.

Consequently the Church does not try to secure her boundaries against earthly kingdoms. She is by definition worldwide, because she is the visible sign of humanity's reconciliation with God. She has no wish to exercise sway over the secular world. She is not concerned to convert it *en masse,* but she does send her members into it. In this sense she bears witness to the ultimate salvation in Jesus Christ.*

VIII. Mark
10:35-45
Gospel
2nd cycle

Here we have the third prediction by Jesus of his passion and death (cf. Mk 8:31-33 and Mk 9:30-32). This prediction, like the preceding ones, produces different reactions among the apostles. There were some who hoped to hold office in the coming kingdom (vv. 35-40); but all realized that they were concerned in the ascent to Jerusalem, and had to face the test of the cup to be drained (v. 39), of service rendered to the brethren (v. 43).

a) In the exchange with the sons of Zebedee, Christ presents his passion in terms of two themes which Mark is the only one to associate: *the cup and baptism.* They both indicate very well Jesus' awareness of his role. In the Old Testament the cup describes the judgment of God on sinners (Ho 5:20; Na 1:6; Zp 3:8; Jr 6:11; 7:20; 42:18; 44:6; Is 51:15-22). It is a cup that must be drained to the dregs (Jr 25:28; Ez 23:31-34). It has a sacrificial value (Nb 4:14; 7:23; 19:25; Zc 9:15). All this implies that Jesus foresees himself undergoing in a sacrificial manner the judgment of sinners (cf. Is 53:10). In isolation, rejected by the sinful world, he nevertheless wants to die for this world, and thus to remove the great weight that unbelief has laid upon it, preventing it from seeing God's will.

The baptism symbol conveys the same teaching (cf. Lk 12: 49-50). It indicates the judgment of God foretold by the prophets, into which the world will be "plunged." Water, fire and wind

*See the doctrinal theme: *faith and human progress,* p. 236.

will overwhelm this world and bring about a new heaven and a new earth. Jesus is actually substituting himself for the universe, and taking upon himself the purifying judgment that will usher in the new era.

Drinking this cup however and being baptized with this baptism are things reserved to one person only: the suffering Servant, the Redeemer. Into this incommunicable role the disciples can never enter. That is why the question in verse 38 presumes a negative response. The disciples can never be suffering servants and saviors in the sense that Jesus is.

Yet, they can become associated. They will indeed drink the cup of martyrdom and be baptized in suffering. In this prediction Jesus does not intend to describe the manner of death for John and James. A very late legend has James drink a poisoned cup and has John baptized in boiling oil.

Jesus' words are concerned not only with suffering in general, but with the sacramental economy. It is this latter which associates the Christian with the passion of Jesus. We die with him in baptism and enjoy the fruits of his resurrection in the Eucharist. By martyrdom and the sacraments the disciples can share his life.

b) The incident of the two sons of Zebedee seeking a *throne* at the side of Jesus in his glory (v. 37) is more understandable in Matthew's context. Here it follows Jesus' prediction to the apostles that they will judge the tribes of Israel (Mt 19:28) as assessors of the great judge (Mt 25:31).

At this point in the public life the apostles had become aware that it was to the Son of man himself, rather than to a nationalist Messiah, that God would confide the judgment and condemnation of the Gentiles (Dn 7:9-27). Daniel's prophecy had envisaged the Son of man (Dn 7:9-10) as surrounded by a tribunal seated on thrones. The apostles thought of course that they would be the tribunal, as the request of James and John shows. They realized that Jesus would be delivered to the Gentiles (v. 33; this is the only time they are mentioned in the Passion predictions). The judgment of the Son of man would however chastise them for their crime. The apostles hoped to be associated with this divine revenge.

We can imagine the pain of Jesus in encountering such ideas. He begins by pointing out that suffering is the only road to the thrones: drinking the cup and being immersed in trials (vv. 38-39). He then says that it is for God in any case to determine the hour of judgment and the composition of the tribunal (v. 40). The duties to be discharged in the final times depend absolutely on divine choice, and will be stamped with the paschal mystery.

c) What he has said to James and John, Jesus goes on to generalize for the benefit of the other ten. He concentrates on the theme of *service* (vv. 41-45). He reveals his own awareness of his role. He is Messiah and Son of man, but he is also the suffering Servant delivered for the multitude (v. 45; cf. Is 53:11-12). He is the leader, confronted with death, which is about to vault his mission. But he has confidence in God, realizing that his achievement is to be that of the servant of Yahweh. He wants his apostles to undergo the same psychological development. If he himself is to be the suffering Servant they must discover the meaning of service (vv. 43-44).*

d) Verse 45 is one of the most important texts in Mark's Gospel. Practically speaking it is the only synoptic reference to Jesus as a *ransom*. Both text and idea are doubtless original. This would not be the only instance where Jesus is inspired by the theology of the suffering Servant and the redemptive value of death (Is 53:10 and 12; Ps 48/49:7-9, 15; Dn 7:14). Ransom describes the payment a man gives someone in compensation for a right. There is one thing for which a man cannot offer ransom: his own life. Death will not accept compensation (Mk 8:36-37), unless God himself arrange that (Ps 48/49:9 and 15; cf. Is 52:3). Jesus becomes the ransom for men who are not alone mortal but guilty (Is 53:10). This substitution, being voluntary ("giving his life"), is for that reason sacrificial, and it is furthermore universal ("for many"). These two nuances are particular to Mark and have no biblical antecedents. There is also a third. It is this "Son

*See the doctrinal theme: *service,* p. 199.

of man," the transcendent judge of Daniel 7, who, instead of judging and condemning, will ransom the guilty. He will in a fashion take upon himself their lot and their condemnation. Where in Daniel 7:14 he is someone to be served, here in Mark he gives service to the accused. Jesus is aware that he is destined for exaltation after the manner of the Son of man; but he realizes the service and sacrifice that will lead to that exaltation.

Our gospel then presents the passion and resurrection of Jesus in terms of its meaning for Christian life itself. One "must" drink the chalice in order to sit on the thrones: one must be baptized in trial in order to judge the earth: one must serve in order to lead. Suffering takes its place in the life of the disciple, not alone the physical and psychological suffering that is part of the human condition, but the same rejection and abandonment that led Jesus to the cross.

The isolation that becomes the Christian's lot in our secularized world can be looked upon as participation in this passion, particularly as we celebrate the Eucharist.

IX. Luke 18:1-8 Gospel 3rd cycle   Jesus' teaching concerning prayer in this passage can only be understood in its eschatological context. The passage, we should note, follows the eschatological section Luke 17:22-37. It concludes with a reference to the Lord's return (v. 8). The phrase "without ever ceasing" (v. 1) is characteristic of eschatological waiting for the day of the Lord (Lk 21:36; 1 Th 5:17; 2 Th 3:13; Rm 1:10, etc.). The phrase "do justice" which is repeated four times in our text (vv. 3, 5, 6, 8) suggests the day of "vengeance," when those affected will finally reach salvation (Is 61:2).

Understood in this way, the parable of the unjust judge and the obstinate widow teaches the necessity to pray without ceasing, even when the Lord seems slow in coming and deaf to our appeals.

We have two characters in the parable. On the one hand a judge devoid of faith or justice (v. 2). He is not concerned with administering justice, above all where someone as weak as a widow is concerned. He is so lax that he finally gives justice in order to have peace and escape possible trouble (v. 5). On the other hand we have the widow, weak, but convinced of her right and determined to maintain it (v. 3).

Jesus' argument is simple (vv. 6-8a). If an unjust judge finally gives the widow her due, how much more will not God, who is just, give justice to his elect who are at the mercy of their adversaries.

The lesson also is that God gives justice promptly (v. 8a) but after a long *delay* (v. 7). Christians then, in prayer, must allow for the delay which God demands. They will pray "without intermission."

No longer is Christian prayer to be an appeal for immediate intervention and vengeance (as it is still in Rev 6:10). It accepts the patience of God, so that sinners may have time to be converted (2 P 3:9-15).

Prayer of petition does not consist in expecting God to accomplish what we ourselves fail to accomplish: give us bread, give us peace, give us healing. God is not a stop-gap! Prayer is basically a protest, protest because war triumphs over peace, because a few rich trample upon the masses of poor. It is entry into communion with the God of patience. In such communion the cries of protest are gradually translated into action.

B. DOCTRINE

1. Theme of Faith and Human Progress

Modern man is deeply conscious of the historic task he has to accomplish on earth. His powers are gradually reaching the point of real mastery over the material universe, and what he has to do is create the secular city that will give a home to a human community of brothers.

Many of our contemporaries combine this ideal with harsh criticism of religion. It has proved, they argue, the great source of alienation for human beings. It naturally tends to favor established order and to preach resignation to the disadvantaged.

A proper understanding however of Christianity refutes this criticism. Faith does not make for evasion. It bids the Christian assume his proper responsibilities in pursuit of the very ideal that is proposed. Facts bear this out. Great numbers of Christians lend a very willing ear to the calls for human progress. Very recently the Second Vatican Council devoted a large part of its deliberations to the major problems, often seemingly more profane than religious, of twentieth century man. Christian reticence in this domain is a thing of the past.

One question of course does indeed present itself. It is usually formulated thus: for all that the construction of the secular city is a task of great importance, by contrast with the Kingdom inaugurated by Jesus Christ which is of another order, is it not stamped with the mark of the transitory? In precise terms, if we contribute to the construction of the secular city, are we also contributing to the construction of God's Kingdom, and if so how? Are they two opposed ideals? Are they parallel? Or are they perhaps closely articulated, one with the other?

The answer to this question is of immense importance in formulating our notion of the Church's mission. Nowadays it has become imperative for our daily Christian lives that our views be lucid and without illusion.

Man's conquest of the earth in Israel

The creation account according to the priestly tradition (which was formulated certainly after the Exile) describes how God created man and woman in his image and likeness. Having blessed them he said: "Increase and multiply, fill the earth and subdue it; have domination over the fish of the sea, the birds of the air, and all animals that roam the earth" (Gn 1:28).

This is the view of the human mission that belongs to the regime of faith. Israel perceived that its God, Yahweh, is veritably the Totally-Other, the creator of all things visible and invisible, whose sovereignty nothing escapes. But her insight also led to recognition of man's own grandeur. In God's plan, which the history of the earthly paradise was meant to reveal, man is called to dominate the universe. The divine order into which he is admitted presumes a contribution from him in the accomplishment of the creative task.

But the man that we really find on earth is not paradisal man: he is a fallen creature. Jealous of God, he tried to become God and achieve by his own resources a mastery over the universe equal to that of God. He sinned. He did not accept his creatural condition, and God expelled him from Paradise. Man's subjugation of the earth seemed to be altogether compromised. Death, the result of sin, would always jeopardize it.

Yet, one day the divine plan for humanity must be accomplished. Yahweh is faithful. Prophetic teaching led Israel to turn her gaze to the future. A man would come, by means of whom God would restore everything, even more marvelously. The lost paradise would not be matter for regret. Under a new heaven and a new earth, man would be truly the king of creation. The new Adam would succeed where the first one had failed.

Thus Israel was well aware of the role God had determined for man; but she did not consider this role compatible with man's actual state here below. To envisage compatibility a further insight would have been necessary, a realization of the value of accepting the human condition. The Virgin Mary alone, who was without sin, sensed that this acceptance extended to death itself, and that man's domination of the universe in these terms was possible here below. It was not really necessary—on the contrary—to escape the human predicament.

Jesus of Nazareth, king of creation

The decisive stage in awareness of the meaning of man's domination of the universe was reached with Jesus. At last it became clear what man's destiny was.

His life showed what could be the dimensions of the human experience. First of all, member of the human family is henceforth the very Son of God, and all other human beings are called in him to share God's own life. Man's yearning for the absolute is fulfilled beyond all expectation. God builds his Kingdom with the cooperation of the Incarnate Word and of all men who have become his adoptive sons. But an essential condition of this contribution to the Kingdom is man's fidelity to the creatural state. Jesus gave us the definitive example of this by his obedience unto death, the death of the cross.

So, in Jesus, the ideal of human domination of the universe is realized. We have a dimension of the absolute, and the realization is definitive, because he is Son of God and all men in him can become children of the Father. But the realization is of the earth too. A way of obedience unto death has been revealed. The authentic way of promoting humanity is the way of love that entails the total gift of self. If man is to be master of creation, it will be by following this way, which summons the utmost creatural resources he can muster.

Jesus entered history, and injected into it a life-giving principle. There is nothing of established and unalterable order about the created universe; rather is it to be viewed as a challenge, a program and a task. The mission allotted by God to man in the universe is one that must be accomplished here on earth, and the path leads by way of death. Jesus opened to man the gate of the Kingdom, and he also showed the eternal dimension of man's lordship over the universe. Simultaneously he freed man from sin, from all, that is to say, that walls man off from discerning his true destiny. He set the wheels in motion for man's contribution in creation.

Human progress and the Church

Jesus established the true relation between religion and civilization, between the building of the Kingdom and that of the secular city. Many generations of Christianity had to elapse before the consequences of this became clear. The whole history of the Church is one of a global and continuous effort to safeguard the transcendence of the salvation acquired in Jesus Christ, and to make man aware of the immense possibilities open to him.

From the beginnings onwards it is clear that human progress actually depended on the gospel. It was only realizable in the context of Christian faith. Human resources were those of fidelity to the creatural condition: their efficacity depended on the link with Christ. Thus it came about that the Church tended to express the Good News she was charged to transmit as moral precepts. During the period when she was confronted with the task of training whole nations in the faith, she set up a vast network of institutions where the mark of religion was stamped on all sectors of life, individual and collective. Eventually it became evident that human progress was more than a means directed toward a supernatural end. It represented an end in itself. For man, the creature, the way of obedience to death which reveals the true secret of human progress is not just a religious tenet. It is an insight into the verity of human nature itself, and sets up an order of values that provide their own justification.

This was a decisive turning point, and we find it accepted in good theology from the 13th century onwards. Saint Augustine had only accepted human values in their relation to the great human choice: for or against the God of love. Saint Thomas introduced the distinction between natural and supernatural that enabled man to see the dimensions of his creatural liberty. Faith does not destroy nature: it discloses the meaning of nature. The result was to be a gradually growing resentment of the Church's tutelage. Man became enamored of liberty, and more and more aware of the possibilities open to him.

So that nowadays the problem for the Church has come to be this. How to restore her tutelage in the proper sense? How do we convince the dispersed Christians of the modern world that it is their link with Jesus Christ that makes them efficacious campaigners for human progress? We begin to see that dimension of the Church that too often fails to be appreciated. In a world of dispersed Christians she should be, no longer an institution, but the leaven in the mass. She is composed of individuals. She becomes an institution when she assembles these; but she does not cease to exist when she does not assemble them. The individual members continue to be united by the personal ties that the Church has formed. They communicate to one another their individual experiences. They would be powerfully aided in this if the specifically ecclesial ties were more evident in their daily lives. That is a good argument for having priests just as involved in secular life as the laity are.

Evangelization and human progress

Evangelization really means witness to the resurrection, engrafting the mystery of Jesus Christ into the spiritual pilgrimage of any people or any culture. It presumes that people will be open to the Good News to the extent that, explicitly or implicitly, they will see its relevance to their own search, and their own way of life.

Toward the work of evangelization, there is a radical difference between the attitude of modern man and that of his predecessor under the sacral regime. The latter was naturally attuned to "religious values," to everything that pointed to the "divine," that was salvific. The former is concentrated on "profane values," on everything that stems from exclusively human resources.

If the sign of the resurrection is to be properly presented to men of our time, it will be necessary for us to meet them at the point that concerns them most, the ideal of human progress. It will no longer be a question of acquiring a new idiom to communicate with another people, whom we wish to mold to the Word and to our institutions. It will no longer be a matter of translating the Scriptures, providing a liturgy that is Indian, Chinese or African, and adapting our catechesis to categories other than Western. The crucial task will be one of opening all men, within the confines of their own cultures, to the Good News of salvation, precisely in the context of their great ideal: the molding of human destiny.

This is something entirely compatible with Christianity, because in the humanity of the man-God human destiny has actually been fulfilled. It is through the eyes of faith that the true nature of man can be discerned, and that concepts such as human progress and human freedom come to have meaning. Conversely, genuine contribution to human progress can be profoundly significant also in the order of faith.

Doubtless there must be an inevitable confrontation between Christian wisdom in this domain and that of atheistic humanism, which sees salvation in terms of human progress only. The Good News of salvation calls for total self-renunciation. Based on such an attitude, the enterprise of human progress finds its proper level, and disposes all men to accept their state of sonship from the hands of the unique Mediator.

Importance of eucharistic initiation

Just because it is his mission to work for true human progress in an environment where the Church can no longer assemble the faithful, the modern Christian stands in greater need of the Eucharist than his predecessor. He is no longer led by the hand; his link with Jesus Christ must be a personal one, forged through all the ecclesial channels, above all through sharing the Bread and the Word. It is indeed particularly fortunate that just now, when ecclesial tutelage has reached its lowest ebb, and when evangelization is beginning to be associated with human progress, that a liturgical reform of quite unprecedented dimensions is taking place in the Church.

There are however two fundamental needs that must be fulfilled if this reform is to bear fruit properly. In the first place all eucharistic celebrations should be so structured that catholicity is constantly in evidence. The Christian must physically experience the universal brotherhood that has been made real in Jesus Christ. Secondly, liturgical celebration should be disencumbered by the elaborate vestments that set up barriers against modern man. We need more sobriety perhaps in our styles of sacralization. We need to give prestige to the Word. It should always prepare people for their responsibilities in the building of the Kingdom.

2. Theme of Service

When the Second Vatican Council questioned itself about the proper manner of presence for the people of God among men today, one phrase caught the attention of everyone: "the Church, servant of the world." It epitomized the truth that the Church could no longer have tutelage over human progress: that the historical circumstances which had placed her in the past in this position were now changed. The world, by rejecting her tutelage, was simply reminding the Church that her function is to serve. It goes without saying that, if this is true for the Church in general, it is doubly true for those exercising ministry in the Church. When the Council discussions were concerned with the functions of bishops and priests, the word service was always recurring.

As we are reminded in today's formulary (1st reading and Gospel, 2nd cycle) the theme is essential to the very notion of Christianity. "The Son of man has come not to be served, but to serve" (Mk 10:45). This the Council, by constantly stressing the theme, was doing no more than literally returning to Christian origins. Nothing is so likely to create a proper understanding of messianic intervention and the mission of the Church.

Service however is more than an affirmation of an attitude. It must characterize institutions as well as persons. The conciliar affirmations, if they are to become more than empty formulas, must issue in quite radical reforms in the institution itself, and in the various offices associated with it. It is not indeed surprising that the postconciliar Church has been undergoing a series of "crises." They were entirely to be expected.

Service of Yahweh in Israel

In the Greek world the idea of service was disparaged because it meant bowing to others. It suggested the slave at table. The Greek ideal was one of power: terms which designate roles in society are always honorific. Public services or services to the gods are described by the noun *leitourgia* and the verb *leitourgein*, from which any suggestion of abasement is absent.

Faith, in Israel, gradually accustomed people to the notion of dependence. Yahweh is the Totally-Other, and man is basically dependent on him. Prophetic teaching gradually set up the religious ideal of the poor man, who, like a slave, owes everything to the generosity of the Master and accepts being led by him. The cultic worship of Yahweh too had dimensions other than those of pagan liturgies. To be pleasing to God, cult must express obedience to the precepts of the Covenant. Thus the Septuagint translators, when using Greek liturgical vocabulary to describe the cult of Yahweh, the priestly service in particular (see, for instance, 1 S 2:11, 18), give it specific nuances that belong to the regime of faith. The effect of this attitude is to be seen in the relative betterment in Israel of the slave's status. A man bound to servitude always remained a man. He could become a confidant or even an heir. Service of another was not regarded as degrading.

The Jews resembled the Greeks however in avoiding the vocabulary of service when designating state or religious functionaries. Such officials were set apart from, and above, the people, and enjoyed power and dignity. During the time of Jesus they were treated with veneration, were greeted with strict protocol, and given titles of reverence that stressed their superiority of rank.

Jesus of Nazareth and service of the other

The contrast to this introduced by Jesus is very evident. The gospels tell how the Twelve during his public ministry were concerned with knowing who was the greatest (Mk 9:34; Lk 9:46; 22:24). He replied by using the vocabulary of service, of slavery even. "If anyone wants to be first he must make himself last of all and servant of all" (Mk 9:35). Again, more precisely still: "For who is the greater, the one at table or the one who serves? The one at table surely? Yet here am I among you as one who serves" (Lk 22:27). Unmistakably, the language used is that of "*diakonia*," service at the table of one's master. In Matthew 20:27 we have the affirmation: "anyone who wants to be first among you must be your slave." The disciple's attitude, following Jesus, must be one of service to others, giving his life for them, for love.

This is the sign too that is to distinguish those who discharge functions in the messianic community. There were many obvious examples of functionaries, but he uses none of them. Of the priests who served God in the Temple he says not a word. Of the scribes and Pharisees he has this to say: "Everything they do is done to attract attention. . . . They love the place of honor at banquets and the first seats in the synagogues, being greeted obsequiously in the market squares and having people call them Rabbi. You however must not allow yourselves to be called Rabbi, since you have only one Master and you are all brothers . . . the greatest among you must be your servant" (Mt 23:5-11). Nor does the role of the disciple resemble in any way that of the civil official: "You know that among the pagans their so-called rulers lord it over them and their great men make their authority felt. This is not to happen among you. No, anyone who wants to become great among you must be your servant. . . . For the Son of man himself did not come to be served, but to serve and to give his life. . . ." (Mk 10:42-45, today's Gospel, 2nd cycle).

The model then is not to be the civil leader, or the guardian of the law, or the segregated priest. It is to be the slave who serves at table. Saint John tells us that Jesus himself could find no better way of demonstrating to his disciples how love lay at the root of his messianic intervention than by serving them at table at the very hour of his supreme sacrifice. And of that table service, we should note, the most significant moment is the washing of the feet (Jn 13:1-17).

Mutual service and the Church

Deaconship, with all that this implies, carried great weight in the organization of the primitive Christian communities. It is the key to the understanding of all functions and all relationships.

Given the great diversity of persons, it could of course take many different shapes. But, because it was always an expression of brotherly love to the point of giving one's life, it built up communion and furthered the common good. For the same reason it supposed a particular gift of God and was a response to grace. It was an expression in the community of the charismatic action of the Spirit. "Each one of you has received a special grace, so, like good stewards responsible for all these different graces of God, put yourselves at the service of others" (1 P 4:10). The relationship between deaconship and charism is extremely close. Responsible service to the community implies the Spirit's action, and the charism is for the good of the community. "The manifestation of the Spirit to each is for the common good" (1 Co 12:7). Each member of the community then is regarded as called by the Spirit to give of his best. That contribution is to be one of service to the others. Such was the principle of organization in the primitive communities.

Deaconship of this quality could have no guarantee of permanency of course. It could only be maintained by constant awareness that Christ was always present among his own, present to serve. It was paradoxical enough to run counter to all natural inclination. Living faith was necessary to sustain it, a faith that could clarify this most profound of the insights of the New Testament. Where this faith became impaired, as indeed it did often enough when transplanted into pagan soil, deaconship lost some of its quality. Jewish institutional forms, and indeed some pagan ones, made their appearance once more in the Church, particularly where it became associated with power. The faithful no longer conducted themselves as brothers, each fulfilling his role of service.

Were Christians but to be brothers again and ready to serve according to the original pattern, the ecclesial institution would automatically become diaconal once more. In any case it is remarkable how the importance of the theme of service at Vatican II was constantly associated with the brotherhood that ought to characterize the people of God.

The service of humanity and the Church as servant of the world

Originally, it was at the moment when the Church turned to the Gentiles, that the primitive ideal of service as an expression of brotherly love gained full stature. Mission, the greatest work of ecclesial deaconship, was born. Whenever service becomes restricted to the boundaries of the ecclesial community, it runs the risk of being impaired. Though the first Christians were all Jews, the moment they extended their service to the Nations they realized the true meaning of Christianity. The concept of mission really developed out of mutual services rendered to one another by Jew and Gentile. The events at Antioch are our evidence. If mission is to be authentic it must always be the work *par excellence* of deaconship.

The lessons of history confront us. From the 4th century onwards the ecclesial institution tends to lose its diaconal structure. With the official conversion of the Roman Empire, masses of men

204 GUIDE FOR THE CHRISTIAN ASSEMBLY

and women came into the Church, who for the most part had no idea of the responsibilities by baptism. It was inevitable that religious institution should begin to overshadow the ecclesial Communion. Subsequently the breakdown of civil institutions forced the Latin Church to assume tutelage of the whole west, and develop numerous ecclesial institutions to that end. Throughout this period, at least on the institutional level, service in the image of the slave who serves at table was lost sight of. Mission consequently tended to be degraded into propaganda or proselytism. This was not the fault of the many individual persons who continued to bear witness to the charity of Christ. But the institution had come to direct mission as a military campaign is directed.

In our day an important change has come about. There is no question of Church tutelage over humanity in those terms. Her business will be to return to the original ideal of service and become the servant of the world. She must be the leaven in the mass, and scrupulously avoid any suggestion of power. She must embrace her vulnerability, and bear witness to love for all in the image of the table slave.

Liturgical initiation into service of humanity

This ideal of service that Jesus has given us must of course be sustained by initiation. Our natural inclinations are not any more directed than those of the Greeks to see our relation to the other in the image of the table-slave. Our initiation to the new commandment is only accomplished bit by bit, through constant reconversions and unexpected insights. All ecclesial assemblies should have this as their object, particularly the eucharistic one. And it is obvious that this does not happen automatically. Saint John thought it well to replace the institution narrative in his Gospel with that of the washing of the feet, so that there should be no ambiguity whatsoever about the ideal of service. And as it is our business, again according to Saint John, to imitate Jesus, we should always, at every epoch, be endeavoring to provide conditions in which the ideal can be practiced.

Among those conditions, in the situation in which we find ourselves now, two should be singled out. In the first place it is absolutely imperative that the Word proclaimed should touch the concrete lives of the faithful, and enable them to see how the ideal of service can permeate every area of their lives. How often, in our celebrations, does not everything seem altogether irrelevant to the real responsibilities of those present. Secondly, the assembly itself should somehow demonstrate the effect upon a man's life of this image of table-service. The faithful present should be made to *feel* evangelic charity, and want to express it in service. What has been done to date in these areas is no more than inchoate.

THIRTIETH SUNDAY

A. THE WORD

I. Exodus
22:20-26
1st reading
1st cycle

These verses were added to the Code of the alliance, under prophetic influence doubtless, particularly after the deuteronomic reform (Dt 10:18-19; 23:20-21; 24:10-13, 17-18; 27:19).

The legislation was promulgated at the end of a long struggle by the prophets for *social justice*. Economic disturbances were brought about at the time by the change from a rural economy based on family and traditional structures to an urban one where the isolated individual could no longer depend on the resources of his clan. Strangers, widows, orphans and numerous poor were dying of hunger, and no one in society rallied to their aid.

We can welcome the tests as the beginnings of that social legislation that was to be the mark of civilized peoples. They also point the way for projects of international aid to the poor, an area where the rich nations still have a long way to travel.

II. Jeremiah
31:7-9
1st reading
2nd cycle

The "oracle of consolation" (Jr 30-31) was compiled by the prophet, in all essentials, during the years after 622. Josias was undertaking an important religious reform, which he succeeded in extending even to the northern kingdom (Israel), which had been provisionally reconquered by a weakened Assyria (cf. 2 K 23:15-19; 2 Ch 35:18). Hope began to grow that the exiles of 721 could return to a restored kingdom of David. This is Jeremiah's topic. Later, however, passages concerning the return of Judah, itself conquered and exiled, were added to the oracle. Our reading belongs to the first redaction.

His description of the *restoration* of Israel in the north gives the prophet an opportunity to introduce a series of themes and images connected with the people's hope. Our passage has three such images: the restoration will be like a vast assembly (v. 8), a reconciliation between a father and his first-born (v. 9), and a consolation given by God after a trial has been endured (v. 8). It is noteworthy that this is the first occurrence in Scripture of the theme of consolation (cf. Is 40:1).

Chapter 31 of Jeremiah had been very prominent in Jewish liturgy. Since, apart from apostolic preaching, the first Christian communities were wont to hear only the Old Testament as God's Word, it is not surprising that they would relate such passages to some saying of Jesus, or episode in his life.

In any case we find Jeremiah 31 in the background of Luke's grouping of some parables (Lk 15). He gives us a sort of Christian homily on the ancient text. Thus Luke 15:4-7 alludes to Jeremiah 31:10-14, and to the joy of those reassembled; Luke 15:8-10 in parallel to Jeremiah 31:15-17 (theme of the woman searching for what she has lost); Luke 15:11-32 refers to Jeremiah 31:9, 18-20 (the Father finding his beloved son).

III. Sirach	After a very elaborate analysis of spiritual
35:12-14,	sacrifice (Si 35:1-9), the author considers the
16-18	liturgical acts performed by people who ex-
1st reading	ploit their neighbor, yet hope to have God's
3rd cycle	favor by their religious conformism.

He imagines a temple scene where a rich man offers numerous sacrifices in order that God will be blind to his injustices (v. 10), while the poor man can only offer his complaint (vv. 12-18). What we have then is a sort of contrast between two *types of sacrifice*, like the contrast between those of Abel and Cain (Gn 4:1-10), of Elias and the prophets of Baal (1 K 18:20-40), of the

Pharisee and the publican (Lk 18:9-14). Ben Sira leaves God to "judge" between the sacrifices and to decide between the oppressor and the oppressed. God's judgment is clear. By granting the prayer of the poor man he shows what sort of sacrifice he desires.

Today too we have Christians who make their Church contributions from ill-gotten gains, and think their participation in the mass will be sufficient salve for their conscience without mending their ways.

IV. 1 Thessa-	This passage is taken from the thanksgiving
lonians	which forms the introduction to the first letter
1:5-10	to the Thessalonians. It describes the welcome
2nd reading	given the apostle by the Thessalonian commu-
1st cycle	nity and how the Good News has spread there.

Paul is struck by the zeal the Thessalonians have shown in imitating him, becoming themselves models for other believers. One can almost say that growth in the Church follows a pattern of concentric *imitations*. The Old Testament recommended believers to imitate God: they should be holy as God is holy (Lv 19:1-2). In the teaching of Jesus we still have traces of this (Mt 5:48; Lk 6:36). The real characteristic, however, of New Testament doctrine is that men can be imitated too because they have become signs of God. Thus, obviously Christians are recommended to imitate Jesus (Lk 14:25-35; Mt 10:38; 16:24), but Paul does not hesitate to tell them to imitate himself (1 Th 2:14; 1 Co 4:16), and he expects the Gentiles to imitate Christians (v. 7).

Our reading emphasizes a condition that is necessary for all mission. Methods associated with power and propaganda should be eschewed, and we should be solely concerned with the purity and visibility of the signs we offer to the world. It is when the non-Christian can discern in the life of the Christian something that touches the inner spring of his own spiritual thrust, that the Good News is proclaimed.

V. Hebrews
5:1-6
2nd reading
2nd cycle

This is the beginning of the long contrast that the author draws between the levitical priesthood and that of Christ. Not alone does Christ fulfill all the conditions required for any high priest (vv. 1-4); his priesthood is strikingly superior. The proof is God's own oath and Christ's eternal sonship (vv. 5-6). The two arguments are put forward in two scriptural citations, that will recur a good deal later on: Psalms 109/110:4 and 2:7.

Among the qualities required for a high priest are that he be "taken from among men" (Nb 8:6; He 2:10-18), and "established" (Tt 1:5; Ac 6:3; 7:10; 27:35; Ex 2:14; He 2:28; 8:3) to offer sacrifices for men (Lv 4; 5; 16). This exaltation does not prevent him in any way from receiving the weak and the strayed (Lv 5:18; Ez 40:39), because he himself shares their weakness. Finally, and most importantly, the high priest is called by God as Aaron was (Ex 28). This condition is preeminently fulfilled by Christ, who did not arrogate the privilege to himself (v. 5), who never sought his own glory (Jn 5:41; 8:50, 54; Rm 15:3; Ph 2:6).

Over and above these conditions however are two others, much greater, verified in Christ. The perpetuity of his priesthood (v. 5) is assured by his eternal sonship; and his priesthood "according to the order of Melchisedech" sets him above traditional criteria (vv. 5-6).

VI. 2 Timothy
4:6-8, 16-18
2nd reading
3rd cycle

Here we have an extract from a sort of farewell discourse by Paul to his disciple. This is a literary *genre*, the elements of which are admirably illustrated here; satisfaction because of having fulfilled one's mission (vv.

6-7; cf. Jn 17-6, 13; Ac 20:20-21), the indication of proximate departure (vv. 6-7; cf. Jn 13:33; Ac 20:22-25), a fairly pessimistic
estimate of the present situation (vv. 16-17; cf. Ac 20:22, 29-34),
and absolute confidence in God's help (v. 18; cf. Jn 17:13;
Ac 20:24).

Paul is practically certain that he is about to face his final
judicial trial; and one of the harshest aspects of his captivity is
that he must do so alone. But even under trial he remains faithful
to his mission; this has been an opportunity to speak with his
pagan judges and proclaim the gospel. How could *trial* be an
obstacle to his mission when it gives a chance of evangelizing.

Furthermore, his trial enables him to share the sentiments of
Christ on the cross and pardon those who desert him (v. 16).
There can be no question of discouragement. Salvation is assured
to the one who walks with Christ.

VII. Matthew **22:34-40** *Gospel* *1st cycle*	Jesus has just dealt with the Pharisees' trick-question concerning tax (22:15-22) and answered a question by the Jews about the resurrection of the dead (22:23-33). He is now asked about the greatest commandment (22:34-40).*

We have three different accounts of this interrogation about
the commandments of *love:*

(1) In Luke (10:25-28) the lawyer himself mentions the commandment. The point about "the greatest commandment" is not
raised because such a typically rabbinical matter would have no
interest for Luke's readers.

(2) Here in Matthew the question is put with dubious mo-

*See the doctrinal theme: *double love,* p. 244.

tives, but the answer of Jesus is so unequivocal that no one intervenes.

(3) Finally, in Mark (12:28-34) the scribe approaches Jesus with good intentions and a genuine wish to be enlightened.

At verse 34, Matthew indicates by quoting Psalm 2:2: *principes convenerunt in unum* that the pharisees were meeting together. Thus an atmosphere of conspiracy and hostility is established at once. Immediately afterwards Jesus repeats two commandments, not one (vv. 37-39). Mark simply gives the drift of the commandment, and Luke combines the two precepts in one. Matthew, in giving two, immediately adds that the second is like the first.

Christ's version of the first commandment follows Deuteronomy 6:4-5, but according to the formula of Jewish morning and evening prayer. The second is taken from Leviticus 19:18.

Matthew's final sentence "On these two commandments hang the whole law and the prophets also" (v. 40; cf. Mt 7:12; 5:17) is peculiar to him. It means that the whole edifice crumbles if these two precepts are suppressed, and is a clear allusion to the Pharisees who prefer the rest of the law to charity and duties to God. The key to the whole law is love and without it the law cannot be observed.

VIII. Mark 10:46-52 Gospel 2nd cycle   The cure of the blind man at Jericho is recounted by Mark with a couple of details that are ignored by the other synoptics. He speaks of one blind man only and he names him (v. 46) where Matthew mentions two, unnamed, and Luke one. Mark perhaps has exact information in this instance that the other evangelists did not consider necessary to tell their readers. The exclamation of the blind man in addressing Jesus is in fact rather different in the three gospels: "Lord, Son of David" in Matthew 20:30, "Son of David, Jesus" in Mark 10:47, and "Jesus, Son of David" in Luke 18:28. Apparently these exclamations are related to pious formulas or liturgical acclamations used by different primitive communities. Mark's formula looks like it is the original.

Verses 49-50 we find in Mark only. They give a particular atmosphere to the whole account, setting it in the context of a catechumenal ritual.

Initiation to faith begins with the manifestation of Jesus in a man's life. Christ must "pass that way" (Mt 20:30). The manifestation is mysterious. The person on the road to faith, represented here by the blind man, does not see Jesus. He has an intuition of the Lord's presence in events (v. 47a), but he already expresses his faith by relying on God's salvific initiative (v. 47b). The world round about him immediately threatens this turning to God (v. 48a), and it requires all his courage to maintain his resolve (v. 48b).

At this stage the catechumen receives attention from people who reveal to him the call of God and invite him to be converted to "rise up" or come alive, and "cast aside his mantle or "strip off the old man"; vv. 49 and 50). Then begins the final interpellation: "what do you wish . . . ?" (v. 51). What we have is a definitive engagement in the form of question and answer so that the absolute liberty of two parties to a contract is made clear.

Finally comes the restoration of sight, a vision of faith (vv. 51-52) which leads the catechumen straightway to "follow" Christ "on the road."

The passage from blindness to sight is the perfect image for the passage from flesh to spirit, from selfishness to outgoing. There are five stages in this development. The turning towards God at the bidding of conscience in spite of worldly obstacles, the answer to Christ's call on hearing his word, the offering of self to the Master by conversion and stripping off the old man, the communion with Christ in the vision of faith, and finally the following of Christ throughout the world and being a witness of the Kingdom.

IX. Luke 18:9-14
Gospel
3rd cycle

The parable of the Pharisee and the publican has received divers interpretations, which, though not altogether wrong, fail to clarify the basic lesson. Its eschatological import has been stressed, for instance, above all because of the final verse (14b). At the last judgment there will be an exaltation of the humble and an abusement of the proud. However, this sentiment is so often on the lips of Jesus in the evangelists (Lk 14:11; Mt 23:12) that it can be regarded as a sort of refrain which punctuates all the major teachings.

Then the parable has been taken as teaching on prayer. Prayer must be humble, based not on personal merit but on God's initiative. Luke for instance juxtaposes two pieces on prayer (18:1-8 and 18:9-14) to form a minor euchological treatise. It is not impossible ineeed that he may have "re-read" the texts with this in view, but it is hard to explain why he stresses, in verse 9, the change of audience as if to distinguish the two incidents.

The main point of the parable is obviously of course the lesson that a penitent sinner is more pleasing to God than a proud man who thinks himself just (Lk 16:15). Behind the characters of the piece we can discern a contrast between two types of justice; that of the man who awards himself an accolade because of works accomplished and that which God grants the penitent sinner. It is an early broaching of the great Pauline theme of justification by faith (Rm 1-9 and Ep 2:8-10).

The prayer put on the lips of the Pharisee by Jesus is a model actually that can be paralleled in contemporary rabbinic documents. The worshipper makes no petition (this would be unworthy) and merely expresses thanks for the certainty that he is on the road to final slavation. Jesus' audience must have recognized themselves as they listened. There was nothing to criticize in the formula.

The inspiration for the publican's prayer is Psalm 50/51. It suggests a profound despair that the audience would consider perfectly natural, because to them the publican's predicament was insoluble. How could he obtain pardon without changing his occupation and without reimbursing those he had despoiled? The case was completely desperate and justification impossible.

Jesus' conclusion is altogether contrary to his hearers' views. God is the God of those in despair. The one who obtains *justice* is precisely the one who has no right to it (v. 14) because he has not even mended his fault.

The contrast between the "just man" who believes he can justify himself, and the one whose only way of obtaining justice is to throw himself on God's mercy (cf. Lk 16:15; 14:15-24; Mt 9:10-13), prepares the Pauline doctrine, where God is the giver of justification to those who cannot justify themselves (Rm 3:23-25; 4:4-8; 5:9-21). It is the cross of Christ which justifies (Rm 5:19; 3:24-25; Ga 2:21), and the instrument is baptism (Tt 3:5-7; Rm 6:1-14; Ep 4:22-24).

Justification is an actuality here and now. It is not the result of human effort, depending upon human resources; but neither is it something exclusively eschatological, dependent upon God's intervention. The Christian is justified by faith in Jesus Christ, the one who is at once the substantial gift of the Father and the man among men who was able to respond in a manner pleasing to God.

The idea clarifies the whole concept of adoptive sonship which we acquire through the living link with Jesus. We are justified because our faith in Christ allows us to approach the Father as adoptive children. The salvation which crowns our expectation is an absolutely gratuitous gift of God, but it becomes in us a source of filial activity. It enables us to maintain a transcendental fidelity to the new law of love.

It is in the eucharistic celebration that we have our highest experience of the justification we have received. All those assembled realize that they are answering a divine summons to salvation, that their common act of thanksgiving has meaning only by virtue of the ecclesial link with Christ that makes them members of his Body. When we share the Word and the Bread, the grace that was manifested once for all in Jesus Christ, especially in his death on the cross, begins to work. It makes us aware of the overwhelming grandeur of our filial state. We are actually God's partners in the building of the Kingdom, and signs of that justification in Christ which must forever dazzle the eyes of men.*

*See the doctrinal theme: *justification,* p. 221.

B. DOCTRINE

1. Theme of Imitation of God

Men have always imitated models and modern man is no exception to the rule. But the models change visage, or name. The extent of imitation varies. It may be exterior merely (the hair-do or clothes of a movie star), or at the other extreme it may be concentrated on spiritual or moral style (imitating a master of wisdom for instance). But the reason for imitating is invariably the same; it gives some sort of expression to the universal. Something becomes tangible and approachable, and consequently provides security. If we can have within our grasp the "exemplar" of an action or an attitude, we feel we are touching something solid. The exemplar appears to have generated some "value" or "universal" and provided concrete means of attaining it.

Christianity makes the imitation of Christ a pivotal matter. It has actually been the subject of a celebrated spiritual classic. If Christians of our day do not feel altogether enthusiastic about this little book, it is just because they feel that the horizons of the topic are vastly wider than the book allows. No one has any doubt about the centrality of the theme. Christ is the Way, the Truth and the Life, and we must all try to follow in his footsteps.

A problem arises perhaps concerning the exact content of imitation. What do we mean by imitating Christ? He is not in the first place a master of wisdom. He is the Incarnate Word, who died and rose again for all humanity. He is the unique mediator of universal salvation and imitation of him cannot be confined to imitating his behavior. He lived at a time and in a culture that is no longer ours, so that a slavish copying of what he did and how he reacted would be quixotic. There is plenty of reason then for attempting to plumb the real meaning of imitation. We shall be dealing with something that is altogether crucial in our faith.

Imitation of Yahweh in Israel

Ancient pagan religions attached great importance to the imitation of divine models. In their quest for the absolute, men, who find themselves in a fluid and precarious existence, will only find security in actions that seem to bring the gods to earth. There is a constant thrust to achieve contact with the divine archetypes, to penetrate to being itself, apart from which all seems empty and chaotic. Imitation seems the means *par excellence* of divinisation. Liturgies are developed which offer ways of access. In ritual men can share mysteriously in divine activity; they are snatched from the hazards of existence and rooted in the stability of the gods. All important activities in life become ritual so that they can have meaning. If the ritual is scrupulously observed, a man can truly "mime" a divine act and absorb the energies it deploys.

It was natural then that the Israelites should see imitation of Yahweh in terms of cult to begin with. Cult imitates a divine model. As faith deepened, however, this whole concept was destined to be altogether transformed. Yahweh is the Totally-Other, the Inaccessible. Between him and the creature the gulf is unbridgeable. Cult does not divinize. The one way of salvation is fidelity to the Covenant. Yahweh will gratuitously save those who depend on him for everything and faithfully observe his Law. Yet because man is created in the image and likeness of God, the fidelity demanded by the Covenant has some resemblance to Yahweh's own action. And it is actually by meditation on Yahweh's action that Israel gains more and more insight into the concrete requirements of the Covenant. The path of Yahweh is always one of fidelity and love, and the prophets never cease calling upon the recalcitrant people to follow him in this path.

In the hinterland of all this however is a vague awareness that the moral ideal of imitation of Yahweh is never going to fulfill man's deepest aspirations. The negative feelings about sin are revealing. It is man's dream that he can somehow have a dimension of the absolute in his response to God. But is not this negatived by the creatural condition? It was out of the yearning to bridge this impasse that messianic hope was born.

Christ and the perfect imitation of God

Israel's hope was fulfilled in the intervention of Christ, beyond all expectation. Yet it was the very unprecedented character of the fulfillment that brought about rejection by the Jews. Let us examine why.

Jesus actually put himself forward as the perfect imitator of the Father. His response to the divine initiative was the adequate one. He is indeed the Messiah, the one who can communicate with God as genuine interlocutor. Saint Paul will rightly describe him as the Image of the Father. But at the same time he demands from himself and from his future disciples absolute self-renunciation, that obedience unto the death of the cross which is the condition of universal brotherly love. What is essential is absolute fidelity to the creatural condition, acceptance of the human predicament. In order to imitate the Father, Jesus does not seek to elevate himself in any way from the creatural state. On the contrary he views this state with the maximum of lucidity and embraces it with the maximum of obedience.

It is because he is man-God, the incarnate Word, that he can reconcile the two extremes of the paradox: the Image of the Father and the full creatural state. Because he is the Son "he can do nothing of himself that he does not see the Father doing" (Jn 5:19); whatever he says is "what he has seen with his Father" (Jn 8:38). Because of the hypostatic union the perfect harmony of his activity with that of the Father overflows into his humanity. Thus he is the man who imitates the Father perfectly, without ceasing to be man. This is the secret of human salvation.

The great expression of his imitation of the Father is the event of the cross. We recall that pagan man in his attempt to imitate divine models sought security. He sought through his liturgies to evade profane time and space. Now, there is no such attempt at evasion, no grasping at security in human terms. There is simple acceptance of the event that leads to lucid self-renunciation, the event that immerses in radical insecurity. In the sacrifice of the cross Jesus carries imitation of the Father to its peak point; he reveals the essential nature of double love, which is the source of salvation.

The Church and imitation of Jesus Christ

What Jesus accomplished once for all on the cross he continues to accomplish in his Church through the members of his Body. Salvation history and that of imitation of the Father has been begun in the New Adam. It goes on through generation after generation, but the shape it takes will depend on the quality of active contribution by Church members. For the members, imitation of the Father necessarily comes by way of imitation of Christ. There is no salvation except in Christ, and he who wishes to be saved, or play his role in the salvation of humanity, must follow Christ in his Passion (Jn 13:36 and 1 P 2:21).

What do we mean by this imitation of Christ? It will be necessary first of all to become conformed to his image, which presupposes ecclesial intervention in baptism. This is what introduces us to Christ's Body and enables us to act as adoptive children of the Father, through the link with Christ. The Church's function however does not cease there; it will be constantly required for our proper development. To act as adoptive children we must be always in touch with the sources of interior grace and be modelled by the sacraments and the Word.

The effect of ecclesial action upon us is constantly to protect us against the temptation of evasion, to make each one open to the event and to what God wishes from him. These will be the events of daily life, of whatever kind, which prove a challenge to our faith and are our means of demonstrating acceptance of the creatural condition. Imitation of Christ does not consist of following a predetermined schedule. It means a total acceptance of what happens; it means traveling the road of the Passion, which, is the Event *par excellence*.

Our imitation has nothing to do with conformism. There is no question of trying to reproduce exactly this or that attitude of his. It means taking his lucid view of reality, being open as he was to the event. In a way it is more inventiveness than imitation. The event will always be unique; so too the believer's reaction will have to be. We should always be asking ourselves whether our response has this quality.

Imitation of the Father and missionary witness

Just because modern man has ceased to be the religious creature he used to be, Christians in their witness are sometimes tempted to subordinate their imitation of the Father to the service they must render humanity. There are indeed colossal human tasks confronting us all; peace, world development, social and international justice, etc. If we are to have impact as Christians, must we not first assume our responsibilities in the collective effort for which modern man knows himself to be equipped?

This is a subtle temptation of which we must beware. If we succumb, Christian witness runs the risk of losing its whole *raison d'etre,* and indeed it loses its savor even for modern man himself. If imitation of the Father is to be the essence of our witness, we must behave as sons of God, and at the same time show superlative acceptance of the creatural condition. We must demonstrate that Jesus Christ the man gives an eternal dimension to human activity, without ever changing its human quality. For that matter we are often wrong in thinking that modern man is so preoccupied with earthly responsibilities that he has smothered his yearning for the absolute. He just differs from his predecessor in channeling his sense of the absolute into the human tasks themselves. For him they are not purely "temporal" tasks. When we assume our due responsibilities in this field, we should show by our attitude the true state of things. Far from wishing to curb the deployment of purely human resources to the full, the child of God will be absolutely open to the task of human progress.

We should also remember that the men of our time will only appreciate the quality of our work for human progress, if we show a scrupulous respect for the rules of the game. The task depends not alone on the inspiration behind it, but also on the manner of its execution at various levels; political, social, economic, etc. Here we Christians, like everyone else, should undergo the necessary training. If not, we can have little hope of accomplishing the ultimate objectives.

Imitation of the Father in the eucharistic celebration

The great eucharistic prayer is concluded by a joint recitation, on the part of celebrant and faithful, of the Our Father. All express their desire to imitate the Father by imitating the Savior: "As we have learned from the Savior . . . we dare to say " "Father, forgive us our offenses as we forgive those who have offended against us." Which is to say "Father, allow us, in Jesus Christ to extend to all men the pardon You have granted us."

The eucharistic celebration should as a rule make everyone conscious of the unending actuality of God's pardon. We should feel the urge to make his gesture towards us a blanket for all wrongs. When we partake of the Eucharist, we are established in the charity of Christ, which is the perfect imitation of the Father. This result will not come automatically. Proclamation of the Word will be highly important; Scripture readings and the celebrant's homily must make the message actual. The actual structure of the celebration is important likewise. All present should be conscious of their diversity in unity, should feel the dimension of openness, and take their group as a microcosm of the whole.

2. Theme of Justification

A people's spiritual odyssey is a profoundly complex proceeding. It is an adventure that engages the very depth of their being and colors the whole texture of their daily life. In search of the great goal men will turn in various directions. Some directions will seem promising; other trails sooner or later will vanish in nothingness. Throughout the whole pilgrimage a subtle bond gets forged between the group as a whole and the individuals who compose it, particularly certain individuals. Religious leaders get thrown up, who provide a new insight about the road to be traveled. The community will either follow them or reject them. Language is affected by the whole development. Terms are coined to describe experience and the idiom is powerfully enriched. Or on the other hand the religious terms themselves may grow old and tired and finally disappear.

When this quest finally penetrates to faith, the effect upon religious language is particularly noticeable. It seems indeed to be transformed utterly. The vocabulary of justice and justification is a case in point. Jewish history indicates that the journey towards faith was long and arduous, and language only adapted itself gradually to the insights. Likewise the spread of Christianity throughout the world was destined to reshape the religious language of many peoples.

Divine justice and human justice in Israel

Man's natural desire for security was translated, in all primitive societies, into a scrupulous respect for the norms and customs which traditionally governed both social relationships and relationship with the gods. To assure a sacral stability, the community would exercise judiciary power over its members. It exacted respect for law and justified the innocent. Thus juridical and moral norms governing behavior were developed in an essentially religious context.

It was so originally in Israel; but the gradual growth in faith slowly transformed this context, so as to make it almost unrecognizable. To begin with Yahweh was the supreme Judge; he rewarded the good and punished the wicked. What initiated the Jew to the order of divine justice and enabled him to share the holiness of God was observance of the Law. Deeper insight in faith begins to change the language about justice and justification. The basic structure was maintained; but an order of justice that answered to security needs begins to yield to an order of mercy that answers to faith. The religious horizons of Israel are widened.

The disconcerting discovery came, when it was realized that the event was the point *par excellence* of encounter with God. Yahweh is the Totally-Other and the Creator of all things. Man has no valid rights before him. Everything that Yahweh does for his creature is a gratuitous expression of benevolence. He alone can save man, and it becomes more and more clear that salvation is a gift beyond all human reach. God's intervention to deliver man from sin is not a recompense for merit, but a demonstration that he is a God of mercy, tenderness and pardon.

The recognition of the Totally-Other God goes *pari passu* with the realization that man cannot merit salvation. Such justice as can be achieved by observance of the law is empty by contrast with the salvation Yahweh has reserved for his people, and which alone can fulfill them. Man realizes that he is indeed a creature of paradox. The relation to God that is kindled by faith, and which is man's proper destiny, cannot be reduced to the moral order. Divine justice and human justice stand in contrast to one another. Only abandonment to God can bring a man to salvation. Thus all eyes are turned to the messianic future; who is the one who can resolve the paradox?

Jesus of Nazareth and the justice of the Kingdom

The Messiah's intervention did not, in that sense, resolve the paradox, but rather intensified it. It is true that the order of faith and the moral order have not a common basis; but when the latter is brought to perfection in the new law of universal love, it opens the way to the order of faith and salvation.

By contrast with the formalism and hypocrisy of the Pharisees, Jesus reveals the unexplored riches of the authentic mosaic tradition. He has not come to abolish the law, but to fulfill it. The fulfillment is universal brotherly love, into which the law is transmuted, when it is observed with fidelity to the event, and constant acceptance of the will of the living God. The Beatitudes are the charter of the New Covenant. It is only for the poor, the gentle and the humble that the new law of love becomes possible. These are the people who do not seek to quench their thirst for the absolute with any created good, who do not seek to possess anything, but abandon themselves to God in absolute confidence.

Jesus demanded this total abandonment; but he also announced the advent of the Kingdom. Man was given salvation, the Father's gratuitous gift. If he had to abandon himself to God, it was in order to become God's adoptive son and have his yearnings satisfied. Fidelity to the new law of love is the fidelity of a member of God's own family .

The Father's Kingdom is inaugurated in the person of Jesus. The absolute renunciation he demands from himself, full acceptance of the creatural condition, he demands from his brethren too. Thus speaks the Savior of the World. The one who proclaims himself Savior of humanity is the very one who experiences the human predicament at its utmost depths. This could only be possible for the Son of God. God so loved the world that he gave his only-begotten son, and in him found the perfect creatural and filial response.

Justified by faith in Jesus Christ

It took the primitive community many years to see all the implications of Jesus' intervention. At first apostolic preaching stresses the eschatological dimension of the Kingdom that goes on being awaited. Saint Paul's early letters reflect this mentality where the order of judgment prevails. Very soon however Christians began to see the real meaning of their link with the Risen Christ. Instead of the Kingdom to come, they see the Kingdom that has already come, and must be built here on earth. Christian waiting is translated from passivity into mission. All believers are called to be God's partners in constructing his Kingdom.

It was under Paul's influence that the vocabulary of justice and justification received a specifically Christian coloring. Justification, salvation that is, is an actuality here and now. It is not indeed the product of human justice, based on human resources, but neither is it a purely eschatological entity. The Christian is a man genuinely justified by faith in Jesus Christ. He is justified, because this faith makes him an adoptive son, and opens for him the way to the Father. His justification is God's gift, but it becomes for him the principle of filial activity.

The justification of all peoples in Jesus Christ
The terminology of justice and justification comes from Jewish religious experience. It served to clarify, in the hands of Saint Paul, the nature of the salvation we acquired in Jesus Christ. But its importance is not confined to this. The very development of this terminology describes the stages by which one comes to faith, and it is of great pedagogic value. The actual words of course are relatively unimportant; but the expression of the meaning they enshrine, in any new idiom, is a matter of the utmost delicacy.

All peoples evangelized by the Church are already at some stage in the spiritual quest, and it is the missionary's task to assess this correctly. The proclamation of the Good News must meet this precise moment. All the spiritual quests, when we examine the language that expresses them, are invariably attempts to articulate in some way the moral and religious orders. In the non-Christian ones, we can discern a notion of collective and individual morality, through which it is hoped human aspirations will be fulfilled. Moral conduct has an immediate religious reference; salvation will come by this means. The traditional pagan always sought thus to insert himself into the cosmic harmony, the stability of which was assured by the sovereign deities.

From this to the faith in Jesus Christ there are two stages, that we know from the history of Israel to be successive. First must come the recognition of the Totally-Other God, the God of faith, with all that this implies by way of adjustment in normal life and culture. This will gradually bring about an awareness of the radical distinction between the religious and moral orders, however closely they be linked. The religious order is essentially one of mercy. Man does indeed have an intuition that salvation depends on God's gratuitous initiative, that, at this ultimate level, moral performance is really without efficacy. His awareness of sin sharpens his sensibility; he sees that it is the ultimate blindness. When the first stage has been absorbed, then comes the second. This is the recognition of the mystery of Christ in whom the order of faith is thoroughly accomplished. It is only in him that the relationship between the religious and the moral orders is properly articulated. In him a new people is enabled to make a specific contribution to the building of the Kingdom.

Our experience of justification in the Eucharist

The Christian awareness of justification is deepest during the eucharistic celebration. Those assembled are conscious of responding to a divine summons to salvation, conscious that their thanksgiving depends on the ecclesial link with Christ that makes them members of his Body. The marvels of God can be properly changed only by the children of God.

Sharing the Word and the Bread proves the best channel of the grace manifested once for all in Jesus Christ. It should constantly draw the faithful towards conversion from their sin, and towards conduct as children of God in the tenor of their daily lives. It should summon them to that total interior poverty, with which as adoptive children they must follow the first-born Brother in the way of obedience. But at the same time it makes them conscious of the grandeur of their filial state. Because they are justified by faith in Jesus Christ, they are God's partners in the building of the Kingdom, and they must honor that responsibility here below. The Eucharist too will strengthen the bonds of universal brotherhood that are symbolized in the assembly itself. It is such bonds that will bear witness to their constant fidelity day after day. This ecclesial sign must never cease to glow before the eyes of men.

THIRTY-FIRST SUNDAY

A. THE WORD

I. Malachi 1:14- The anonymous (malachi means "messen-
2:2, 8-10 ger") author of the collection under this name
1st reading lived during the 5th century, after the recon-
1st cycle struction of the temple, but a little prior to
Esdras' reform. The people had expected
everything from this new temple, but in fact nothing had
changed. The prophet, in the name of the people, inveighs vehe-
mently against the clergy (Ml 1:6–2:9). He considers them responsible for the political and moral decadence. They do not offer
sacrifice with hands sufficiently clean to win divine benevolence.
The shortcomings of the priests however do not excuse the laxity
of the people (v. 14), and the second pamphlet is directed against
these (Ml 2:10-16). Clergy and people have in fact taken shelter in
cult from the strictures of the prophets. Malachi seeks to bring
them forth from this ghetto.

The attack upon the Levites recalls the particular *covenant* between God and Levi (Dt 33:8-11; cf. Jr 33:18-22). This tribe had
engaged to render not alone liturgical service, but also to teach
the law (v. 7). The Levites however have betrayed their mission,
and scandalized believers by lax interpretations. They have led
the people into attitudes contrary to the law (v. 8).

Chatisement will come swiftly. Whenever the covenant is vio-
lated, the priests lose the respect of the people. Their influence
wanes and their prophetic role is challenged (v. 9).

227

II. Deuteronomy It is rather extraordinary to find the most
  6:2-6 explicit affirmative about the love of God in
  1st reading a legislative context. They are furthermore
  2nd cycle relatively numerous, either in the heart of the
  legislative code itself (Dt 13:4; 19:9), the
introductory discourses (Dt 5:10; 6:5; 7:9; 10:12; 11:1, 13, 22),
or the final exhortation (Dt 30:16, 20). Verses 4-5 may well belong to the most primitive redaction of Deuteronomy.

a) The *love of God* enjoined is primarily concerned with cultic fidelity. To love God means in the first place that one does not worship other gods (cf. Dt 6:5, 14-15; 11:13, 16-17; 13:2-3; 30:16-18). The cultic relations of the people to God are indeed often described in terms of love (cf. Ho 1-4). Thus the Deuteronomic emphasis is normal.

However, in Deuteronomy, we have also the exercise of love towards God by obeying his precepts. It should be remembered that today's reading gives us the most fundamental affirmations in Hebrew ethics. Furthermore, the insistence that love of God must be expressed not alone exteriorly, but interiorly ("with all the heart, with all the soul" . . . v. 5; cf. Dt 10:12; 11:13; 13:3) envisages a total, personal love unknown in previous legislation. Finally, the precept is formulated in the second person singular (v. 5; cf. Dt 10:12; 30:6) in order to stress the personal aspect still more. This interpretation makes the love enjoined by Deuteronomy the sort of "love" that was normal in contemporary near-Eastern contracts between a suzerain and his vassals. It required fidelity, loyalty and obedience. The note of affection then, in reality, is not present. The Deuteronomic concept of the love of God is still too close to juridical and cultic origins to be comparable with the New Testament concept, or even indeed with that of Hosea or Jeremiah.

b) Our passage constitutes the beginning of the Jewish prayer; Schema Israel (Hear, O Israel) which was recited by be-toward such peoples the *love* that God himself was constantly ready to give.

IV. 1 Thessa-   Paul continues with the description of his
     lonians   apostolic ministry. Having established his link
     2:7-9, 13   with the prophetic tradition of the Old Testa-
     2nd reading   ment (1 Th 2:1-6), he now discusses the par-
     1st cycle   ticular character of his mission to the Gentiles.

a) An unusual *tenderness* characterizes Paul's evangelization of the Thessalonians. He finds himself at a loss in language. He feels the gentleness and warmth of a kind superior (v. 7). The concerned affection of a mother (v. 7), tenderness that goes the length of offering one's life (v. 8). Most of this language is hellenistic, showing no trace of Old Testament sources. It is a clear indication of the distance between his debt to judaism, and what he derives from his missionary experience, in communicating God's love to the Gentiles.

b) The most important thing in the passage is the image of *spiritual paternity*. It is a theme that will be developed more explicitly still in 1 Corinthians 4:14-21, but here the main lines are already determined in his mention of fatherhood where the Thessalonians are concerned (v. 11). He also borrows from the Old Testament the image of a nurse (vv. 7-8; cf. Ex 4:22; Ho 11:3-4; Is 49:15; Si 4:10) to describe his mission there. Determined as he is not to play the role of philosopher or propagandist, to distinguish his preaching from pedagogy in the ordinary way (1 Co 4:14-21), he sees his missionary activity as a transmission of life, the life to which God summons men. This becomes the source of his best imagery.

Furthermore, he associates his person with his message. By his attitude, his sufferings, his zeal, he himself is a transmission of the gospel, a summons to life. In that sense he is ready to assimilate himself to a father or a mother. He is like them a giver of the divine gift of life. No paternalism is suggested. This is a fatherhood that claims nothing for itself, that refers everything to God, the unique source of life.

V. Hebrews
7:23-28
2nd reading
2nd cycle

Here we have the conclusion of the proof of the superiority of Christ's priesthood to the levitic. In particular it emphasizes that Jesus does not stem from Levi, but belongs to the order of Melchisedech (Ps 109/110). His priesthood depends on his quality as Son and Lord (Ps 2:7). It corresponds to God's oath (v. 28).

In the verses preceding our passage (vv. 20-22) the oath has already been mentioned. The author does not now discern it in the promises to Abraham (He 7:6-7), but in the promise of Psalm 109/110:4, which is here cited for the fourth time in Hebrews 7 (cf. v. 21, and the references in vv. 24 and 28). But in this instance the reference is abbreviated, and Melchisedech is no longer mentioned. The main interest has become, not Melchisedech, but the *oath.* The Lord has sworn (v. 21).

The lines of argument are normal.

(1) A priesthood guarantee by divine oath is the pledge of a covenant greater than the former, which was not based on any oath of God (vv. 20-22).

(2) A priesthood associated with such an oath cannot but be eternal (cf. Ps 109/110:4; vv. 23-25, a repetition vv. 15-17). The eternity of the Risen Lord guarantees the eternity of his priesthood (v. 24), by contrast with the transitory character of the former priesthood. Christ's priesthood then is always operative, always making intercession for us.

(3) The new priesthood is that of Christ in glory (vv. 26-28), the priesthood of the Son (v. 28). Because the Son is forever exalted, the priesthood is once for all inaugurated, and eternal.

Men are not capable of carving out a path to God. The organization of a cult, where genuine encounter does not take place and where there is no radical deliverance from sin, is doomed to failure. Christ brings men into real communion with God. By his ascension and enthronement as Lord his human nature is in a real sense drawn into godhood, and this was wrought in the very impasse of death and surrender of existence. The Christian when he shares the Eucharist, which is the commemoration of this moment, and is under the presidency of ministers who guarantee its link with the Lord's death and enthronement, is assured of the impact of this priesthood in his own life. He has achieved the genuine encounter with God which transforms.

VI. 2 Thessa-   Paul is allaying the misgivings of his audience
   lonians   about the manner and time of the Lord's
   1:11-2:2   coming. Christians of Jewish origin saw this
   2nd reading   event as a gathering of the nations in
   3rd cycle   "assembly" with Christ (Mt 24:31; 2 M 2:7).
                    The Thessalonians, however, are confused by
prophecies, and affirmations attributed to Paul himself (v. 2), concerning the imminence of the Day of Yahweh.

The attitude recommended by the apostle is one of *prayer* above all (v. 11). This is the only means of avoiding the confusion raised by false rumors. It makes a man aware of the power of God at work in his life. It begets confidence, and enables the true awaiter of the Kingdom to read correctly the signs of the times.

VII. Matthew   This passage is the introduction to the male-
   23:1-12   dictions on the scribes and Pharisees (Mt
   Gospel   23:12-32). From the second verse onwards
   1st cycle   Jesus confronts his adversaries. They usurp
                    the chair of Moses. The Law had provided
that only the priests should teach and interpret the Word of God

(Dt 17:8-12; 31:9-10; Mi 3:11; MP 2:7-10). By so doing they have brought about a radical change in religion. For faith in the Word they have substituted intellectual procedures, for obedience to God's plan juridical and casuistic procedures. In cursing them, Jesus is rejecting such an ungodly concept of religion.

Verses 8-10 are peculiar to Matthew. They are connected with the previous verses by the *soubriquet Rabbi;* and there is a ternary rhythm, punctuated by the words "Master," "Father," "Teacher" (or, better perhaps, "Director"). It is not so much the titles that Jesus condemns, but the kind of religion they suggest, that of exegetes and professors. One cannot reach God by relying on professors.

The two final verses are misplaced in this context (cf. Mt 20:26).

What Jesus is concerned with here is the *hypocrisy* of the scribes and leaders of the synagogue. This consists essentially in deceiving others by religious gestures or assumed sacral prerogatives. Honors are arrogated which indicate that one is God's representative (vv. 6-7). Such a one seems to render worship to God, but actually he is merely aggrandizing himself (v. 5), perverting the most religious practices away from their meaning as acts of faith (cf. Mt 6:2, 5, 16). The hypocrite will minister to his own egoism with his theological knowledge. He will use casuistry to select among precepts those that suit his convenience, to impose commandments on others from which he dispenses himself (v. 4; cf. Mt 23:24-25).

The chief sin of the hypocritical scribes is that they usurp the place of God by assuming a power they do not deserve (vv. 8-10; cf. Mt 15:3-14), drawing to themselves a faith and confidence that should be shown only towards God.

The brand of hypocrisy that Jesus denounced has always remained a temptation throughout Church history. We can discern its influence in the attitude of clergy to laity, but perhaps more still in that of the faithful towards other human beings. Today's gospel has a moral for us all.

The important thing to remember is that the Church can never regard herself as the definitive goal. She proclaims the Kingdom, but she is not yet the Kingdom. She can never make herself the center of her own preaching. The world must strive not towards her, but towards the Kingdom. She should never then bind the faithful with insupportable burdens; she should be concentrated on building the future. She should eschew all pride. Her responsible officers should scrupulously avoid all the usual means by which people seek power; diplomatic intrigue, political pressure, honorific titles, etc. At all times the Church must realize that her business is to serve.

A Church that becomes forgetful of her own sin inevitably becomes hard of heart, preoccupied with her own justice, the herald of misfortune and catastrophe. She deserves the maledictions that were directed against the proud scribes. Good and evil are in fact juxtaposed in the hearts of all; it is only the mercy of God that has maintained the Church in existence.*

VIII. Mark 12:28-34 Gospel 2nd cycle   Jesus has just encountered the principal *demarches* made against him by the Jewish sects. Specifically, he has evaded the trap laid by the Pharisees concerning the tribute (Mk 12:13-17), and he has answered the question about the resurrection of the dead (Mk 12:18-27). Now he is approached by a scribe concerning the greatest commandment. Where Matthew suggests a hostile bias in this episode (Mt 22:34-46), Mark curiously enough implies good dispositions on the scribe's part, and a desire for enlightenment. He is the only one to place on Jesus' lips a eulogy of the man (v. 34). One inclines to the

*See the doctrinal theme: *hypocrisy*, p. 238.

view that the synoptics wanted to combine a number of polemic episodes in a single section. Mark may have done this more awkwardly than the others, and allowed some details to stand, that were authentic no doubt, but contrary to the otherwise polemic purpose.

Jesus answers the question by affirming the two commandments of *love* (vv. 29-31), though he was asked for one only. The text of the first comes from Deuteronomy 6:4-5, but according to the version used for Jewish morning and evening prayer. The second follows Leviticus 19:18.

Mark's account makes the precepts distinct, whereas Matthew and Luke either combine them or just give one. Mark has not reached this stage, but follows the Jewish practice of juxtaposing the two as a resume of the law. He is the only one to recount the scribe's commentary on the two. Then, where Matthew has the affirmation that love is the key to the law, he has Jesus tell the scribe that it is the key to cult that is pleasing to God (v. 33; cf. Am. 5:21; 1 S 15:22).*

IX. Luke
19:1-10
Gospel
3rd cycle

Luke is the only one to give us the Zacchaeus episode. It fits in very well with his views about riches, and about Jesus' relationship with sinners. It is the last of a series of episodes which stress Luke's personal attitudes. We have the parable of the Pharisee and the publican. Both pray in the Temple, but only the publican is justified (peculiar to the third Gospel, Lk 18:9-14). Then there is the incident of the "small" children whom the disciples snub as unworthy to participate with the adults. Jesus welcomes them (Lk 18:15-17). The "rich man" cannot enter the Kingdom because he clings to his

*See the doctrinal theme: *double love*, p. 244.

riches (Lk 18:18-27). The blind man of Jericho, illumined by
faith, is cured, by contrast with the disciples who "do not understand" the words of the Lord (Lk 18:31-43).

a) In the Zacchaeus episode we have all of these emphases
conjoined. Jericho, which houses Zacchaeus, is a city accursed
(Lk 18:31-43). He is a rich publican (Lk 18:18-27 and 9-14),
small of stature (Lk 18:15-17). These characteristics, for Jesus,
are titles to the salvation he is bringing sinners and the *weak*.
The crowd understands him in this way and murmurs: "He has
come to eat with sinners" (cf. Lk 5:30; 15:2).

b) Still however, at least for Luke, there remains an obstacle
to Zacchaeus' salvation; his *riches*. Luke regarded actual poverty
as a prerequisite for the Kingdom. It was the obstacle that the
"rich man" could not overcome (Lk 18:9-14). Zacchaeus however
removes the obstacle himself. He repays fourfold all of his debtors and gives half of his goods to the poor. Fourfold restitution
is contemplated in one instance only in the law, and that extremely grave (Ex 21:37). By extending it to himself Zacchaeus
is punishing himself very rigorously and exhibiting magnanimity.
The gesture of giving half his goods to the poor is one that Luke
expects from all the rich who want to enter the Kingdom. In the
Acts he stresses the magnanimity and significance of this.

c) Verse 9 was probably the original conclusion of the episode, that given by Jesus himself. The house of Zacchaeus receives
salvation because the conditions are fulfilled. The title that he
gives Zacchaeus, *son of Abraham,* makes this concrete. It was a
title reserved to themselves by the Jews as being the only heirs
to the promises (Lk 3:8; Rm 4:11-25; Ga 3:7-29). Zacchaeus, if he
is not actually a Gentile, has been affected by paganism. Jesus
then is widening the concept of a son of Abraham, and laying the
basis of a theme that Paul was to develop. It is not carnal membership of the line of Abraham that gives true sonship, but the
faith properly lived. We have a preview of the great Pauline
themes about the seed of Abraham, the predominance of the

B. DOCTRINE

1. Theme of Hypocrisy

It is frequently alleged that hypocrisy is more common among Christians than among other men. No one questions the nobility of the Christian ideal, but people do wonder why Christians profess to follow it, while continuing to perpetrate the same injustices. They pretend to be better than they actually are. Why for instance is lying so very prevalent among Christians?

The situation does indeed seem paradoxical. If there is a single point on which Jesus seems altogether intractable, it is certainly this—hypocrisy. Pharisaic hypocrisy that is, the attitude of people who thought themselves superior, and were thought superior, as the spiritual guides of Israel (today's gospel, 1st cycle). The gospels would lead us to believe that the greatest obstacle blocking us from the road Jesus wants us to follow is precisely hypocrisy. How then explain that something so roundly condemned continues to be evident among Christians, more evident perhaps than elsewhere? Is it in fact perhaps the greatest temptation that besets believers, the temptation guarding the last hurdle we must surmount in order to understand the mystery of Jesus Christ?

It is highly important for us to have a proper understanding of Jesus' violent reaction to this vice, and to ask ourselves what relevance his invectives could have for us, now. What is at stake is proper insight about our faith. The theme is also very timely, in a world where men are more than ever sensitive about honesty in attitudes and behavior.

The prophets and hypocrisy in worship

The quest for happiness in traditional pagan religions was always spelt out in terms of security. The great desire was to touch as much as possible the stable sacral world. Cultic procedures seemed the best way of doing this; such rites seemed to escape the fluidity and vicissitudes of history. Cult of the gods became a value in itself and the rites were something to be performed with scrupulous exactitude. The rite itself would provide the sacral security provided all its details were deserved. Formalism in liturgies consequently was *de rigueur*. The rite itself was the meaningful thing; its link with moral performance was not perceived. The established order of moral conduct was governed by custom and law.

Under the regime of faith another insight was gradually developed. Yahweh continued to expect liturgical cult from his people; but he also made moral and social demands of deeper and deeper import for the daily conduct of life. Cult was not agreeable to him except insofar as the other obligations were honored, so that it ceased to be thought of as a value in itself. Rites continued to have their importance but formalism in cult soon comes to be denounced as hypocrisy by which Yahweh is not deceived. "These people honor me with their lips." The prophets keep repeating that what the living God requires is sacrifice of the heart. Fidelity to the covenant is to be demonstrated above all in the conduct of life.

The great prophetic achievement really is not so much the stress on the moral requirements of the covenant. It is that they launched Israel on an unprecedented road of interiorization and integration of daily existence. They should be regarded in this domain as authentic champions of human liberty. The proper goal of human liberty was not the security the pagans sought. The moral fidelity which the prophets promoted is fidelity in confrontation with the event, and consequently a constant voyage of discovery. It was natural that such a doctrine should lead to the discrediting of lip service and the illusory security this offered. Any believer who followed this path was no more than a hypocrite.

Jesus' denunciation of pharisaic hypocrisy

The violence of Jesus' denunciation is at first glance rather surprising. The Pharisees, comprising all the scribes and doctors of the law, plus a certain number of priests, must have formed a group of about six thousand at that time. Their purpose was to preserve among their members a fervent fidelity to the law. They were looked up to by the people as spiritual leaders. It was here that Jesus encountered the most intractable opposition. Other groups like the Sadducees or the priestly caste opposed him too but for more or less opportunist reasons. It is to the Pharisees, regarded as faithful observers of the law, that Jesus addresses the most cutting rebuke possible, the charge of hypocrisy. He does so in such terms that there can be no doubt that he regarded his essential message as being at stake.

We must not forget that the Pharisee was a personally involved believer. He was very well aware that fidelity to the covenant could not be reduced to ritual cult, that there were precise moral requirements. He knew the most important precepts of the Law, those concerned with justice and mercy. However the fear of being lost, of having to appear empty-handed before God; the reluctance to follow the path of self-renunciation; pride in a word, a very subtle pride, led this man to reintroduce the old notion of security into the very structure of faith. In search of this security nothing could be more simple than to degrade fidelity to the faith to legal observance. Inevitably the consequences followed. The Pharisee automatically took himself to be better than others. His refinements of casuistry reinforced this attitude. Where others found themselves hopelessly entangled and loaded with observances, he was able when necessary to manipulate the essentials of the law. His hypocrisy is manifest. He lies to himself and he deceives others. He seems to manifest genuine fidelity towards Yahweh, but his brand of religion is really foreign to the concept of faith. Instead of leading men to God, he is turning their gaze toward himself. His object is to be noticed, even when he has ceased to realize this himself.

It is the perversion that explains Jesus' violence. Nothing is more foreign to the religion of love than legalism of this kind and its consequences. There is no more corrosive temptation. Once it is admitted, the dynamism of faith is strangled, even while the appearances are maintained. Jesus felt it to be essential that this be unmasked.

The permanent risk of hypocrisy among the faithful

Hypocrisy among Christians is still more reprehensible than among the Pharisees. It comes at the time of fulfillment, where the Pharisees belonged to the time of preparation. True, they prevented the Jewish people from crossing the threshold that would lead to recognition of the veritable Messiah. But contortion of the proper image of the Kingdom that Jesus inaugurated is a greater crime. Christians are no more immune to the risk of hypocrisy than the Jews were. The subtle pride that leads to it is still at work.

It was the hypocrisy of the spiritual guides that Jesus denounced. In the Church too the hypocrisy most to be feared is that of leaders. Remember the Antioch incident between Peter and Paul. "His (Peter's) custom had been to eat with the pagans, but after certain friends of James arrived, he stopped doing this and kept away from them altogether for fear of the group that insisted on circumcision" (Ga 2:12). Paul, in these ambiguous circumstances, does not hesitate to charge him with hypocrisy. In fact an essential dimension of Christianity was at stake, its universalism. Peter's attitude was countenancing the view, very widespread among disciples of the Risen Lord, that only converted Jews, who observed the Law, were genuine Christians. They were superior to others. The damage was aggravated by the fact that Peter was considered by all the first of the apostles, the authoritative interpreter of the wishes of the Lord. To yield thus to the Judaizers is, for Paul, a betrayal of what Christ accomplished. Nothing less is at stake.

Today, as then, the greatest possible danger is precisely what Saint Paul denounced. Often enough we talk rather subjectively about hypocrisy, as if conscious perversity were essential to the notion. This is not at all true, at least not always. Some Pharisees, who listened to Jesus' denunciation, must have thought themselves wronged. Their intentions after all were good. It is probably that Peter at Antioch thought he was acting for the best. The hypocrisy in question is really something objective. Anyone in the Church who by act or word disseminates a false idea of what Christianity is, and misleads others, is a hypocrite. The idea he disseminates may seem to offer more security, but it jeopardizes the whole dimension of universalism.

Hypocrisy and proselytism

In the denunciation of the Pharisees there is one sentence which no missionary should ever forget, "Alas for you, scribes and Pharisees, you hypocrites. You who travel over sea and land to make a single proselyte and when you have him you make him twice as fit for hell as you are" (Mt 23:15). To understand this seemingly enigmatic sentiment, we have to see it in the general context of the denunciations.

During the time of Jesus, the most zealous Jews of the Diaspora labored very assiduously to make proselytes and swell the ranks of the chosen people. It was understood that in order to serve the living God a necessary preliminary was acceptance of the mosaic law, above all the precept of the circumcision. Following the pharisaic lead, entry to judaism meant that outsiders had a quantity of customs and observances imposed on them that were altogether foreign to them and indeed to the essentials of faith. The true visage of Yahweh was being obscured. However the worst aspect, the one that Jesus emphasizes, was that the new state of the convert Gentile was worse than the first. The legalism with which he was confronted, as a prerequisite for following the living God, seemed to him more insupportable than to a native Jew. In many cases he had to begin to dissimulate.

It is evident from Church history that this sort of thing can always recur. Whenever mission becomes proselytism and the Church a synagogue, converts find that their last state is worse than the first. They should have been shown that the mystery of Christ is actually the fulfillment of the spiritual quest of their own people and that Saint Paul's law of liberty is basic. In fact they were uprooted from their cultural tradition and made to follow laws and customs that had more to do with western civilization than the essentials of the faith. In such an atmosphere western Christians inevitably began to feel superior to their brothers in Asia and Africa. Just now this particular balance is rather better than it used to be. But the temptation to hypocrisy is a subtle one and none of us should ever feel that we are immune.

The denunciation of hypocrisy and the eucharistic celebration

In Christian tradition the link between rite and life has always been so close, that cultic conformism is invariably condemned as unworthy of the believer. The fact that moral doctrine has tended to prevail over dogma in sermons indicates the anxiety to make the assembled faithful model their lives on the faith they were celebrating. Nevertheless it is possible that there has not been sufficient emphasis on the more subtle forms of hypocrisy that Jesus and Paul denounced. We have often enough, heaven knows, had a recrudescence in the very bosom of the Church of these pharisaic and judaeo-Christian attitudes. They are ubiquitous and never-ending, and they always jeopardize the basic gospel message.

Leaders in the Church must indeed exercise particular care. In their case hypocrisy becomes particularly grave. As Jesus pointed out, pharisaic hypocrisy involved others in the lie. The truth of Christianity does not admit any compromise or any limitations. Those who have the duty of proclaiming it must acknowledge that they are sinners, launched on the great adventure of love, which is without horizon. Hypocrisy can have no place there.

gard oneself as central. One deliberately chose a "justice" that was of God, not of men. One accepted the creatural condition, with all this meant in terms of relationship to the Creator and to other men.

Thus Israel's experience led to insight about love of God and love of one's neighbor. If Yahweh loves his people, and displays particular benevolence towards the little ones and the poor; if he maintains fidelity in spite of sin on the part of his faithful, man's duty is to follow this example in dealing with his fellows. It is by following God's example that one comes to know him. One cannot love God without being interested in men, respecting them, being concerned about the poor and disadvantaged.

But, in the very concept of the neighbor, we can discern the limits of Jewish universalism. Because of Israel's conviction about being a people apart, her consciousness of election in terms of privileges, the neighbor had to be one of the chosen people. Her attitude towards the Gentile was different. She recognized God as Creator, master of the destiny of all nations, but not to the extent of universal fatherhood. She did not learn the lesson of brotherly love without limits. Without total renunciation the lesson cannot be learned.

The indissoluble link, in Jesus, between the two loves

In Jesus, the two loves came together. The inadequacies of the old covenant were surmounted. The true dimensions of human salvation were clarified.

The key to salvation, it became clear, was love; not any sort of love, but love that was immersed in the mystery of God. The basic principle of this love is the perfect reciprocity between Father and Son, which is expressed in the person of the Holy Spirit. It was in the name of this love that the Father sent the Son to reconcile all humanity into his own Family.

Jesus was the perfect exponent of this love. He loved the Father with the love with which he was loved, and thus became God's partner in the realization of the divine plan for humanity.

Because of the Incarnation this love was spread to all humanity, who were his brothers. In the Father's Family the same law governs all relationships. All are recognized by the man-God as adoptive sons.

Such are the dimensions of the love manifested in Jesus Christ. By his Incarnation the love he demonstrated became rooted in humanity. Filial love for the Father and universal brotherly love were fused in his way of obedience even to the death of the cross. The total self-renunciation required by this obedience springs from filial love that is creatural, and from a total acceptance of the other, in all his otherness, even if he be an enemy.

It was by demonstrating this indissoluble link between love for the Father and love for men that Jesus brought about salvation. He invites us, in him, to enter the Family of the Father, to live there as sons, and to find there our fellowmen as brothers. It is thus that we come to see what our creaturehood really means, and what its possibilities are. When Love became incarnate the order of creation was seen for what it truly is in the mind of God.

The Church the sacrament of double love

The link with Christ is of primal importance for every man. It is the only avenue to saving love. Our destiny is to love God with the filial love of partners and all our fellowmen as brothers. Love of such quality is only possible for the man-God, and we can only reach it on this earth by joining ourselves to him as unique mediator. This we do by entering the Church which is his Body. Our baptism gives us the capacity, provided we take the means, of loving as he loved.

We should be very clear about this. The love to which we are summoned has a definitive exemplar. We are asked to love *as* Jesus loved. We go before the Father as adoptive sons, realizing that to him we owe everything, including our filial state, and that our filial response makes a contribution to the divine plan. We realize too that all men are our brothers and that we must cement bonds of brotherly love with them. This will require from us a fidelity to the creatural condition that excludes sin; because the kind of double love we have to manifest is impossible without self-renunciation. It is also impossible without full respect for the order of creation and a desire to promote it.

The commitment then is one that exposes us to all sorts of demands that we can never previously anticipate. It is an adventure of which we cannot chart the way. The order of creation is not something fixed and established. It is something that must be constantly shaped, something that must be invented as it were day by day. The requirements of yesterday are not going to be those of tomorrow. Where love is concerned, we can never go on automatically repeating ourselves.

The witness of love in the world now

It has always been the task of the Church to exhibit to men the love which saved the world. Being as she is the Body of Christ she never ceases to be a sign of this, but at any given time the intensity of the sign will depend on the fidelity shown by believers. The Church must be present to the people to whom she exhibits the sign, and must always be concerned about the actual means to be employed.

What are these in our world now? Like all men indeed at all times, modern man dreams of more peace and more justice. But he is much more conscious of the need to muster all human resources for this purpose. If we will the end, we should will the means, and mere good intentions are not sufficient. Precise plans have to be made, on the individual and collective level, that will tackle the problem at its roots in all its complexity.

The witness of love in the world today must be particularly concerned to articulate supernatural charity with man's creatural responsibilities. This charity which is infused into each Christian soul can become the source of a great dynamism in the human sense. One who, following Christ, loves God and all his fellow-men will feel the urge to bring about a transformation in human relationships. That transformation calls for lucidity and inventiveness; it requires the dedication of individual liberty and responsibility. From this aspect it seems that we do need a re-evaluation of traditional procedures in Christian charity, especially collective charity.

On the other hand, in a world which is preoccupied with service to humanity only, the Christian must beware of settling for an ideal of universal brotherhood that falls short of the gospel. God must always be part of the evangelic ideal. Self-renunciation is essential to it, and the only basis for this self-renunciation is the relation between creature and Creator. What the world needs more than anything else is the witness of double love. If we Christians fail to love God with the creature's filial love, we cannot really love our fellowmen as brothers. We shall very quickly find ourselves turning from the gospel towards other alleged solutions.

Eucharistic initiation into love of God and men

The link between the two loves is best cemented in the eucharistic assembly. The initiation here is always on-going. When we respond to the Father's initiative of love by giving thanks, we feel the urge to bind ourselves to those who are our brothers in Jesus Christ. The actual celebration consists of a fraternal sharing of the same bread, and is a constant reminder of the duty of mission, which is the expression *par excellence* of love for all men.

All ecclesial assemblies have in fact as purpose the proper disposition of the members towards God and towards all men. The two thrusts must always be in evidence; they provide a basic "structure" for everything the Institution does. Whether it be a eucharistic celebration, a simple liturgy of the Word, some Catholic Action meeting, etc., there is never question of emphasizing now the love of God, and again that of men. Everyone present is always summoned to deepen the quality of his double love, that of God and men together.

claimed by the prophet in the heart of Gentile territory. Jezabel
lives in luxury and riches (1 K 21): the Sarepta widow in very
great deprivation. Elias pronounces the curse of death on one (1
K 21:17-24), but bestows the blessing of life and abundance on
the other.

a) The episode is principally a narrative of *faith*. Elias had to
have faith to ask for sustenance from a widow who had so little
left (vv. 11-13). His faith resembles that of Abraham. He does
not know what will be the end of this crisis; but he has faith in
God who disposes all things.

The widow likewise shares his faith. She does not look beyond
her act, or speculate about its possible result. She relies on the
commandment of God that has come by the mouth of the prophet
and trusts in the promise.

b) The account is also revealing concerning the *universalist*
dimension of the prophetic Word. Elias does not address himself
solely to the members of the chosen people: he offers salvation
to the poor of other nations too (cf. Lk 4:25-26). In this domain
our reading is an excellent preparation for the striking Pauline
passages about Gentile access to salvation by faith alone, without
the works of the law.

III. 2 Maccabees The story of the nameless mother and her
    7:1-2, 9-14 seven children suggests probably the city of
    1st reading Jerusalem, which had been already repre-
    3rd cycle sented in Jeremiah 15:9 as a mother with
seven children.

a) Our reading could very well be a commentary on
Jeremiah's passage. That which men have destroyed in Sion
God will rebuild. *Trial* has its meaning, provided at least that the
children of Sion remain faithful to the law. The figure seven is
always a sign of divine blessing.

The law for which the seven brothers and their mother are ready to lay down their lives was one of high importance for the Pharisees. The martyrdom-narrative may very well have served to propagate the doctrine of this intransigent sect as a counterblast to the pagan customs of the time. Salvation is assured indeed, but it means that one's fidelity will be tried.

b) Salvation here is seen in terms of *resurrection* (vv. 9-14). Doubtless the author is contemplating the restoration for Sion of her dead children before the inauguration of the eternal Kingdom.

The resurrection of the people of God was no more than an image for the Jews. Death signified exile and suffering, life the return from exile (Ho 6:1-3; Ex 37:1-14; Is 51:17; 53:10-12). The book of Maccabees takes a new turning by contemplating individual resurrection for the future citizens of the Kingdom. Yet the resurrection continues to be partial only; the wicked will not share it (v. 14).

In fact it is from the concept of retribution, so deeply embedded in biblical thinking, that this faith in the resurrection springs. The just are destined for life and death cannot rob them of this reward. The wicked on the other hand are doomed to death. They may seem for the moment to escape it, but the final struggle will herald their dissolution.

The resurrection contemplated is also a terrestrial one; the new life will be lived on earth. That is the principal shortcoming in this passage.

That resurrection became more than an idea is evident from the Sadducees' attitude when they raised the question (Mt 22: 23-33). It indicates the sort of hope entertained by those faithful who had to surrender their lives. A gift is recompensed by a gift. One must be ready to surrender life in order to believe that it will one day be restored. The one who has never given will not expect to receive.

IV. 1 Thessa- Paul is allaying misgivings among his corre-
lonians spondents concerning the events at the end of
4:13-18 the one posed by many Jews. Would the dead
2nd reading be present or not at the inauguration of the
1st cycle Kingdom? Most believed in a restoration of
the people; but did not have any clear idea of the connection between this and individual resurrection.

a) Paul gives the usual Jewish answer of the time. The dead
would be present at the restoration, having previously arisen.
This *resurrection* however has now a new dimension; it will be
"with Jesus" (v. 14). Paul bases this affirmation on faith (v. 14);
God, who has raised Jesus from the dead, will also raise up those
who die "in Jesus." He then appeals to a "World of the Lord"
(v. 15), which is undoubtedly a particular teaching of Jesus (not
the apostle's own idea). According to this, the dead and the
living (who enjoy no particular privilege) will rejoin Christ at
the first moment of the Parousia. They will accompany him as he
proceeds to inaugurate the definitive Kingdom.

b) For the Jewish events of resurrection of the body and advent of the Kingdom, Paul thus is substituting; resurrection,
Parousia, being "with" the Lord, and the definitive advent of the
Kingdom. The expression "being with the Lord" (cf. Jn 14:3;
17:24) should be taken in the strongest sense. It is not merely a
matter of living "in company" with the Lord, but of sharing his
privileges. The parallel New Testament expressions are: *"to reign
with Christ"* (Rev 3:21; 20:4-6; 5:10; 2 Tm 2:12), "take a meal
with him" (Mt 26:29; 25:10; Rev 3:20), or again "have part with
him" (Jn 13:9), "be with him in paradise" (Lk 23:42-43).

Thus the Pauline concept is that not alone will the dead arise
to become the citizens of a marvelous Kingdom; they will share
the Lord's reign. Christ took on the humble mortal state of men;
in return he will share the glory of his Lordship with the risen
dead. Not alone will the Christian have access to future glory;

he will participate in a real fashion in the special glory of the
Risen Lord.

V. Hebrews **9:24-28** *2nd reading* *2nd cycle*	Here we have the conclusion of the exposé concerning Christ's sacrificial role as a perfect fulfillment of the Expiation ceremony (cf. Lv 16:11-16). The author has shown how Jesus introduced all humanity to the Holy of holies,

near to God (vv. 11-13); and how, as priest and victim of the cult
in spirit and in truth (v. 14; cf. Rm 12:1-2), his sacrifice has
cleansed and consecrated the believer. He follows the ritual of
Leviticus 16 by concentrating on the two important themes of the
Expiation ceremony; the solemn entry of the high priest to the
Holy of holies (vv. 24, 26, 27b) and the expiatory sacrifice itself.

a) *Christ's entry* to the Holy of holies is no longer punctuated,
as was that of the high priest, by the annual cycle of festivals. He
has entered once for all (v. 26) into an eternal "now" (vv. 24 and
26), whereas the high priest was governed by a recurring cycle.
Furthermore, the Holy of holies into which he has entered is
something much more authentic than that of the temple (v. 24).
He does not enter for some moments only as the high priest did,
but for always. The prayers and petitions of men now have a constant mediator, who is always before the face of God. The high
priest's mediation before Yahweh was occasional only. Finally,
whereas the high priest's entry enthroned Yahweh for a single
year, Christ carries in his person the universal lordship. When he
issues, as the high priest used, from the tabernacle, and rejoins
the people (v. 28), it is to exercise over them a definitive kingship. And the assembly of the just awaits the appearance of the
new high-priest and Lord with much more fervor than did the
Jewish assembly their high priest. His appearance is so much
more glorious than that of the Jewish priest as he issued from the
Holy of holies after the enthronement of Yahweh (cf. Si 50:5-7).

b) It is not the material circumstance of having shed his blood that makes the expiation of Jesus definitive. It is the fact of offering his life. The act has the value of the person who acts, and the oblation of Jesus has a double value. Because he was the son of God, the value of his sacrifice transcends that of the former ones. Because he was the perfect man a dimension, unknown to former sacrifices, is added.

Because its author is concerned to establish a close parallel between the ceremony of Expiation (in which the readers cannot now participate) and Christ's sacrifice, the letter to the Hebrews concentrates on one efficacious aspect only of the blood of Christ; that of purification and expiation. The theme was stressed at the very beginning of the letter (He 1:3). It purports to show that Christ, by his death and resurrection, effaces and remits sin, not in an exterior fashion, like the blood of goats (v. 25), but radically. He was the first man to live a life free from sin, the first Lord to abolish the reign of evil.

**VI. 2 Thessa-
lonians
2:16–3:5
2nd reading
3rd cycle**

Paul has just given thanks to God for the confirmation in holiness of the Thessalonians and their fidelity to traditional teaching (2 Th 2:13-15). He now implores the grace of God for his correspondents (vv. 16-17), commending some personal intentions to their prayers (vv. 1-2) and endorsing them to persevere (vv. 3-5).

a) The believer inevitably encounters struggle and challenge. But his fidelity finds strength in the *grace of God* which provides comfort and assurance (vv. 16-17).

b) The apostle asks his correspondents to pray first of all for the success of evangelization, which he sees as a glorification of the *Word* (v. 1). He often is concerned with prayer for his ministry (cf. 1 Th 5:25; Rm 15:30-33; Col 4:2, 18) which he sees as an athlete's race in the stadium, in an image that is dear to him (cf. Rm 9:16; Ph 2:16; Ga 2:2; 5:7; 1 Co 9:24-25). The Word may indeed encounter obstacles; but we should pray that it be accomplished as soon as possible. Then he asks for prayer for the *freedom* of his ministry (v. 2; cf. further 1:10; Rm 15:31). Just now it is the object of persecution and of Jewish opposition (cf. 1 Th 2:15-16).

c) Paul's own prayer for the Thessalonian Christians (vv. 3-5) expresses *confidence* above all, confidence in God who will strengthen them and guard them from the "Evil One" (a term which probably characterizes Satan, and his enterprise of domination over the world, cf. Mt 13:19, 38; Jn 17:15; Ep 6:6; 1 Jn 2:13-14; 5:18-19). The best weapon they can use in resisting the Evil One is obedience to his directives (v. 4).

VII. Matthew 25:1-13
Gospel
1st cycle

The parable of the ten virgins is not now in its original context. Verse 13 does not provide an adequate conclusion, because the exhortation to watch does not correspond to the content of the narrative. All the virgins, wise as well as foolish, slept (v. 5). Furthermore this conclusion repeats Matthew 24:42 and seems to come from Mark 13:25. Matthew has actually placed the parable in the context of the eschatological discourse (Mt 24), and the consequent interpretation does not seem to be the original. Jesus never likened himself to a spouse and no allegorization at all is necessary to discern the primitive meaning of the parable.

a) It is probable that Jesus took advantage of some real occurrence in order to remind his audience of the *imminence* of the Kingdom and to spur them to greater vigilance (cf. in Mt 24:39 the suddenness of the deluge; in 1 Th 5:1-5 and Mt 24-42 the unexpected entry of the thief; in Mt 24:48 the unexpected return of the master).

The sudden arrival of the bridegroom is indeed an extremely realistic contemporary detail. Often the negotiations between the two families were long drawn out as an indication of the parents' interest in their progeny. Almost always the bridegroom did not appear until the guests were beginning to tire. It was a custom admirably suited to suggest an imminent advent for the Kingdom, that would take people unawares.

b) Very early the Church transformed the piece into an allegory of the *espousals of Christ and the Church*. The bridegroom becomes a figure of Christ (cf. Mt 9:15; 2 Co 11:2; Ep 5:25) and his judgment a decision about requirements for sharing the wedding banquet. This however strains the original parable where there is no mention of a bridegroom. Early Christians however saw the ten virgins, foolish as well as wise, as a figure of the Church-spouse. The Church, before the fulfillment of the marriage, is made up of sinners as well as the just. We have similar images in the net which takes in the less good fish as well as the good (Mt 13:48), the banquet hall where the wicked are assembled with the good (Mt 22:10), the field which produces bad and good growth (Mt 13:24-30). This allegory then sees the Church as a procession of people wending their way towards the Lord. Some keep their lamps of vigilance lit, while others neglect to nourish their faith. The former refuse to allow their attention to be withdrawn by countless futilities. They have chosen Christ and take the necessary means to maintain fidelity. The latter are content with purely sociological membership of the Church.*

c) It is also possible that Matthew is adding another personal nuance to the parable by placing it after the eschatological discourse. He is providing an answer about the manner of participation in the Kingdom. He distinguishes two broad categories; those who belong openly to the people of God (Mt 24:45–25:30), and those who are preparing themselves for the Kingdom without knowing it (Mt 25:31-46). Among those in the first category again he distinguishes the responsible leaders (Mt 24:45-51), next the members, women (Mt 25:1-13) and men (Mt 25:14-30). This parable of the ten virgins would thus be addressed to Christian *women*, to remind them as a group of the

*See the doctrinal theme: *vigilance,* p. 260.

duty of vigilance. He often uses the procedure of pairing a "feminine" parable with a "masculine" one (cf. Mt 24:18-19; 9:18-26; 13:31-33). This indicates awareness on the part of the first preachers of diversity in their audience.

VIII. Mark The two episodes in this passage form a con-
12:38-44 clusion to the discussions between Jesus and
Gospel the sects. They are closely connected one with
2nd cycle the other. The malediction on the scribes who
plunder widows (vv. 38-40) is followed by the
blessing of the widow (vv. 41-44), and both groups illustrate the parable of the vineyard workers (Mk 12:1-9). The leaders of the people are about to be deprived of their privileges. The Kingdom will be offered to others, to the poor that is to say.

The contrast between *rich and poor*, or here scribes and widows, is usual in Christ's eschatological discourses. It corresponds to the procedure in the beatitudes, where the contrast between poor and rich indicates the imminence of the Kingdom, and the reversal of inequalities. There is question not so much of passing judgment from a moral point of view on this or that social situation. The emphasis is on the reversal, the change, that will be brought about in the final times for people who will share the very life of God. From this point of view the passage is an excellent introduction to the eschatological discourse which follows immediately (Mk 13).

The widow gives from her poverty, by contrast with the rich who give from their power and privilege. She contradicts the principle that one only gives what one has; she actually gives what she does not have.

Have we got here an image of God? If God be someone who gives only from abundance, surely he would be better represented by the rich donors than the widow with her mite; and the importance of the widow's gesture for Jesus would be puzzling. Can we say that God too gives from poverty? Yes, if we reject certain theistic notions, and concentrate on the acts of God as manifested in Jesus. Being God in this sense means serving and giving; giving not from what one has, but from what one is. Jesus, poor and enslaved, is not just an episode of divine life. He is manifesting the very state of godhood. God did not come from on high, like a rich tourist nowadays, albeit sympathetic, into underdeveloped countries. He became a slave because poverty for him was the expression of divinity.*

IX. Luke
20:27-38
Gospel
3rd cycle

Jesus continues his discussion with the Jewish sects, by replying here to the Sadducees concerning resurrection. They regarded bodily resurrection as absurd, and cite the case of the widow who successively marries the six brothers of her first husband. Jesus, in responding, indicates that marriage has nothing to do with life in the Kingdom and affirms the reality of bodily resurrection. The two sentences are quite mysterious, both by reason of their content ("they are as the angels"), and the use made of biblical texts that do not seem relevant to the argument.

a) How does Jesus find confirmation for *bodily resurrection* in Exodus 3:6? The text contemplates the God of Abraham, Isaac and Jacob (v. 37) as the God who made a covenant with them and protected them. This God is a God of the living (v. 38), and consequently can hardly be conceived as covenanting with and protecting the dead. God affirms himself the Savior of Abraham. Were Abraham definitively dead, this would be meaningless. Abraham thus, and the patriarchs, will be resuscitated. What is true of them is true of all members of the chosen people. The covenant must mean that people will enjoy God's protection

*See the doctrinal theme: *gospel and riches,* p. 266.

against the only ultimate enemy, death. It is true that all this can scarcely be found in the text Jesus quotes, Exodus 3:6. What he does is use the text against the background of faith as it had developed in Israel.

b) Jesus' second affirmation is still more mysterious. In excluding conjugal relations from the quasi-angelic state of humanity after the resurrection, he seems to be disregarding needs associated with bodies as we know them. He is not in fact taking any position about the nature of *angels*. Nor is he saying that the resurrected body becomes angelic to the point of losing corporeity. This would be a terminology foreign to Jewish anthropology. His allusion to the angels is meant to indicate that human language cannot describe the nature of the resurrected body.

B.   DOCTRINE

1. The Theme of Vigilance

There do not seem to be natural roots in human psychology for the biblical doctrine of vigilance, and modern man does not differ from the ancients in this respect. Hope of fulfillment for the ancients depended on the security offered by cosmic stability and immemorial laws about individual and social life. There was no reason for vigilance. Man's task was to seek perfect harmony with the archetypes, established once for all by the gods when the cosmos began. The thirst for the absolute which troubles the hearts of men could only be assuaged by cyclic recurrence. In such a climate the event, with its novel and unforeseen aspects, is quite simply rejected; there is a constant urge to evade it, to cancel its reality.

Modern man's attitude to the event seems to be different; but really it is not. He has the same urge to cancel its reality. But he cannot now evade it. His increasing mastery over the data of nature and over man himself enables him to "possess" the event, to bring it within foreseeable limits. Here too there is no room for vigilance in the biblical sense, only for foresight. True, there is no myth of a recurring cycle to give validity nowadays to human existence. All are faced with the complex task of transforming the world and building structures which make it habitable for human beings. To surmount the great challenges nowadays to human happiness, hunger, war, injustice, there is continual need for ingenuity. But, in theory anyhow, the time will come when nothing can disturb universal security.

The gospel of the first cycle invites us to deepen an essential attitude of Christianity: vigilance. The word should not be lightly used, for the issue is grave. Deprived of its biblical implications, vigilance holds no particular interest for the Christian.

But when properly understood it illuminates an aspect of our faith, the permanent relevancy of which one cannot overstress.

Vigilance and the regime of faith

From the moment, in Israel, when the regime of faith appeared among men, vigilance began to have meaning. The event began to assume realistic proportions, inconceivable in pagan terms. The series of concrete happenings, individual and collective, so stamped themselves on human existence that this seemed the only valid area of investigation in the quest for fulfillment. Without doubt, confronted day by day with the march of events, Jewish man found himself more and more deeply disjointed. He was involved in a dramatic adventure, the key to which escaped him, and he had not, by himself, the resources to gain the fulfillment he sought. A corollary though of this realization of "poverty" was the extraordinarily fruitful discovery of a "Totally-Other-God," who saves by intervening at the level of the event, the dramatic adventure in which man is actually engaged. The God of Israel reveals himself as the Existing, the Living One *par excellence*. Only he can save the people he has gratuitously taken to himself. He leads them day by day. He meets them on the concrete historical plane; but can only fulfill them if they are faithful according to the terms of the covenant he made with them in the desert. Yahweh comes; he does not cease to come. One should anticipate his comings even when they are not responses to human expectation, particularly when they are not. One should anticipate them by being vigilant, by watching lest we fall into temptation.

Not today or yesterday did Jewish man serve his apprenticeship to vigilance. Throughout her long history Israel had shown herself stiffnecked, preferring the pagan securities, even those of slavery, to the discomfort of encounter with the living God. Sin however is not the total explanation. Being under the regime of faith brought about considerable interiorization, both individual

262 GUIDE FOR THE CHRISTIAN ASSEMBLY

and collective; but it was only gradually that Israel reached the depth of self-emptying required by faith. Her gratuitous selection implied privileges, and her difficulty was to avoid interpreting these in terms of security. The prophets were always having to intervene to correct the inevitable misunderstandings that arose.

The city of Jerusalem is a case in point. It is clear from the prophetic texts of the first week of Advent that the Jerusalem which pleases the heart of Yahweh, where there is perfect encounter between him and his own, where all the nations find their place, is other than terrestrial Jerusalem and its temple of stone. These were liable to fail in their mission and be destroyed. The awaited Jerusalem, in the time of fulfillment, is one where all justice will flourish, where the call which comes from God the Father and Savior will find hearts unceasingly vigilant, always ready to listen.

Intervention of the Messiah and Christian vigilance

In the gospels the theme of vigilance is far from accidental. In those texts, parables and discourses, which speak of the proximity of the Kingdom, it is always present. There is even insistence about vigilance, to the extent that in the person of Jesus proximity has become actuality. The happening which is the historical intervention in the world of Jesus of Nazareth manifests the "Lord who comes" in such fashion that all our energies must be mustered to confront it. Vigilance reaches its peak point. It summons us to a precise involvement: following Jesus, being present when the bridegroom passes and joining in the cortège. Expectation is fulfilled; but that itself is a stumbling block. It obliges man to empty himself to the point of obedience unto death. To follow Jesus is to bear his cross too. Hearts are prepared by vigilance for the comings of the Lord; but this means that the believer is plunged into the tensions which freewill will cause. He is always summoned by God, and finds no true support except in turning to the merciful Father. Vigilance means the aspect faith assumes when it has the clear vision of empty hands.

Jesus has given us the example. All through his time on earth, he lived under the sign of that vigilance he requires from his disciples. His nourishment is to do the will of the Father who sent him among men. Nor is this will made clear for him through the medium of private revelation. For him, like every man, it was a matter of discovering in the procession of days the path he must follow here below. It was not determined *a priori,* clear from the first day. Always he examines the events; but he does so with that sovereign realism which is proper to him, and whatever it costs him, he engages himself with perfect fidelity and obedience. Gradually the Passion looms on the horizon; because Israel will not agree to follow a Messiah who proposes such a demanding road, that of love without limits, of total renunciation.

So Jesus is the Vigilant One in the fullest sense. But because he is Son of God this very vigilance discloses him to the eye of faith as the Lord who comes. Aligned as he is with the will of his Father, Jesus, in the very moment of his response, reveals the plan of God and the true import of his interventions among men. With Jesus and in him the vigilance of faith affirms its true identity: it is the welcoming of God's today in human history, a welcome, it should be added, which engages all the energies of human liberty restored to its true state.

The vigilance of the Church and the temptation of the synagogue

The primitive Church was strongly insistent about vigilance: we should be in readiness for the return of the Lord. Since his Pasch is now an event of the past, his return must be imminent. It is however an object of faith and therefore unforeseeable: it will surprise like the unexpected visitation of the thief. Hence the absolute necessity of vigilance: Christians must keep vigil, live every moment virtuous lives, and strive not to fall into temptation.

We notice that the first generation of Christians retains a horizontal and temporal notion of the Lord's return, even while insisting on the aspects that only faith could discern, which subsequent experience would delineate more sharply. In the year 70 an event occurs, which has strong repercussions on the concept of the Lord's return, and consequently on the Christian notion of vigilance: the destruction, that is, of the city of Jerusalem. So prominent a place did terrestrial Jerusalem have in the religious world of the first Christians, that its destruction was unimaginable except in direct relation to the end of the world. However the return of the Lord did not coincide with this evidently divine intervention. So it is that the return of the Lord is always an actuality present in life, its immanence and its unforseeable character emphasizing the fact that it is transcendental. So it is too that God's today in human history means the annihilation of all particularism, even when that is based on the privileges of a chosen people.

The vigilance of the Church, as she holds herself ready for the return of the Lord, is especially related to her catholicity. At every moment she must go to meet the Lord who comes, demonstrating the power of universal charity which animates her. She must watch so as not to fall into temptation, and the temptation which besets her always is that of the synagogue. It was on this point that the Council of Jerusalem, the first council of ecclesial vigilance, declared itself. The temptation of the synagogue is the temptation to particularism. Link Christianity to a people, a group of peoples, a particular culture where the Church is already spread, and we are immediately according privileges which they do not actually have to an enclave or group of people. Has not the idea been widespread in the Church that the mission to non-Christians is exclusively the business of the white races? Even today, traces of it remain.

Evangelization of the world under the sign of vigilance

Two major questions, both challenges to the Church's catholicity, are posed to the People of God in these days. Firstly, does the Church build her unity by embracing all the diversity of human beings and the tensions that diversity implies? Secondly, is the Church capable of adapting herself to a secularized world, and propagating the good news of salvation in a manner that will be relevant to it?

To answer these challenges with deeds the People of God must display exceptional vigilance. Particular churches will be more and more diversified. This is an irreversible trend, largely favored by Vatican II in response to the signs of the times. All the vigilance of our faith will be required to avoid stifling the process uselessly on the one hand, and on the other to prevent ecclesial differences from solidifying into walls of separation. Nowadays, too, efforts are being redoubled to reevaluate the content of our faith for accommodation to the modern mentality, or to demonstrate the importance of service to the world in the task of evangelization. Here again all the vigilance of faith is called for—to forward the efforts on the one hand, and on the other to ensure that the mystery of Christ is faithfully transmitted.

The kind of vigilance demanded in the evangelization of our actual world calls for daring in the first place. To be in the actual world and to witness true Catholicity, the Church everywhere needs a radical change, which has scarcely yet begun. The shockwave engendered by Vatican II still awaits the proper results; much courage and imagination will be needed to accomplish necessary reforms. Individual churches will not bear witness to Church unity unless they develop a reciprocal exchange of life and energy; unless dialogue and intercommunion govern the growth of their interior life.

Our initiation to vigilance in the eucharistic celebration

A primary function of the Christian liturgy is to rescue Christians from their torpor, to rouse them from the sleep where they always run the risk of being blanketed in security. It is now all the more necessary, because the modern world in which Christians like others are immersed certainly does not tend to develop the vigilance of faith.

Yesterday, in a Christianized world, it was possible to be content with reminding the faithful of the rules to be observed in their moral conduct. The air they breathed was, in principle at least, impregnated by the faith. Today that is not so. Every influence in the surrounding world turns people, Christians as much as anyone else, to the search for security. Everything makes them blind to the mystery of human liberty in its daily confrontation with the unforeseeable in human history. So then, it is essential that the eucharistic celebration, and above all the Liturgy of the Word, should provide the basis for permanent initiation into the vigilance of faith.

2. Theme of the Gospel and Riches

Nowadays Christians are to be found above all in the comfortable countries, among the more comfortable classes. We cannot blink the fact. They own a considerable amount of material wealth and are certainly the richest religious group in the world. At first sight anyhow, this accords ill with the gospel. Let us take two texts only; "In truth I tell you it will be difficult for a rich man to enter the Kingdom of Heaven. Yes, I tell you, it is more easy for a camel to pass through the eye of a needle than for a rich man to enter the Kingdom of Heaven" (Mk 10:23-24). "Woe to you, rich; for you have your consolation." These seem to indicate absolute condemnation.

In any case, there is no way of escaping a question of major significance. Christians indeed seem to have an uneasy conscience in this area. They know from experience the dangers associated with riches, and feel intuitively how well founded Jesus' strictures were. Some actually worry about how to fulfill their Christian duty, since they do not see an easy way of getting rid of their goods.

Could it be that the only true Christians are those *elite* who have chosen a life of poverty? Another group, not without occasional misgivings, try to convince themselves that, in order to contribute to human progress, some accumulation of worldly goods is essential. They reason also that material wealth does not perhaps have the same meaning now that it had in Jesus' time.

How far do his comments have relevance in the contemporary situation?

Today's formulary (1st reading and gospel, 2nd cycle) gives us an opportunity to deepen our insights about this problem. It is really quite urgent. Throughout the world the poor await unambiguous testimony from Christians. Are we prepared to give it, and on what conditions? We should like to consider that question in the light of salvation history.

Riches in Israel, a blessing but a danger too

The Jews, like every other people, regarded material prosperity as a blessing, a sign of divine favor. The patriarchs, the kings who pleased Yahweh, Job himself after his trial, are all seen, even in the most recent texts, as crowned with riches. The origin of the belief is not far to seek. Riches give security and independence; and with the Jews as with others, happiness was seen in such terms.

Deeper insights under the regime of faith modified this. To begin with, material wealth was never of course seen as the ultimate good. There were obvious limitations; certain blessings like love and wisdom, which could not be purchased, were preferred to it. Prophets and sages went further. Wealth in itself was a blessing, true; but very often it was accompanied by grave dangers. It was better to beware of it. How many times did not wealth lead to injustice. "Woe to those who add house to house and join field to field until everywhere belongs to them" (Is 5:8). How many times did it not lead men to impiety. Rich men tend to rely on their wealth, to believe they can become equal to God. They begin not to recognize wealth for what it is, God's gift and thus are led to wickedness.

We find indeed a deep contrast running through the Old Testament. On the one hand we have all the vocabulary of wealth, abundance and satiation used to characterize God's attitude towards men. On the other, prophets begin more and more to use the vocabulary of poverty to describe the requirements of the covenant. They develop misgivings about the illusions and dangers of wealth, and teach that the Good News of the Kingdom to come will be proclaimed to the poor. They at least have learned dependence and openness through experience.

The New Covenant and the condemnation of riches

The prophetic trend already begun is carried to its culmination by Jesus. No one else has ever described more graphically how money can become a pitiless master. He never describes wealth as a divine blessing. His criticism is quite radical. Wealth is an insurmountable obstacle practically, because it means possessing rather than renouncing, and total renunciation is necessary for entry to the Kingdom. Wealth makes us blind, insensitive to the Word, forgetful of the essential thing. Similarly, on poverty, he carries to the ultimate the prophetic teaching. He blesses the spiritual attitude towards God and men that it engenders. He is always recommending his disciples to act like waifs, poor sinners, seeking the Father's mercy. This is the price that must be paid if one is to follow the gospel; one can only become neighbor to the other by losing everything.

Luke, among the evangelists, is the one who goes furthest in condemnation of riches. He is absolutely intransigent. If one has possessions, one must sell them in order to follow Jesus. The beatitude, which in Matthew is one of "poverty of spirit," is one of poverty simply with him; and it is accompanied by a malediction on the rich. In his gospel numerous other episodes carry this emphasis. It would be wrong I suppose to think that the other evangelists softened the teaching of Jesus in this matter; but it would also be wrong to think that he went beyond that teaching. The gospels, in their very diversity, form a single whole; and Luke's insistence is a very forceful reminder that the gospel will not be really lived unless some anyhow actually do renounce their goods.

If we ask the question what measure of material wealth is compatible with fidelity to the gospel there is certainly only one answer. A wealth that is shared. Jesus never required the destruction of "dishonest money" or any material goods; he simply recommends that they be distributed to the poor. This is to restore wealth to its proper purpose; it is destined for all men. Seen thus, it becomes the gift of God, something that can play a positive role in the building of the Kingdom.

Poverty and riches of the people of God.

As we read the acts of the Apostles we find that one of the major preoccupations of the first disciples was the preservation of a unanimous attitude concerning riches, that conformed to the Lord's Word; "The faithful all lived together and owned everything in common; they sold their goods and possessions and shared out the proceeds among themselves according to what each one needed" (Ac 2:44). Of course, as exegetes point out, the author is using a variety of sources to describe the Jerusalem community. It is clear that all did not react on this issue in precisely the same way. Some sold their houses, but others kept them. From the very beginning then we have some difference in practical performance. What they all did have in common was a rejection of riches as commonly understood, riches as the goal of possession.

What was the subsequent development? Whenever in Christian communities wealth began to lead to injustice and impiety, a constant danger, the finger of denunciation would be raised. The care of the poor was also a constant preoccupation in local churches. This continued throughout the early centuries, during the period when the marginal status in society of Christians kept them faithful to the original attitude. It was not so subsequently. Once society as a whole became Christian, from top to bottom of the social ladder there was much more compromise. The intransigent attitude of the gospel ceased to be the norm; and, just as in the Old Testament, it was maintained only by the protest of single prophetic figures, who had to encounter challenge.

The Church's privileged position after the 4th century led to the gradual enrichment of the Institution itself. True, ecclesial wealth was used to alleviate the misery of the poor and to embellish places of worship. But some churchmen also used it for less noble purposes, and were not above the lust for power and gain. Generosity to the poor often came from abundance, not from the widow's poverty that is commended in today's Gospel (Mk 12:44).

The actual requirements for evangelic witness

Everyone today is so conscious of the malign flavor of money and property, all the more so because it is now so collective and anonymous, that, whether Christian or not, they expect from the Church an unequivocal protest. Otherwise they fail to see in her the gospel. It is indeed imperative that the Church divest herself of money-power. She will lose power certainly as a result; but she will become more sensitive to the poor throughout the world. The Word by itself is not sufficient. All members of the Church are required to act in a manner that speaks.

Modern man is an extremely keen critic of the genuineness of spiritual and religious values. He knows what money can do to them. He is invariably dubious when he sees power tactics applied to evangelization, when the charitable institutions that serve the poor seem too rich, when the chink of money resounds around the altar itself. He has had far too bitter experience of what wealth can do.

There is one question which grows more and more urgent and which concerns the majority of Christians. The riches, we have seen, that are compatible with gospel teaching are riches that one shares, not riches that one hoards. And riches nowadays have become something collective rather than individual. If a nation is rich, its members are rich. The sharing that is essential concerns all humanity, because men everywhere are being drawn closer to one another. It seems then that our Christian responsibility necessarily becomes a political one. Whether it be a matter of redressing inequality as between social classes, or between rich nations and poor, equitable sharing, in analysis and execution, calls for the concerted effort of all men of good will. The prophetic witness of those who have chosen voluntary poverty will achieve its full intensity, when it is properly articulated with the more general project that concerns everyone now. That is the radical reform of systems where the distribution of wealth is still too often a prerogative of the few.

The Lord's Supper and the sharing of goods

In the first letter to the Corinthians, Saint Paul takes up the matter of the eucharistic celebration. It is revealing that the occasion should have been a wrong attitude about wealth on the part of his correspondents. "The point is when you hold these meetings it is not the Lord's supper that you are eating. Since when the time comes to eat, everyone is in such a hurry to start his own supper that one person goes hungry while another is getting drunk. Surely you have homes for eating and drinking in? Surely you have enough respect for the community of God not to make poor people embarrassed?" (1 Co 11:20-22).

Paul, it should be noted, is not a social reformer. He is not asking the richer Christians to share their goods with the poorer. But he does find it unthinkable that people can come together for the Lord's supper where there is no evidence of sharing. He is certainly convinced of one thing. If Christians gathered round the Lord feel a deep, ritual experience of sharing, they will return to their ordinary lives changed in some way.

The lesson is clear, and just as valid now as it was then. The eucharistic celebration should always be a reminder for each person present that he must somehow renounce all his goods in order to follow Christ. Often enough we have appeals for this or that charitable purpose; and too often everyone goes away with tranquil conscience, because they have contributed from their abundance only. We need perhaps more imaginative proclamation of the Word, or structuring of the celebration itself. The faithful should be made to realize that the only riches that can be regarded as a gift of God are the riches one shares, and this should impel them towards the decisions that are necessary in our world.

THIRTY-THIRD SUNDAY

A. THE WORD

I. Proverbs 31:10- This eulogy of woman seems to be a late addi-
13, 19-20, 30-31 tion to the book of Proverbs. The structure is
1st reading alphabetic acrostic, a late style not yet fully
1st cycle studied. Doubtless it is characteristic of the
bourgeois milieu of the period. The woman
demands a good deal for herself, but also for her assistants, of
whom she has many. She is docile insofar as she finds that her
finger is always in the pie.

The author of the eulogy sees the ideal *woman* as someone
who has blossomed as she toiled. She is one whose tact, that rare
and precious thing, so much more important than beauty, is conspicuous as a gift of God. Her fidelity contrasts with the behavior
of adulterous women depicted by the Wisdom writers. Her
common sense preserves her from the triviality so common
among women of the time.

At the time this eulogy was written women were still in an inferior position in Jewish society. The walls of the house for instance were regarded as a bulwark to protect her, as the source
of life, from wicked outside influences. Yet the Jewish wife was
never so strictly sequestered as in some other cultures. The married state was a real partnership, and, in the more comfortable
families anyhow, the mother held responsibilities that gave her
high prestige.

II. Daniel This is one of the most important texts of the
12:1-3 Old Testament on the topic of bodily resurrec-
1st reading tion. The context however is obscure and the
2nd cycle exegesis difficult. The author refers to a campaign by a northern king against Israel and

273

some Gentile nations. There is no question of conflict between Jews and Gentiles. A Gentile is warring with Jews who find themselves allied with Gentile nations (Dn 11:40, 43). The result is adverse. The Gentile allies take to flight and Israel faces the enemy alone (Dn 11:44-45). She is in great distress (v. 1); but there is a guardian angel whose help is highly efficacious, the great prince Michael, who will preside over the final resurrection.

The author seems to envisage those Jews who will be living when history comes to an end, and also the case of those who will be *dead*. In both cases it seems that resurrection will be granted only to those who are inscribed in the Book, those that is who will have practiced justice. Others will perish.

III. Malachi 3:19-20 *1st reading 3rd cycle* This is the conclusion of the third and last discourse of the Book of Malachi (2:17–3:22). The discourse was put together between the announcement of the return from exile and the reform of Esdras. It is addressed first to unbelievers (2:17–3:5), then to the lukewarm (3:6-12) and finally to believers (3:13-23). The believers had encountered a very difficult situation on their return to Jerusalem. They are astonished that God is not rewarding their fidelity more promptly. In their disappointment there is a great temptation to collaborate with the pagan world around them.

a) To encourage them the prophet proclaims the proximity of the *judgment,* for the wicked a furnace (v. 19), but for the good a "sun of justice." This expression seems to be borrowed from Phoenician mythology, where one month of the year (corresponding practically to the month of October) was devoted to sun worship. It indicates perhaps in a cryptic fashion a date foreseen for the people's salvation.

b) Following Isaiah 10:16-17; 30:17; Zephaniah 1:18; 3:8 and

Amos 5:18, *fire* is very prominent in descriptions of the day of
Yahweh. It was natural that the prophets should see it as an instrument of judgment, since God had promised never again to
use water in chastisement of humanity (Gn 9:12-17). The New
Testament follows this imagery faithfully enough (2 P 3:12); but
spiritualizes it by making fire the purifying element that ushers
in the final times (Ac 2:1-4; Mt 3:11). In any case the main purpose of the symbol is to suggest the reality of God's presence in
man's life.

IV. 1 Thessa-   Timothy, on his return from Thessalonica, in-
   lonians   forms Paul that the community is avid for en-
   5:1-6   lightenment about the Parousia, the time and
   2nd reading   the manner. Thus the apostle takes up the
   1st cycle   question of the moment of the Lord's coming,
   one which was frequently enough posed by
the faithful (v. 1; cf. Ac 1:6-7; Mt 24:36).

a) Jewish tradition had made the *day of the Lord* a day of
revenge and triumph over enemies. Paul, when he takes up the
theme of light and darkness, so long associated with the day of
Yahweh (Am 5:18-20; Ze 1:15; Jl 2:2; 4:15), stresses rather the
moral aspect (vv. 4-5; cf. Rm 13:12-13). The "Son of light" is not
likely to be taken unawares when the day of the Lord comes.
Being a "child of day," the dawning of the day cannot surprise
him.

b) The *light-darkness* contrast in the Bible frequently indicates the opposition between the world of the good and that of
the wicked (Am 8:8; Jr 4:23-24; Is 3:20), or again the actual
world and the eschatological future (Is 60:19-20; 30:26). When
a man who has been a son of night is converted and becomes a
son of the light, he is preparing for the day of the Lord.

c) The great contrast between *sons of light* and *sons of
darkness* comes doubtless from the environment which regarded
monastic seclusion as the assembly of the sons of light, who had

thoroughly severed connection with the sons of darkness. In any case a recently discovered treatise from the library of Qumran has the significant title: "The war of the sons of light against the sons of darkness."

The sons of darkness are said to sleep, while the sons of light remain awake and sober (v. 6). The former fail to see the meaning of events, while the latter practice vigilance and have that mastery over themselves which is necessary to know God (cf. 1 Co 15:34; Rm 13:13).

Under the regime of faith Israel did indeed give value to the event as the great point of encounter with God. However in envisaging salvation, Yahweh's great intervention that is to save his people, the concept of the "Day of Yahweh" was not a day in history, but the day to end history. Between profane and sacral time, the time of man and the time of God, there was a sort of dichotomy.

Jesus modified this concept profoundly. The Kingdom that he brought is one which is built here below in the pattern of daily life. For him there is only one time for man, profane time. Man must live that to the full, as the place where God intervenes to save.

Paul's thesis is that, instead of desperately looking towards a "day of Yahweh," it is better to live all our days with God in the light. This is Matthew's teaching too. His answer to the question about the coming of the Son of man consists of the vigilance parables (Mt 24-25).

V. Hebrews
10:11-14, 18
2nd reading
2nd cycle

These verses are from the conclusion of the central portion of the letter to the Hebrews (5:11–10:18), which concerns the superiority of Christ's priesthood to the levitical. Here the author recalls two of the arguments he has used to demonstrate this.

a) Unlike the Jewish high priest, Christ has penetrated to an *eternal sanctuary* (vv. 12-13). This entry symbolizes his ascent to the Father, beyond the sky which Jewish cosmology represented as a tent (Ps 103/104:2). Christ then has gone beyond a "tent" that was not made by man (He 9:11), creation that is; and he is seated above this.

At this point he develops a new idea. Christ's sacrifice confers on him messianic investiture (v. 13), something to which the high priest could not pretend. For the first time a priestly act leads to royal investiture.

b) By contrast with the many sacrifices of the Temple, Christ's *sacrifice* is *unique* (vv. 12, 14 and 18). Everything is accomplished once for all. By offering his life and his blood he surpasses all that had been previously accomplished (cf. He 9:9-12). His sacrifice makes those that benefit from it perfect (v. 14), something that no previous rite could do (cf. He 8:7-13). It gives them access to spiritual and eschatological blessings, where the former rites gave access to material blessings only. The very fact that the Savior is "seated" (v. 12), not standing in the sacrificial posture (v. 11), indicates that his sacrifice is not to be renewed. Sins have been effectively remitted. Consequently there is something anomalous in preoccupation with being forgiven on the part of any Christian.

VI. 2 Thessalonians 3:7-12
2nd reading
3rd cycle

Paul concludes his letter by taking up a distressing matter. Many members of the community, disappointed in their misguided eschatological hopes, had turned to futile pursuits. They refused to work and depended on the charity of the brethren for subsistence (cf. previously 1 Th 4:10; 5:14). Paul's treatment of these indigents is summary. The community can be no longer burdened with them (vv. 6 and 14). Their subsistence will be cut off in the hope that their laziness will be cured quickly. But before imposing this sentence, he invites them once more to consider the value of work.

Christian charity can never be made an excuse for laziness. Everyone should live by the fruit of his *toil;* it is part of human dignity that a man does not become a charge upon others. Paul does not elaborate any doctrinal arguments for this view; he simply offers his own example. Is he not an apostle, and does he not for this reason have normative authority (v. 7; cf. 1 Th 1:6)? He has not lived an indigent life nor depended on others for his bread though he had the right (v. 8). On the contrary, in addition to his apostolic work, he has toiled hard day and night.

Paul's toil in this fashion springs from his desire to keep the propagation of the Gospel free from any gain-getting atmosphere (v. 9; cf. 1 Co 9:12-18; 2 Co 11:7; 12:13). He recommends that his example be imitated. In fact the Jews were fond of work, and most known rabbis lived by exercising professional skill. Greeks on the other hand depended often on slaves for the manual tasks that left themselves free for philosophy or leisure. Paul has the good Jew's reaction against this. Not alone is he anxious not to be himself a charge on anyone; he tries to modify the Greek attitude towards work.*

VII. Matthew   Matthew's version of the parable of the
    25:14-30   talents is very different to Luke's (Lk 19:12-
    Gospel   27). It is in the context of the moral conclu-
    1st cycle   sion to the eschatological discourse (Mt 24)
                       and describes Christian life during the period
between the glorification of the Lord and the fall of Jerusalem, and the final Parousia. The new assembly takes the place of the former Jewish one. Its members, each in his own place, are a sign of the coming Kingdom. The leaders of the community (Mt 24:45-51) by their manner of service, the women (Mt 25:1-13) by their vigilance, Christians in general (Mt 25:14-30) by their "stewardship" of gifts received. In general we can say that the first part of the eschatological discourse concerns the divine intervention in the building of the Kingdom, whereas the second part is concerned with man's portion.

*See the doctrinal theme: *work*, p. 289.

It is this context which gives the parable its whole emphasis. All these parables which follow the eschatological discourse were placed here by Matthew to construct a theology of the time of the Church and the assembly. Luke places the talents parable in a different context, and thus gives a different emphasis.

a) Essential to Matthew's account is the theme of *delay* (v. 19), recalling the spouse who delays (Mt 25:5). He has in mind the time of the Church, where Luke is only considering the interval between Christ's death and the fall of Jerusalem (Lk 19:11). People believed in the imminence of the Kingdom, and Christ tells them that before this will come a revolt against the King (his Passion) and the chastisement of the city (the fall of Sion). Doubtless Luke is thinking of Archelaus who had gone to seek the kingship at Rome, and was followed by some Jews who wished to intrigue against him. His horizon is limited to the immediate situation, while Matthew is altogether concerned with the "time of the Church."

b) Another difference between the two accounts can be seen in the *servants* of the master. For Luke Jesus' purpose in the parable is to indicate the attitude of the persons listening. Some believe in him, while others are indifferent or frankly hostile (Lk 19:7, 11). When the Kingdom comes these attitudes will get suitable recompense. The fervent disciples will get the power of jurisdiction (Lk 19:17-19). The indifferent Jews will lose their privileges (Mt 24:24; Lk 19:16). The hostile Jews will be lost (Lk 19:27). For Matthew on the other hand, who is considering the time of the Church after the fall of Jerusalem, the point is the extraordinary disproportion between the stewardship on earth and the promised reward (Mt 25:21, 23, 29). The master distributes talents (interests in the Kingdom that is) according to each one's natural quality; but one talent alone at that time represented a huge fortune. It is consequently wrong to interpret the "talents" as natural gifts to be exploited. We are dealing with the largesse of the Kingdom, of which the Christian becomes the steward, because the Kingdom cannot be built without his collaboration.

Consequently Matthew is giving the parable a new emphasis by making it part of ecclesiology. The disciples are being apprised of their obligation to use the riches of the Kingdom during the time allotted to them, the time of the Church.

God risks his word as a financier risks his capital. He does not hoard it, but hands it to us for good use. The last servant, in his morbid avoidance of all risk, is opting for an illusory security. Uninvested talent is devalued talent; what is not increased is spent. "Burying" the talent, for fear of compromising it, means burying oneself and opting for death.

This severe warning by Jesus to the religious authorities of his time loses none of its point now. To use our treasure, we must encounter the world. A Church afraid to risk her heritage by involvement in the city of man would have lost everything.

VIII. Mark   In 49 the emperor Caligula demanded that his
13:24-32   statue be erected in the temple of Jerusalem.
Gospel   It was possible to avert the sacrilege, which
2nd cycle   in fact was only perpetrated in 70 by Titus;
        but Jewish communities disseminated at this
time writings, which purported to see in Caligula a new Antiochus (Mk 13:14), and feared a winter departure from Sion (Mk 13:18). In the background then of Mark 13 is a Jewish apocalypse that was put together during the anguished period of waiting for the destruction of the temple, and was heavily based on Old Testament texts (cf. Jr 29:9 and Dt 18:7 in verse 6; Dn 2:28 in verse 7b; Is 19:2 and 2 Ch 15:6 in verse 8; Mi 7:6 and Is 19:2 in verse 12; Mi 7:7 in verse 13b; Dn 9:27, 12 in verse 19; Dt 13:2 in verse 22; Is 13:10 in verse 24; Is 34:3 in verse 25; Dn 7:13 in verse 26; Dt 30:3 in verse 27).

Subsequently the apocalypse passed into Judaeo-Christian circles, which used it to express expectation of the Parousia (v.

26) and their particular reading of the preliminary signs (vv. 6, 8, 12, 22). At some stage the text was reworked in these circles. Sayings of Jesus were inserted (for instance, v. 26); but there continued to be a note of apocalyptic frenzy which Mark is at pains to soften in the definitive redaction of the chapter. Thus he adds a part of verse 24 to point out that the coming of the Son of man is not necessarily linked to the destruction of the temple. He adds verses 9-11 and 13b to counter the false prophets who are disturbing people unduly. Finally, he concludes the chapter in verses 28-37* with a personal doctrinal expose.

a) Mark's description of the fall of Jerusalem is very restrained. Matthew stresses apocalyptic images like the lightning (Mt 24:27, borrowed from Is 29:6; 30:27-33; Ze 9:14; Ps 17/18: 14-15; 96/97:4; 143/144:6), or vultures feeding on bodies (Mt 24:28, borrowed from Is 18:6; Jr 7:33; 12:9–15:3). The day of Yahweh, as described in Mark and Matthew, is the judgment of *Jerusalem*, not the final Parousia. Only by analogy is it possible to pass from one to the other, and the tendency of Mark is to warn his readers against this procedure.

b) Assuming however that Mark envisages the fall of Jerusalem only, what is the meaning of the vision of the *Son of man* (v. 26)?

In fact the coming on the clouds of the Son of man (Dn 7:13) indicates, in the New Testament, Christ's resurrection and enthronement as Lord of the world (cf. Mt 26:61-64; Ac 7:41-56, two passages where the sign of the Risen Lord is linked to the destruction of the temple; cf. further Mt 23:38). The expression "they shall see the Son of man" suggests further the vision of the Risen Lord in faith (Jn 16:17). The vision is meant to convince Mark's readers that they need not look to some alleged apocalypse, seeing that in the Lord's resurrection they already have all these elements.

c) There remains the question of the *reassembly* (cf. Ze 2:10; Dt 30:4) affirmed in verse 27 to be the consequence of the coming of the Son of man. We can see here perhaps a reference to the

*See the doctrinal theme: *last times*, p. 285.

missionary action of the Church as she gathers the nations by means of her "angels," who are the missionaries (as in Rev 2:1, 8, 12, 18; 3:1, 7, 14). A number of text insist on this function of the Church, as she succeeds Jerusalem as assembler of the nations (Is 66:18-19; Mt 12:30; He 12:22-23; Rev 7:1-9; Mt 13:30, 47).

Those Judaeo-Christians who inserted verse 27 in the basic Jewish apocalypse doubtless did give an apocalyptic meaning to the theme of reassembly. But Mark, who is opposing the false eschatologies of pseudo-prophets (vv. 9-11), takes it in another sense. It is the whole ecclesial phase of the construction of the Kingdom that is contemplated, with no indication that it is to be brief.

d) Christ evidently used the image of the blossoming *fig-tree* in the biblical sense, a sign of blessing and prosperity (Jl 2:22). It seems possible that he chose this as a symbol of the time of salvation. The burgeoning fig-tree signifies the end of winter, and the nearness of summer with its promise of renewal. In the redaction of the gospel the transference by which it becomes a harbinger of catastrophe seems questionable.

e) Verses 30-32 are important insofar as they reveal that the cosmic catastrophe will take place during the succeeding years. The "generation" of Jesus' listeners will see it. It can only be the fall of Jerusalem, of which the Son of man himself did not know the precise date. Jesus did not see his lordship over the world, that would come about through these events, as a right. It was a *gratuitous gift* of the Father, the result of his free initiative, the gift of love.

IX. Luke
21:5-19
Gospel
3rd cycle

In this preface to his eschatological discourse Jesus gives two categories of signs preliminary to his coming; wars and maladies on the one hand (vv. 8, 11; cf. Mt 24:4-8), persecution on the other (vv. 12-19; cf. Mt 24:9-13).

a) Matthew 24:5 speaks of false Messiahs. Luke suppresses this somewhat, as too obscure for his readers of Greek origin. He alludes to false eschatologies which wrongly predict the end of the world (v. 8; cf. 2 Th 2: 1-8).

Both evangelists refer to Daniel 2:28, according to whom "it must be" that wars and upheavals will precede the dawning of the Kingdom. This phrase should be taken in the sense given to it by Jesus himself when, in justifying his own Passion, he affirms repeatedly that "it must be" that the Scriptures be fulfilled (Lk 9:22, 24; 24:16). There is no question of a *fatalistic necessity*. It is the paschal law, woven into the texture of salvation events, where life emerges from death.

Matthew presents the events in the style of Jewish apocalypse. The earthquakes are reminiscent of the oracles of Isaiah 8:21; 13:13 and Jeremiah 21:9; 34:17. Luke passes this over in silence. His readers were not sufficiently familiar with biblical mentality.

b) Jesus mentions *persecution* at verse 12, as a preliminary sign of the Kingdom. On this point Matthew and Luke differ remarkably. Luke makes use of a passage that Matthew gives elsewhere (Mt 10:17-22). Matthew 24:9-13 contemplates above all the effect of persecution in the community; many dead and much apostasy, many people deceived by false Messiahs, love grown cold. Only a "Remnant" will emerge to be saved. The Remnant for him will be made up of Christians, definitively liberated from Judaism at the fall of Jerusalem.

Luke describes the reactions of Christians to persecution. The faithful will be judged and persecuted by Jews (synagogues) and pagans (v. 12); but they will receive the eloquence and wisdom necessary to answer accusations. In mentioning wisdom, he is thinking perhaps of Joseph or Daniel triumphing over pagan learning (Gn 40; Dn 2). Thus he is broaching a theology that will be thoroughly developed by John, when he reveals the role of the Paraclete (Jn 15:26–16:15).

By way of conclusion he takes two sentences from another context that are highly optimistic. Thanks to their trust (Mt 10:30) and constancy (He 10:36-39), the persecuted Christians will surmount all trials.

Luke then, like Matthew, is giving a doctrine of suffering and

persecution which stresses the link with the eschatological dynamism of the Kingdom. This is the paschal law. Trial will enable
the "Remnant" (Mt) of the "saved" (Lk) who form the Kingdom
to establish themselves. The persecuted will be assured of the
presence among them of God's Word and Spirit.

B. DOCTRINE

1. Theme of the Last Times

Today's formulary gives us texts that combine to form a dynamic vision of God's plan and of Christian life. Faith in Jesus Christ should normally issue in hope of cosmic dimensions; so great is the fulfillment, so endless the vistas of transformation.

Yet, in actual fact, how narrow are the religious horizons of very many Christians. To take just those who try to "live" the faith they received at baptism, how many find it a source of dynamism capable of molding their lives into instruments for the salvation of all men. Too many have no concept of the grandeur of their vocation; their religion is something narrow and individualist. People preserve a religiosity that is more or less authentic; but of the pulsations of a spirit that is limited only by the entire universe, they remain unaware. All realize of course that the commandment of universal brotherly love is basic in Christianity. But how inadequate many feel when it comes to means of applying this precept in order to renew the face of the earth.

The period of history in which we live challenges us to take the measure of this universe to which our faith introduces us. Indeed it is imperative, if we are to fulfill the role we should. The faith cannot be lived casually; certain demands must be answered. If our faith fails to correspond to the historical situation in which we find ourselves, we shall not give the witness before men they have a right to expect from us. The faith itself becomes degraded; it is no longer the salt of the earth.

The wait for eschatological fulfillment

The Jews were a people who loved life, who had the deepest yearning for fulfillment for soul and body in every way. This aspiration was expressed in numerous ways, one of the most usual being the ideal of fulfillment, as the dispersed members of the chosen people gathered in the love of Yahweh.

Under the regime of faith the fulfillment was seen as something that would come about through God's intervention. Yahweh alone is master of his people's destiny; he alone can save them. But because he is the God of love he cannot save men without man's cooperation. Thus he makes a covenant with his people; salvation will depend on an encounter between two fidelities.

Unfortunately however, from the desert experience onwards, Israel showed herself a recalcitrant, stiff-necked people. The pagan way of security was preferred to the spiritual adventure offered by Yahweh. This sin of the desert was destined to be renewed in generation after generation, perpetuating the original sin in paradise.

Prophets arose to denounce the people's infidelity to the alliance, stressing the constant fidelity of Yahweh and his appeals for conversion. The great and passionate quest began, pursued by all the better element. Who would be the man capable of giving a pleasing response to God? When this Messiah came, Yahweh would provide the promised plenitude. Messianic hope was descernible everywhere; it is so all-pervasive in Israel's spiritual pilgrimage that it has been justly termed the "backbone of the Old Testament."

On the day of Yahweh justice would descend like lightning. Fulfillment would be so overwhelming that the new paradise would be altogether different to the present world. There would be a new earth, a new heaven, a new heart that would open men to the action of the Spirit.

The coming of the Son of Man

In the eschatological discourse Jesus uses the themes and vocabulary of contemporary apocalyptic literature to characterize his messianic intervention.

This was an event that inaugurated the last times. The day of

Yahweh had actually dawned, and fulfillment was vouchsafed. The Messiah's work was above all ecumenical; his task was to re-assemble all men "from the four winds," for all are called to be children of the Father. Jerusalem is rejected. She has betrayed her mission by arrogating to herself a privilege where she should have undertaken a responsibility. She was unable to shed her particularism.

The sign of the Son of Man is obedience unto the death of the cross. To enter life eternal one must go by the way of death; because death when confronted in obedience can become the great focus of love for God and all men. There is no greater love than laying down one's life for those one loves.

This means that eschatology in the former sense is completely reversed. The fulfillment that was associated with the final times is something that is actually granted here and now. It is a seed which has but to grow. Jesus does not bring fulfillment ready made; he plants the living seed. The accomplishment of eschatology will come from on high; but before then, there must be a process of growth here below. The impetus given by Jesus must be carried on in the great task where each man makes his contribution.

This is the task of reassembly "from the four winds." The coming of the Son of man is an actuality always present with us, always reminding us that there is only one leader in the project. His sign reminds us that, for us too, growth to fulfillment will only come by means of death and the cross.

The Church of the last times

Since Christ's resurrection the task of reassembling humanity continues apace. The whole cosmos has entered on the decisive phase of its growth towards universal recapitulation in Jesus Christ. The central force in this work is the Church, which is the Body of Christ. She, and no other agency, is properly fitted to carry it out; but the adequacy will always be determined by the fidelity of her members.

Saint Paul reminds us often enough that the test of fidelity is the decision to grow, day after day, in the knowledge of God's will. A fuller discernment of his will in the event is the Christian's great means of planting the mystery of Christ throughout humanity.

The search for his will inevitably leads us to realize what a weight of death lies upon the whole pattern of human existence, individual and collective. We have to confront this with "perfect patience and endurance, giving thanks with joy to the Father" (Col 1:11-12). Our sign must be the sign of the Son of man, obedience unto the death of the cross for love of God and all men.

We must never forget that we continue to be sinners, that we must cry to the Lord from the depths of our misery, that our heart always needs to be converted to the Father's will.

If the Church be equipped with fidelity of this calibre on the part of her members, she will successfully overcome what is for her the most formidable temptation; that of allowing the particularism of old Jerusalem to manifest itself again. The validity of her proclamation of the coming of the Son of man is always proportioned to the extent of her demonstration that Jerusalem in that sense is no more.

The witness par excellence of the coming of the Son of Man

In the great task of universal reassembly the initial impetus was given at the coming of the Son of man. But the building has to be constructed stone by stone, in individual contributions from those who bear witness to that coming. In Christ everything was accomplished. But everything remains to be accomplished, because the plenitude of salvation presupposes growth. The secret of growth is mission.

Today the greatest obstacles to reassembly are the barriers of separation between peoples and cultures. Sin lies at the root of all this. If peoples and cultures are going to encounter each other, like individuals, with full acceptance of the otherness in each other, that will call for self-renunciation. Men, because they are sinners, naturally tend to seek security in their own groups, to be opposed to others, and sometimes to seek their destruction.

Mission, as the expression of the greatest love, which includes the love of enemies, seeks to overcome this obstacle. Its object is real catholicity. It attempts to demonstrate that all men, however diverse, are called to be children of the same Father in the one and only Kingdom. Unless the missionary himself confront death as the Son of man did, this will not be possible.

Today, much more acutely than in the past, we begin to realize the huge dimensions of the missionary task. We begin to see that, while distinct, there is a close connection between it and the enterprise of civilization. The so-called "encounter of cultures" is indeed the most pressing problem for humanity here and now. It has many different aspects, political, social, economic, etc. Ecclesial mission should give priority to all of them.

The Eucharist, a prelude to final reassembly

When Christians assemble for the Eucharist, they are answering a universal summons; and the gathering that they constitute has already the characteristics of the final reassembly. This is so because the bonds of brotherhood forged by the Eucharist depend altogether on what Jesus accomplished once for all. By partaking of the body of Christ we receive all men as brothers; the Christ we receive into our being is the plenitude of this sentiment.

This being so, the Church should see to it that the eucharistic assemblies visibly express what they mean. The seed of brotherhood planted in the heart of each member will then take root deeply, and blossom in his life. He will have felt in his own being some little of the abundance that will characterize the definitive Kingdom; and he will bend his energies to furthering the growth of the Body to its full stature, despite all obstacles.

2. The Theme of Work

The Church is directly concerned with anything that has to do with work. It is God's plan that man should dominate the universe and humanize the earth. Secondly the Good News should first be proclaimed to the poor, whose dignity has been wounded; and many workers throughout the world are among the poor.

Pius XI once made the remark that in the 19th century the Church had lost the working class. It is a revealing remark; because it indicates, that more or less unwittingly, Christians found themselves on the side of the rich and propertied, for whom human labor was more a source of profit than of dignity. It indicates that, on a global scale, Christians were not faithful to their mission.

Even today the dignity of the worker is far from being secure. Injustice continues to reign, and has indeed assumed gigantic proportions, when we consider relationships between peoples. It is imperative that we Christians have a lucid concept of what is required of us in the Church's mission to the world now.

The concept of work in Israel

Basically, Israel had a positive attitude to work; it was regarded as part of God's plan for men. In creating man, Yahweh had given him the commission to occupy the earth and subdue it (Gn 1:28). Man's work would be an extension of God's creation. Respect for work went side by side with distrust for idleness. Work was essentially a community effort, where each one was expected to play his part in furthering the common good.

Unfortunately however work was also involved in the vicissitudes of fallen man on earth. The soil was cursed and resisted the power that man had been given over creation. Work began to seem more a duty than an honor and suffering went with it. Nature continuously jeopardized the toil of man, and, worst of all, death seemed to nullify this toil. Work could become the occasion for exploitation of one man by another. The effects of sin could be seen, between peoples, and between individuals. Before she entered the Covenant with Yahweh, Israel herself had known the slavery of forced labor in Egypt, under pitiless masters.

Sin of course is the cause of all this maladjustment. Yahweh however, when he concluded the alliance with his people, wanted them to be free of sin and its consequences. When that came about, work would be restored to its proper dignity. The Law has many details which reflect this attitude. If a man were fully faithful to the covenant, the ill effects of sin could be overcome; such was the will of God. Man's fidelity would be rewarded by a blessing on his toil; he would enjoy its fruits. Alas, Israel continued to be a sinful people. Injustice continued to be rampant and work was not restored to dignity. That would have to await the dawning of the day of Yahweh.

The New Adam and the dignity of work on earth

Throughout the greater portion of his life Jesus worked with his hands. His father was a carpenter. However, when at the age of thirty he departed to preach the Good News of the Kingdom, he seemed no longer to attach any importance to work. He commends the birds of the air "who sow not, neither do they reap" (Mt 6:26). Only one thing counted; the Kingdom.

The truth was that the very nature of the Kingdom proclaimed by Jesus provided an answer to Israel's problems concerning work. His Kingdom was something that had to be constructed on this earth. It was not of this earth; but it was not necessary to leave the terrestrial state in order to enter it and contribute to its growth. The road to construction of the Kingdom was the road of obedience unto the death of the cross. Suffering and death regained hereby their veritable meaning.

Jesus did not speak of work; but, in inaugurating the Kingdom here on earth, he gave it its proper signification. Work derives its meaning from evangelic obedience to the terrestrial state. In proportion to a man's acceptance of the creatural condition, something that he can do through his link with Jesus Christ; to his readiness to confront suffering and death as the greatest expression of love for God and man, all human values will be restored to their proper dignity. Their passage through death does not mean their destruction, but their transfiguration. So it is with work. The performance of work in our context does not turn a man's gaze towards a new paradise. On the contrary it makes him muster all energy to reinstate work to its proper dignity at the terrestrial level. It is thus that the child of God makes his contribution as partner to the building of the Kingdom.

Jesus Christ, the New Adam, reminds us that man's mission is to subdue the earth by his toil; but that this can only be accomplished with proper lucidity when we recognize that the one thing necessary is the Kingdom. If we can replace work where it should be in the scheme of things, it will regain its proper inspiration. Under the impetus of love, the love of total self-giving, human toil has the capacity to humanize the earth.

Work in the tradition of the Church

The apostolic writings do not put forward any philosophy of work or any program for social reform. The primitive communities were made up of people from every social class, in general the lower classes, including slaves. Revolution was not preached to them. Yet, because they were made free with the liberty acquired in Jesus Christ, a seed was sown among them that was gradually to transform the Graeco-Roman world.

A good deal militated against such a transformation. The culture which Christianity encountered in the Mediterranean did not hold manual work in high regard. It was the province of slaves for the most part. There was exaltation of the values of the Spirit, and a sort of disdain for everything connected with the body and matter. Contemplation was exalted over action, speculation over the transformation of the world. It was only in works of art that matter was humanized. Secondly, once Christianity became the official religion of the Empire, the tendency was to support the established social order rather than put it ceaselessly to question. All this did not make for change, but for resignation.

Nevertheless the seed sown by the gospel was at work. It was gradually to make men aware of the essential distinction between religion and the enterprise of civilization. The two are intimately connected, but have to be carefully distinguished. Eventually civilization came to be recognized for the profane and autonomous enterprise that it is. At this point the modern world began to be born. Work is no longer just a necessity. It is a value in itself with its precise demands. If the child of God is to play his part in the building of the Kingdom, he must do so by playing his part in the humanization of the earth. He must transform the relationship between men, between all men. Action, as against contemplation, is restored to where it should be; and work has its proper value.

The missionary significance of properly valued work

The industrial revolution in the 19th century made human labor one of the most critical issues in the whole history of humanity. An explosive development in technology in the West opened up vistas of man's possible mastery over the universe. But it also brought about, in total environments, and internationally, the most glaring injustices. Economic development served the interests of the few, and of some nations, rather than those of all humanity. The great majority of workers everywhere became aware that they were being exploited.

It was a great irony. At the very moment when modern man discovered the value of work as the great instrument for human advancement, he had to witness the fruits of labor being diverted from their proper ends. He found that the conditions for human toil, so far from being ennobling, were degrading.

The masses of workers had to resort to struggle, and had to join forces. The struggle was inevitable if iniquitous systems were to be replaced, and solidarity was the only way of exercising the necessary pressure. Throughout it all, there was no mention of religion, unless indeed as one of the prime sources of alienation. Among these masses of the poor of our time the Church faces, and must continue to face, the greatest of all challenges, that of atheism.

To meet this, she must place herself resolutely on the side of the poor. To take the part of the poor is to take the part of hu-

manity. In season and out of season she must give her support to
a civilization of work that will be for the benefit of all. Her
members must try to demonstrate in a concrete fashion that faith
in Jesus Christ and practice of the beatitudes does lead to revolution in the good sense. It will make the earth more habitable
for man. We should all derive inspiration from the prophetic
career of Pope John XXIII. His two basic documents on world
peace and world development point the way for us, and the price
that must be paid.

The Eucharist and the dignity of work

To those Jews who reproached him for having healed on the
Sabbath Jesus responded "My Father works always and I too
work" (Jn 5:17). A festive day, that is, is not one on which we
escape the terrestrial state and enter an illusory Kingdom. Work
for the construction of the Kingdom must continue without intermission always. The festive day differs from other days in the
sense that we then work differently, with more intensity. We become conscious of all that work can mean.

In the eucharistic celebration we are at the very nerve center
of construction of the Kingdom. The Word and the Bread initi-
ate us deeper and deeper into the mystery of the gospel. The
Kingdom is already with us, and the whole of creation is involved. It is erected on the principle of love, the love of Jesus
Christ. We learn authentic fidelity to our creatural condition.
We can and should make our contribution to the humanization
of the earth and our filial state will give our efforts an eternal
dimension. We shall have to meet the challenge of death of
course; but if we confront it in obedience, we shall find that this
is what purifies our effort and makes for the transformation of
the universe.

In the immense work-yard of creation, the Eucharist will
clarify for us the decisive steps that we must take. We become
aligned with the great Master, the leader of the work, who died
and rose again for the salvation of the world.

THIRTY-FOURTH SUNDAY
Feast of Christ the King

A. THE WORD

I. Ezechiel 34:11- 12, 15-17
1st reading
1st cycle

Chapter 34 of Ezechiel, called the "good shepherd" chapter, is not easy to interpret. The prophet is writing after the fall of Jerusalem, when Judah is in the throes of complete anarchy (Jr 40-42). The survivors had not learned their lesson, and believed they had only to change politics in order to regain status.

In a first discourse, delivered doubtless about 584, Ezechiel turns to invective against bad shepherds (Ez 34:1-16). He foretells a judgment of God against them, and regrets the absence of a legitimate king (v. 6). These bad shepherds were probably the leaders of bands that were terrorizing the population during the breakdown.

A second discourse, verses 17-22 (and 31?) attacks the rich sheep who exploited the poor. This refers doubtless to the comfortable peasants who refused to aid the proletariat in the cities. These had been reduced to starvation by the siege.

A conclusion in verses 23 and 24 provides a solution. The reign of Yahweh and his prince David will be restored.

Verses 25-31 form a poem of consolation that was composed a full century later. The great themes of Second-Isaiah are taken up. A paradisal future is envisaged when the flock will be reassembled.

Our reading today gives us a portion only of the first discourse (11-12, 15-16) and the first verse of the second (17).

a) At this moment of the exile the people is made up of "worthless" sheep and those who are "scattered." The former are probably the people who remain in Palestine. They are delivered over to the tyranny of the conqueror, or despoiled by his agents. The latter are those who have been deported into exile, or who have fled to Egypt. The future is seen in terms of a *reassembly* of all the sheep round about Yahweh himself, and no longer round the king (v. 11). This gathering will be based on personal relations between God and each member of the people (v. 16). It will no longer be based on external, juridical association with the covenant.

Thus what Ezechiel has in mind is a Kingdom directly under divine direction, which depends on relationships that are essentially religious. Membership will be selective. It will have nothing in common with earthly kingdoms or human institutions. It belongs to another order. Ezechiel does not at this point say so; but the Kingdom could well be extended to all nations.

b) The selectivity of the Kingdom of God will be determined by a *judgment* between "sheep and sheep" (v. 17). Not alone does God separate the chosen people from their enemies; he also makes a division between the good and the wicked.

The eucharistic assembly has these decisive characteristics of God's Kingdom. It is made up of those whom God has already assembled, irrespective of their cultural, political or social origin. It includes the good and the wicked, because it is the sign of mission. It initiates each member into the personal, intimate dialogue of faith that characterizes God and his children.

II. Daniel
7:13-14
1st reading
2nd cycle

Chapter 7 of Daniel is one of the most important apocalyptic pieces in scripture. It seems to have been put together according to the most ancient traditions. We can discern one source, in prose, which concerns the end of the kingdoms of this world (the vision of the four beasts; vv. 2-8 and 11-12). Another, older still, is in verse, and concerns the Son of man (vv. 9-10 and 13-14). Then comes the angel's interpretation (vv. 17-27) regarding both the previous traditions, which reassembles doctrinally Daniel 2. Finally, there are some later interpolations (vv. 8, 11a, 20, 24 and 25a, 21, 22b and 25b), which are subsequent interpretations, sometimes fiercely nationalist in tone.

The purpose of the final redactor is fairly clear. He wants to proclaim the approaching end of the great terrestrial empires, the last of which in particular tyrannizes over the chosen people. He is reestablishing confidence in the possibility of a proximate Kingdom of God by a "Son of man" (v. 13) and a "people of saints" (v. 18).

Probably the *Son of man* vision goes back to Ugaritic mythology. The "ancient of days" suggests the title of some ancient God-sovereign. The "Son of man" could have been a rival god, whom Daniel, ignorant doubtless of the mythological background of these images, reduces to angelic state.

The identity of the "Son of man" for the author is indeed quite puzzling. Nothing suggests that he is thought of as a human being. He is "like" a Son of man (v. 13), and he comes on the clouds, a characteristic of heavenly beings. This seems to preclude any messianic earthly interpretation.

The kingship conferred on the Son of man in verse 14 is accorded to the "Saints of the Most-High" in verses 18 and 22, which suggests that the Son of man stands for these, for the celestial court that is.

Because of such phraseology, unknown elsewhere ("ancient of days," "Son of man," "saints of the Most-High"), and highly ambiguous, the chapter remains a puzzle. It does seem possible to discern a double inauguration of the Kingdom of God. One is on the terrestrial level, the annihilation of the four imperial beasts. The other is on a celestial, the submission of the celestial court to the ancient of days.

Apparently then we are dealing with important evidence of a spiritual current, which was turning popular soteriology away from davidic messianism towards intervention by a transcendent being.

Under the influence of contemporary thinking, the parables of Enoch in particular, Jesus would correct this tendency. He was conscious of fulfilling at once three traditions; the transcendent mission of the Son of Man, the expiation of the suffering Servant, and the Messiahship of the Son of David. He considerably modifies the concept of the Son of Man. He makes the image the sign sometimes of his humiliation (Mt 8:20; 11:19; 17:22; 20:28), sometimes of his glorification (Mt 26:64; Mk 13:24-27). He retains it for the proclamation of a kingdom at once celestial and terrestrial.

III. 2 Samuel   David was an excellent politician. Anointed
5:1-3   king of the southern tribes at Hebron (2 S
1st reading   2:1-4), he at once tried to be recognized as
3rd cycle   king by the northern tribes who had remained
faithful to Saul's dynasty. Through the connivance of Abner he managed to recover his first wife Mical, the daughter of Saul (2 S 3:13), and thus to represent himself as a descendant of Saul. After the death of Ishbaal, the son of the old king (2 S 4), the throne was vacant. Through his diplomacy David was able to take over.

The very fact that the northern tribes made a special pact with David, and repeated the anointing that had already taken place in 2 S 2, is evidence that he is now king of two distinct peoples, not of a single realm. His political awareness enabled him to see that he could no longer reside at Hebron, a southern town. He must have a neutral capital, belonging neither to north or south, and Jerusalem was the obvious choice. It was still at this stage a Canaanite town. His conquest would be an exploit that would reinforce his authority over the tribes, and obliterate the memories of the Gelboe disaster.

The ruse which brought about the capture of the Jebusaean town was seen by contemporaries as a sign of God's particular assistance (we have this interpretation in Jg 4:17-22; 1 M 7: 10-29). It appears that the town was taken without striking a blow by some soldiers who were able to scale the shaft that led from the fortress to the fount of Gibon. This is still visible today.

IV. 1 Corinthians   Our reading is one of the most complex pas-
    15:20-26, 28   sages in this chapter which gives us the Paul-
    2nd reading   ine doctrine concerning the resurrection of
    1st cycle   the dead. Paul is addressing people who be-
                     lieve in the immortality of the soul as a liber-
ation from a material, corruptible body. He maintains the Jewish concept of personal unity. Man is not a dichotomy of soul and body, but a personal being that is unique. Since the resurrection of Christ, he knows that God has destined him for survival.

We have the conclusion of this argument in verses 22-23. Verses 24-28 are a digression; they describe the relationship between Christ's reign and that of the Father. Doubtless he is concerned to show the total submission of Christ to the Father. He does not want the Corinthians to see their relationship in terms of pagan mythology, of gods either hostile or in opposition.

a) To understand the passage we have to keep in mind the main thrust of Jewish apocalypse, where the *messianic kingdom* is thought of as a transition to the reign of God. Only thus could theology resolve the apparent contradiction between the oracles which proclaimed the reign of a Messiah, and those which prophesied a theocracy.

Paul too still sees some succession between the two reigns, the messianic and the theocracy, but he demonstrates that the messianic reign has its own particular function. It will be fairly lengthy because the Messiah must conquer all his enemies (Ps 109/110:1), death included (v. 25). Death and the forces that control the world (the heavenly "powers"; v. 24) must be submitted to Christ's Lordship (cf. Rev 20:14; 1 Co 15:54). For that reason the "end" is not yet, and must be awaited with patience.

b) Concerning the conflict between Christ and the *powers of the world* (v. 24), among them death, the New Testament gives no definite answer. Some texts suppose that the battle has been won in Christ's resurrection (Ep 1:22; 1 P 3:22), others that the victory is constantly in process. Taking the first view, Christians can regard themselves as sharers in the victory of Christ from the moment of baptism. The second, which Saint Paul is presenting here, sees all human life as a constant struggle against the alienating forces of evil. The Corinthians thus must be careful about the spiritual charisms they have (1 Co 12-14), and about their sexual habits. The fruits of the Kingdom are theirs to be sure; but this does not mean that perfection is acquired and victory assured.

As we survey Church history, we see that there were moments when she insisted that she was here and now the Kingdom, and others when she was forced to recognize that she was not so "yet." During periods of the former kind, there is a tendency to absolutize structures, places of worship, hierarchy, as if everything were settled and proven. During the other times the people of God become more aware of all the alienating forces in the world that have still to be dealt with. They see the limitations of all that has been done, and feel the urge to plunge into the great human struggle for a better world.

V. Revelation 1:5-8
2nd reading
2nd cycle

Our reading gives us, except for verse 4, the address to the Churches of the Roman province of Asia, to whom John dedicates the book of Revelation. The text is somewhat modified in the liturgy in order to concentrate attention on the person of Christ.

a) Jesus is given three titles (v. 5). He is *first-born* among the dead, because he is the first man to be exempt from the law of death (1 Co 15:20; Rm 6:9), and the only means for others of conquering death (1 J 5:1-5). He is the faithful *witness*, because he has born witness unto death to the Father's plan, and because in him all the prophecies and promises are fulfilled (cf. Ps 88/89:

28, 38). Finally, he is *prince* of the kings of the world, because he has received all power from the Father (Dn 7:13-14), and manifests this by directing earthly empires, as the book of Revelation will go on to show (cf. Rev 11:15; 17:14; 19:16).

b) Verses 5b-7 constitute a sort of anamnesis of the *salutary* work of Christ. He has shown us his love by purifying us through his death from sin (Ga 3:13; Ep 1:7; 1 P 1:19), and establishing a people who are a royal priesthood (Ex 19:6; cf. 1 P 2:1-10; Rev 5:10; 20:6; 22:5). Verse 6 is interrupted by a brief doxology, usual in the New Testament, in honor of Christ as Savior (cf. Rev 4:8, 11; 5:9-13; 19:1-7; Rm 11:36; 16:25-27; Ep 3:20-21, etc.). Then the author continues his anamnesis by proclaiming the proximate return of the Lord. He will come like the Son of man on the clouds (Dn 7:13). He will be "seen" (following Ze 12:10), and the nations will be converted. These themes are all adapted to the Christian view of the last times (Mt 24:29-31). For a Jew, to "see" the Lord coming on the clouds was to have faith in his transcendent origin. For a Christian it meant believing in his resurrection and his Lordship (Mt 26:61-64; Ac 7:55) and being converted to the Kingdom he inaugurates.

c) The paraphrase "he is, he was, he comes" (v. 8; cf. v. 4) clearly designates the Father. It is an expression of Jewish origin, an elaboration of the phrase "I am," known since Exodus 3:14. It shows that God is not alone in the present but also in the past and future. "He is, he was, he will be" was sometimes a way of naming God. John substitutes "he comes" for "he will be" to stress the fact that the Father is master of a history that he will sanction by his advent as judge.

VI. Colossians 1:12-20
2nd reading
3rd cycle

In this piece attention is concentrated on the primacy of Christ as lord. It is proclaimed in a hymn of two couplets, which commemorate his kingship over the created world (vv. 15-17) on the one hand, and over the re-created world (vv. 18-20) on the other. The strophes are so structured that they correspond:

v. 15: He is . . . first born of all creatures	v. 18b: He is . . . first born of all the dead
v. 16: It is in him . . . all that is	v. 19: It is in him that God . . . all plenitude
v. 16: in heaven and on earth	v. 20: in heaven and on earth
v. 16: created for him	v. 20: created for him

a) Verses 15-20 are doubtless a paraphrase of a primitive hymn (perhaps baptismal). We should note first of all that the first strophe terminates with an enumeration of the powers of creation; thrones, lordships, principalities. The second concludes with a mention of the cross, which is the sign of the new Lordship. Earth and heaven are mentioned in both strophes, giving the idea of totality or universality.

Each strophe furthermore deals with the Word incarnate, not the divine Word.

He is first born of all creation, not in a chronological sense, but a causal one. In creating the world God used Christ as a model (cf. Pr 8:22 concerning Wisdom).

He is also first born in the supernatural order (thus chronologically as well as causally). The pre-existent Christ is contemplated but seen as incarnate.

Finally, the *primacy* of Christ is depicted in three images; the first born, head of the body, and plenitude. These figures, favorite ones with Paul, indicate that Christ's resurrection places his human nature at the head of a regenerated humanity as well as creation itself (Rm 8:19-22; 1 Co 3:22; 15:20-28; Ep 1:10; 4:10, etc.).

b) This christological hymn should be taken not so much as a doctrinal pronouncement, but rather as a passionate *profession of faith* elicited by the gnostic environment. For a Christian, Christ's primacy is everything, and the rest fantasy. Gnostic speculations about a creator God are ridiculous; Christ does all. Adam himself surrenders to him his title as first man. Equally futile are the commentaries about angels now that Christ is here. Paul is really using gnostic vocabulary to combat gnosticism.

The Risen Lord is leader of all those faithful who wish to follow him by sharing the life of the Church. His resurrection establishes him in absolute pre-eminence over the universe, of which he has become Lord. Paul actually says that the angelic powers and dominations had usurped a power over creation which Jesus recovered by the resurrection.

Christ's Lordship however is not to be thought of as in any way similar to that of the angelic powers, something that deprived man of free choice in his destiny. Of all the lordships, only that of Christ does not prove alienating for man or creation. It was in the very pattern of his earthly life that he acquired his lordship. Man can share it, by following his example and working for the spiritualization of creation.

The resurrection makes Jesus lord, because it is the great reconciliation between soul and body, matter and Spirit, earth and heaven. In the eucharist we have the opportunity to experience here and now the victory of the Spirit over matter and the "flesh."

VII. Matthew
25:31-46
Gospel
1st cycle

Matthew has already shown that members of the chosen people must practice vigilance in order to share the eschatological Kingdom (Mt 24-25). In this passage he considers what the destiny of the Gentiles is likely to be in this regard. The Jewish view was of course simple and uncompromising; the judgment of God would confound all Gentiles. Matthew's view of the judgment is considerably more nuanced.

He is certainly the final redactor of this passage, and verses 31, 34 and 41 are certainly from his own hand. Christ would not call himself king, nor would he attribute to himself the role of judge that was reserved to the Father. The other verses are from Jesus but Matthew must be responsible for their grouping. We can distinguish a brief parable of the shepherd dividing sheep and goats (vv. 32-33), and a series of figures where Jesus identifies himself with the "little ones" to whom good was done (vv. 35-40, 42-45). These latter sayings could have had their original context in Matthew 10:42.

a) The separation of sheep and goats (vv. 32-33) is an illustration from Palestinian moral life. Each evening the shepherds would divide the flock thus. It is probable that the parable attributes to Jesus the judicial function of the pastor in Ezechiel 34:17-22. In that case it would be indicating that the *judgment* will not be a division between Jews and non-Jews, but between the good and the wicked. It will be a moral judgment, not an ethnic one.

b) The other sayings added by Matthew are probably from a different context. They are about the welcome given to *little ones* (vv. 40 and 45). The phrase, on Jesus' lips, always refers to his own disciples (above all in Mt 10:42 and 18:6, probably in Mt 18:10, 14). It describes those who have become little for the Kingdom, who have abandoned everything to devote themselves to their mission. Such little ones are now become great. They are united with the Lord in judging the nations, and identifying those who received them (cf. Mt 19:28; 11:11).

By associating this with the judgment parable Matthew is formulating a sort of beatitude concerning the disciples. They are despised by the public, and have made themselves poor to follow Jesus. There will be a reversal of situations. One day these little ones will be judges. And, in company with the final judge, they will receive only those who have received them (cf. Mt. 10:40).

c) Is it possible to give a wider interpretation and see in the little ones, not only the disciples, but every poor person loved for his own sake, without explicit reference to God? Apparently yes, when we remember the insistence that the beneficiaries of the Kingdom were ignorant of Christ. This would scarcely be conceivable of people who received the disciples and heard their message. The works of mercy listed in verses 35-36 are precisely those that Scripture gives as signs of the proximity of the messianic kingdom (Lk 4:18-20; Mt 11:4-5), without limiting it to disciples only. *Charity* appeared to be the essential thing in the Kingdom of God (1 Co 13:13).

Jesus puts himself forward not only as the Son of man expected by the Jews, but also as the pastor of Ezechiel 34. He will not have it that God's Kingdom depends on physical membership of the chosen people and he seeks to define the conditions that will enable someone not of that people to be justified. It is clear that he does not concern himself with the sort of knowledge of God and his Messiah such a person can acquire. That would be an adequate criterion. For him, the only decisive criterion is a man's treatment of his fellowmen, especially the poorest among them, whether or no he have explicit knowledge of God. He is putting forward indeed a new concept of God's judgment. The man who is a brother to his fellowmen fulfills the messianic Kingdom, because his action, whether he is aware of this or not, comes from God.

Thus we have two standards in the judgment, depending on whether it concerns humanity in general, or the members of the chosen people. The former will answer for their efforts to better humanity (cf. Mt 25:31-40), the latter for their vigilance (cf. Mt 25:1-30), which consists in seeing God's presence in the pattern of human relationships. Only faith can give this insight. That is why Christians are signs, and will be judged according to this. Their faith should lead them to make manifest the divine seed at work in every genuine attempt at brotherhood. Thus they are advance witnesses of what will become clear at the judgment, when God will reveal to men that he was always part of their brotherhood and solidarity.

"Vigilant" Christians are united in the eucharistic assembly for this express purpose.

VIII. John   Like the synoptics, John too records this most
    18:33-37   improbable accusation by the Jews against
    Gospel   Jesus; that he usurped the royal title. Doubt-
    2nd cycle less the allegation was made principally in the
hope that Pilate would prove a jealous guard-
ian of the emperor's prerogatives (Lk 23:2). In fact the procura-
tor did inquire about these royal pretensions. However, whereas
in the synoptics Jesus maintains silence (in imitation doubtless
of the silence of the suffering Servant; Is 53:7), here he replies
and his remarks are pregnant with meaning.

Coming from a Roman, Pilate's question could be ambiguous.
In order to answer it correctly, Jesus had to distinguish the
Jewish kingship in the Roman sense and the messianic kingship
from every other kind of royalty. It is only when he has established that the question emanates not from Pilate but from the
Jews that he expresses his thinking without equivocation. The
theme of *kingship*** is central in his reply. Because it is not really
a typically Johannine theme (he refers to it only in 3:3-5), we
might expect John to have it a separate issue. In fact he fits it into
the constant theme of his gospel. He distinguishes that which is
of this world, and that which is not (Jn 8:23; 17:14).

Pilate does not have the faith that would enable him to distinguish these two orders. He simply concentrates on one word
in Jesus' answer. "Then you are a king?" Jesus says yes, and goes
on to the nature of his kingship (a definition that is typically
Johannine). He has "come into the world (Jn 1:10) to give testimony to the truth" (Jn 3:32 and 5:33), to proclaim to the world,
that is, the knowledge he has of divine life. Truth, for John, is the
divine life itself (1 Jn 3:19). Pilate however takes the ambiguous
term as a Roman philosopher would.

What we have then is an affirmation of Christ's kingship that
derives it from his sharing in divine life. Where the synoptics

---

**See the doctrinal theme: *Christ's kingship,* p. 309.

trace the kingship to Christ's messianic function (the Ascension and Resurrection accounts in Matthew and the Acts), giving it a cosmic dimension, he links it with Christ's divine origins.

IX. Luke
23:35-43
Gospel
3rd cycle

This passage relates the mocking investiture of the King of the Jews on the cross (vv. 35-38), and the episode of the two thieves (vv. 39-43). Luke's own hand is particularly noticeable in the second episode.

a) The *royal investiture* takes place on the cross, the improvised throne of the new Messiah. Luke gives us the inscription that was set up on the cross (v. 38), but he does not point out that it was a reason for condemnation (cf. Mt 27:37). Here it serves as a formula of investiture, similar to that by which the Father invested his Son at the baptism (Lk 3:22). Furthermore Luke also adds a detail that was recounted elsewhere (v. 36a; cf. Mt. 27:48), giving a phrase (v. 36b) by which the crowd purports to recognize Jesus' titles to royalty. This is a test that Jesus refuses. He does not want a kingship that comes by way of escape from his destiny. On the contrary, he wants to be faithful to this.

As always in the mosaic law, this royal enthronement has to be recognized by two witnesses. By contrast with the royal investiture at the transfiguration, where the witnesses were the two principal figures in the Old Testament (Lk 9:28-36), and the resurrection, where the witnesses are likewise mysterious (Lk 24: 4); here the witnesses are two common thieves. It is a parodied investiture for one who had to sink to the depths of humiliation to become king.

b) He exercises his kingship over all men, including his enemies, by offering them his *pardon* (v. 34a, 39-43). This note is prominent throughout Luke's whole recital of the passion but at this point it reaches its culmination.

His pardon reveals him as the New Adam, the one who can aid humanity to recover the paradise lost by the first Adam (cf. Lk

3:38). Humanity must accept this pardon from God and not turn in pride to its own resources. Christ has arrived at that point in his earthly career when he can inaugurate a new humanity, freed from the alienation of sin. He offers the good thief a portion with him, because his will to pardon is limitless. His reign has begun over all those who turn to him.

B.   DOCTRINE

1. Theme of Christ's Kingship

Because of concrete repercussions on the role of the Church in the world, this christological theme has been fairly thoroughly exploited in ecclesial tradition. Theological reflection on it has not always been disinterested and on more than one occasion it has been used to buttress an actual ecclesial situation that was no more than contingent but which some wished to perpetuate. Noticeably for instance it has been applied to Church-state relationships in the Christian West, without adequate realization that the Christian West might prove an ephemeral phenomenon. So much so indeed, that the moment ominous cracks began to appear in the structure, a great many people had recourse to this doctrine as a means of repairing the breaches, and arresting the course of history. It is very true that trends in the modern world jeopardize a proper understanding of Christ's universal kingship, by relegating it altogether to the spiritual domain. But this danger does not for a moment justify Christian structures that were very faulty in themselves and gave full rein to clericalism.

When, in 1925, Pius XI instituted the feast of Christ the King, his purpose was to guard against both extremes, modern laicism and the clericalism of previous generations. Yet, so strong at the time was the heritage of the past, that certain Christians regarded the institution as another weapon to be used in defense of the old order against modernism. Consequently, those who were concerned to bring about reconciliation with the world as it was, never felt attracted to the new devotion.

The situation now has been eased. We can regard the feast of Christ the King as a good opportunity to gain proper insight into a traditional doctrine that is essential to Christianity, and extremely relevant to the Church-world relationship now.

Royal messianism an ambiguous concept in Israel

Though the political institution of kingship was confined to a particular period of Jewish history, it had a profound influence on Jewish psychology. It was not indeed accepted without hesitation. The early prophets saw a danger here of assimilation to Gentile nations, and it was often discussed. Not all of the kings were people of the stature of David or Solomon. When, in the post-exilic period, there was a return to the pre-royal structures of priestly theocracy, this was commended. Notwithstanding this however, the period of kings had provided such moments of splendor, assuring political prestige for Israel according to what seemed to be a providential plan, that most Jews thought of the final times in terms of restoration of the kingship.

Messianic hope had made its appearance early in the period of kings, and it was natural that it should develop in this context. The Messiah to come would be a new David. The constant royal dimension given to messianism shows that, in popular religious psychology, the royal function was thought to be representative. A king's action could involve the spiritual destiny of the people. At the same time we note that persons who actually wielded this royal power were continuously submitted to prophetic criticism. When Isaiah gave Achaz the sign of Emmanuel, he conveys that the king is not fulfilling the conditions of fidelity to the covenant, and that a successor must be awaited.

The real ambiguity of royal messianism arises from the fact that it is a vehicle of illusory hope. So deeply tinged with particularism were the chosen people, that all took it for granted that Israel would have a privileged place in the eschatological Kingdom. Insofar as that Kingdom was destined to be terrestrial, her privilege naturally could only be political dominance over other nations.

The universal kingship of Christ

The two liturgical readings given in today's formulary indicate for us the true nature of Christ's kingship. He put himself forward as a King; but his Kingdom is not of this world. It is constructed in this world, but bears no resemblance at all to earthly kingdoms. Throughout his public life he took considerable care that people should not give his mission a political interpretation. Several times people wanted to make him King; but each time he evaded this.

He is King because he is the one mediator of salvation for all creation. It is in him that all things find fulfillment, their true destiny in God's creative plan. It is through love that God creates, and through man all creation is assumed, to be absorbed in divine life. The plan of love was accomplished through the sending of his Son, the man-God; because only such a one could, through his humanity, open the way to the Father's Family. So it is that Jesus is first-born of every creature, King of creation. He alone is the image of the invisible God. The whole creative plan depends essentially upon him.

Creation, because of sin, had become estranged from God. Thus Christ's kingship takes on also the aspect of universal reconciliation brought about by the shedding of his blood on the cross. The accomplishment of creation demands man's acceptance of the human condition, suffering and death included. Such was the obedience of Jesus. It is man's sin that makes of death a cross. The obedience by which Jesus saved creation is the sovereign expression of a love that is stronger than hate.

His kingship is universal. It extends to every dimension of creation. He achieved it by dying on the cross to remit all sins. The first-born of every creature is, by that very fact, the first-born among the dead.

The royal state of the baptized Christian

In today's second reading (3rd cycle), in the heart of his description of Christ's universal kingship, we have from Saint Paul this affirmation; "It is he who is head of the Body, that is to say the Church" (Col 1:18). In other words the kingship is exercised here on earth, in the Church, which is his Body.

The Church shares his kingship, insofar as she is the presence among men of the Risen Lord. Wherever she is implanted, there is rooted the mystery of Christ. And this is the principle that directs the spiritual pilgrimage of any people in God's creative design. In this mystery the stones of awaiting are sorted out from the obstacles; all things disclose their veritable meaning.

The Church's royal state extends to her members too. Such is the dignity baptism confers. We are all called, through our link with Christ, to play our part in promoting God's creation plan for the universe, and drawing all things into the paschal rhythm. Our responsibility is indeed a cosmic one; all that we do, because of Jesus Christ, reverberates universally.

The Church however, because she was conscious of her royal function, has perhaps, in history, been too ready to take this literally. In the Western world she was unable to withstand the seductions of power. The whole of human life, political, social, economic was thought of as an "order," where the Church had supreme discretion because she represented Christ's universal kingship. Strictly secular matters were, true, left to the prince; but the general disposition of human affairs was designed to facilitate religious requirements everywhere.

Christ's universal kingship was expressed by means of ecclesial tutelage and institutions. Missionary enterprise followed the same pattern. We find for instance, at the end of the 15th century, a Pope allotting, as between Spain and Portugal, according to a definite meridian, newly discovered or about to be discovered territories for evangelization.

The inconveniences of such a system soon made themselves felt. In Christian countries people began to grow restive under ecclesial tutelage and wanted fuller liberty. In non-Christian territories, people began to resent the inroads of Western Christian civilization, because they did not feel at home with it.

Nowadays Christian civilization in that sense is defunct, however much the attitude of some people continue to be shaped by it. The pontificate of John XXIII was the great ecclesial act of reconciliation with the modern world. The task that confronts us now is to find some expression, other than the medieval, for Christ's universal kingship. Doubtless we run the risk of being unable to find a formulation that will cover all the dimensions of a world that has grown more and more profane.

Mission as witness to the universal kingship of Christ

We might formulate a major problem confronting the Church in our day thus. Given that modern man is particularly aware of his own capabilities and of his mastery over the universe, how can he be convinced that without Christ he can do nothing?

The possible answer must be provided by Christian witness. We Christians, dispersed among men, must manage to demonstrate the close link between the actual pattern of human life and faith in Jesus Christ. If we are obedient unto the death of the cross, if we practice the beatitudes and give rein to the great impulse of love, we shall be working to restore the created universe to its genuine dignity. Christ's kingship commands the allegiance of all men, and, through man, of all creation. It makes man freer than he was before, less weighted by the slavery of sin and more than ever capable of mastering the universe.

Such is our problem. We must first, ourselves, begin to appreciate the profundity of this link. We need to be re-educated indeed; because very many Christians nowadays no longer really see the need for Christ in the whole texture of life. If they did, the message would get conveyed. The non-Christian would see the Christian as someone passionately concerned about human nature. Penetrating a little further, he would begin to realize that this passion for humanity had been kindled by Jesus Christ at the very moment that he made his disciple passionate for the true God.

The royal banquet of the eucharist

Our royal state as Christians is most keenly felt during the eucharistic celebration. Summoned to share the Bread, our bond with the death and resurrection of Christ is cemented; and our capacity to cooperate in the regeneration of the universe is intensified. Summoned to hear the Word, we have the means, day after day, of deepening our insights. The events of our own lives and of secular life round about us, begin to illustrate the link between faith in Jesus Christ and the whole enterprise of civilization. In this context the importance of the homily becomes very evident.

Then there is the further consideration that the Eucharist is not merely an initiation into these truths. It should be their actual exercise. The members present are joined in a unique brotherhood that has been set up by Christ. The bond between them is an anticipation of the final accomplishment of creation when all things will be reconciled in Christ. The structure of any eucharistic assembly should manage to make this felt.

2. Theme of the World

The connotation of this term for the majority of Christians in our day is the sum-total of terrestrial things as a theater for human activity in the historical sense. Already, in the first doctrinal theme for the twenty-ninth Sunday, we have discussed the ultimate importance, in God's plan, of this great human task.

In the present context we should like to push these considerations further. We Christians have perhaps grown used to a view of the world around us that does not allow for divine grace as an influence. Our style of thinking and acting makes for too clear-cut a distinction between creation and the plan of redemption. We realize of course that sin introduced an element of disorder into creation; we fail very often though to take the supernatural view of all this. We fail to appreciate the unity of God's plan in Jesus Christ. We fail to see how the rupture with God that sin brought about had repercussions on the order of creation, and actually obscured the true purpose of creation. The "world" is something of which sin has distorted the real meaning. All creation is involved in man's supernatural destiny; the natural and the supernatural in this context are merely two different facets of one and the same thing.

When Scripture speaks of the "world" it is always of the world in the total sense. We should never be led by the distinction, which the Church gradually formulated between natural and supernatural, into forgetting how closely these two orders are related. Nowadays particularly, when there is such a readiness everywhere to embrace the "world" in its natural dimension, we Christians must be careful to preserve the supernatural insights concerning it that are rooted in the Bible and tradition.

The meaning of the actual world for Israel

The basic reaction of Israel towards the world in which she lived was to celebrate its goodness. Yahweh had created all things for man's happiness and all creation was a living parable of his power and fatherly love. The believer, who contemplated what there was to see, could not but be seized with admiration.

Yet there was misgiving about the elements in creation that militated against man's happiness. Why the floods, the droughts, the earthquakes, the countless diseases and calamities; why suffering and death? Jewish monotheism precluded any recourse to dualism. Of this we have no trace in the Bible. The only possible explanation was man's sin. The world is always a prominent concept in salvation history. Yahweh uses it as an instrument to show his goodness; but he also uses it as an instrument to punish. Man's sin has actually placed the world under Satan's sway; death has made his entry. Man who, in God's creative design, was to fulfill the world by subduing it, instead of being faithful to his destiny, has involved the world in his sin.

Consequently the actual world, insofar as it shares man's guilt, is a fallen one. If death be the consequence of sin, then deliverance from sin must mean deliverance from death. Thus messianic hope for salvation becomes hope for "another" world, a "world to come." Because the present world is subject to sin, it is marked out for judgment. On the day of Yahweh a cosmic cataclysm will plunge sin and the universe of death into chaos. To replace it, Yahweh will create new heavens and a new earth.

To sum up, Israel never solved the puzzle of ambiguity in the actual world. Her only escape was to turn her gaze to the future and hope for a new creation. Ceaselessly she found herself confronted by the obstacle of death, and she never surmounted it. Sin was the reason for this bafflement.

Jesus, conqueror of the world, liberator

When Jesus came, the ambiguity of the actual world became a crucial point of reflection, as is evident from the New Testament, above all the fourth gospel. The world had been loved first; God so loved it that he sent his own Son. Yet the world did not receive the Father's envoy; it responded with hate to the overtures of divine love and it sent Jesus to the cross. Yet it was for this world that Jesus died, in order to free it from slavery. He did so deliver it, wiping out sin. In one and the same gesture he conquered the world in its evil aspect, and renewed it at its roots. The Kingdom he inaugurated was not of this world; but his disciples did not have to quit the world. It was there that their work had to be done.

By Jewish standards this was a totally new concept. The world to come is not juxtaposed with the actual world; it does not chronologically succeed it, but it has its roots in the actual world. It is this actual world which is ransomed and delivered from slavery in Jesus Christ. Death, that rock of scandal for every Jew, becomes the instrument of ransom. Paradoxically, it appears as the focal point of love. This was the meaning that human wisdom could not reach.

The world in other words for which man was made, which he had the mission to subdue, to recapitulate, to fulfill, was this actual world. True, it carried the mark of sin; it had made death the great weapon of Satan. But when Jesus died on the cross, in total self-renunciation for the love of all men, he showed that salvation comes by means of death. *This* was the transfiguration. The road leading to it was one of obedience which he was the first to travel.

The only world that is, is this actual one in which man finds himself. Love is the secret of its deliverance and sin the secret of its slavery. With the advent of the Messiah, Jesus of Nazareth, men came to realize what love was.

Separated from the world in order to free the world

Like Christ, the Church which is his Body can affirm; "I am not of this world." She is the sacrament of the Kingdom, and thus a sign that the world of sin has been defeated. Her members are "separated" from the world in a very real sense, because they share Christ's victory over sin. Their separation however is not a sociological one. They are in the world in that sense. The difference lies in the fact that they are delivered from the power of Satan and thus can work to deliver the world. They can gradually restore the world to its proper state, draw it into the paschal rhythm of passage from death to life.

That is not to say that Christians cease to be sinners. On the contrary the world continues to draw them, and they succumb. This is the endless tension. The member of Christ's Body has all the means, in Christ, to save the world and bring it life. But he is also a member of sinful humanity, and can lead the world to a blind state, where God is excluded, and terrestrial aspirations reign supreme.

For a long time this anguishing tension between the Kingdom and the world of sin has been a main focus of theological reflection. Augustinian thought has played a preponderant role in the West. The bishop of Hippo spoke of two cities; "Two loves built two cities. Love of self that excluded God gave us the terrestrial city. Love of God that excluded self gave us the celestial. One has its glory in itself; the other in the Lord" (*De civ. Dei* XV, 2). Augustine's thought was religious in a formal sense and it would be a betrayal of that thought to try to determine, in the actual world, the frontiers of his mystic cities. "In the actual world they are intertwined and intertangled (X, 32). Augustinian thinkers have not always been so nuanced as their master; they relegated everything that was not subject to Church direction to the "terrestrial city." As time went on, the confusion was compounded. Men became conscious of a further tension, that between religion and the enterprise of civilization. They grew more and more resentful of ecclesial tutelage in areas that concerned human resources only. Their legitimate struggles for independence were countered by people who invoked, wrongly, the historic contrast of Augustine.

Witnesses of Christ before the world

It may be that nowadays one has to be careful about Augustinian language; but the truth with which he was concerned is essential to Christianity. If we have to distinguish between religion and the enterprise of civilization, this does not dispose of the biblical distinction between the Kingdom and the "world." It just means that we should define our terms. Specifically, we should beware of taking the term "terrestrial city" in the Augustinian sense. With that proviso, it is imperative that we have constant recourse to Scripture, if we are to be true witnesses to the Risen Christ in the world of today.

Today, the Good News must encounter men precisely at the point where they feel themselves to be masters of their destiny. We Christians know that our non-Christian brothers do not possess the evangelic key to the construction of the city. Yet we are sensitive to the "values" of the secular city and we see the Gospel at work when the secular world is unaware. Do we forget that Satan too is at work? Does not modern man purport to find his own salvation? Do not all the grandiose projects put forward emanate ultimately from atheistic paganism? When all is said and done, modern man is no nearer than his predecessors to the insight that salvation depends on self-renunciation.

The missionary today must have no illusions. The world he encounters is a sinful one; and despite all his sympathy with it his message will be opposed. We Christians have come into the world to bear witness to the truth, to indicate by our lives and by our language the true destiny of man. We can be encouraged by the fact that the Spirit is at work in the heart of every man who is looking for the Savior; but our path is beset with perils. The world we encounter hates us. It will persecute us and mobilize all its forces to oppose us, or ensnare us in its toils. Let us never be surprised. Since Jesus, this is the way things are.

The missionary then today is a person challenged by the unbelieving world. He must however be careful not to extend the area of challenge attributable to the Prince of this world. When the modern world tells the Church that she is uncontemporary, this is not Satan's doing. Perhaps indeed we should take it as a "sign of the times." The very point at which the Good News must encounter modern man, the center of gravity, is this matter of human progress. The Christian version of this is that the secret lies in the Gospel, and requires self-renunciation. The world's version is different. It sees human progress in terms of man's own endowment, his capacity to work out his own salvation. Here lies the dilemma; and confrontation between the two wisdoms seems inevitable.

The eucharistic assembly of the liberators of the world

The sharing of the Word and Bread is the great ecclesial act of participation in Christ's victory over sin. The assembled faithful continue to be sinners; but sin has ceased to exercise decisive sway over them. The more we hear this Word and share this Bread, the more we find ourselves divided from the sinful world. Our presence in it becomes the presence of liberators.

The Eucharist has this effect because it is the memorial of the cross. Jesus is the liberator because he was obedient unto the death of the cross. The world that has to be liberated is our actual world. It will be delivered from sin, and pass to regeneration, by the road of death and the cross. We Christians will play our part in the liberation, because the Eucharist involves us in the sacrifice of the cross.

TABLE OF READINGS